THE VEDAS

WITH

ILLUSTRATIVE EXTRACTS.

ADDRESSED

TO

THOUGHTFUL HINDUS.

[*The most important Hymns are quoted in full; extracts are also given from the Brahmanas, and the claims of the Arya Samaj are considered in an Appendix.*]

THE BOOK TREE
SAN DIEGO, CALIFORNIA

First published 1892
The Christian Literature Society
Madras, India

ISBN 1-58509-223-1

Cover layout & design
Lee Berube

Printed on Acid-Free Paper
in the United States of America

Published by
The Book Tree
P O Box 16476
San Diego, CA 92176
www.thebooktree.com
We provide fascinating and educational products to help awaken the public to new ideas and information that would not be available otherwise.
Call 1 (800) 700-8733 for our *FREE BOOK TREE CATALOG*.

FOREWARD

This book is an overview of *The Vedas*, the holy book of Hindus. The most important Hymns are quoted in full; extracts are also included from the Brahmanas, the part of The Rig Veda that guides the Brahmans, the highest class of priests, in Vedic ceremonies. Also included is a section on the *Arya Samaj*, a later westernized version that is shown to be inaccurate, covered in The Appendix.

The Vedas is one of the oldest and most important of the world's holy books. There are four Vedas: the Rig Veda, Sama Veda, Yajur Veda and Atharva Veda. The Sama Veda and Yajur Veda consist almost entirely of selections from the Rig Veda. Of the four, the oldest is the Rig Veda, first composed about 1500 B.C. It was not written down until about 600 B.C. because *The Vedas* were considered too sacred to be written down—they could only be passed down orally through generations of Brahman families. In their complete form *The Vedas* were not written down until near the end of the third century B.C.

The Vedas are primarily composed of hymns, poems, incantations, and rituals from ancient India, mostly written in beautiful metric verse of three or four lines. They include invocations to the "One Divine" and also to the divinities of nature, including the Sun, Wind, Rain, Fire and the Dawn. A number or prayers are also included, covering such areas as marriage, progeny and prosperity, plus domestic rituals and magical formulas. They have an immense spiritual value, being the "Bible" of the Hindu religion. Beyond this, however, they offer a unique snapshot of normal, everyday life in India as it occurred four thousand years ago.

These books have also served as a valuable tool in the study of Sanskrit, being the oldest known texts in that language. Scholars in comparative linguistics have found them useful because our modern Western languages are known to have descended from Sanskrit.

The first three Vedic books were used by Hindu priests as ritual handbooks. The Rig Veda was meant to call directly on the gods by reciting the hymns aloud. The most frequently mentioned was Indra, the god of war and weather. Agni, the god of fire, is also mentioned prominently.

Next to the Rig Veda, the last one, the Atharva Veda, is the most important. It is attributed to a rishi, or sage, called Atharvan and was possibly compiled as late as 500 B.C. It contains hymns and magical incantations often directed to lesser gods that were believed to effect the health and happiness of people, offering them homage to induce them to abstain from doing harm. Long life and recovery of illness was often the aim. Because this book deviated from the others, it was not at first readily accepted—much like the Book of John in the Western Bible. Only later was it adopted as a ritual handbook by the Brahmans. It became useful because ordinary Aryan people could use the hymns for simple rituals, addressing lesser gods, that did not require the mediation of priests. Most of the magical spells are found within this section.

All told, *The Vedas* have had a compelling influence on other religions from around the world, most directly on Buddhism, Jainism, and Sikhism. And those individuals searching for ancient wisdom on their own will, sooner or later, always come to *The Vedas*.

Paul Tice

Prefatory Note.

—◆—

THE following compilation is a greatly enlarged edition of
Vedic Hinduism, published in 1888. Since then the translation
of the Rig-Veda by Mr. R. T. B. Griffith, has been completed, and
through the kindness of the author a free use of the work has been
allowed. It is strongly recommended to the student of the subject.
The title, &c., are given below :

*The Hymns of the Rig-Veda translated with a Popular Com-
mentary*, by Ralph T. B. Griffith, formerly Principal of Benares
College. 4 Volumes 8vo. Published by E. J. Lazarus and Co.,
Benares. Price Rs. 16 in 16 parts; Rs. 19-12-0 in four Volumes.

The Sanskrit Text, with Sayana's Commentary, edited by Max
Müller, can now be obtained for £8-8s. Though it should be carefully studied by competent scholars, few are able to do so, and the
work is expensive. The translation of Mr. Griffith gives a fair
idea of the contents, and the Commentary often throws great light
on the text.

Next to the above, Dr. John Muir's *Sanskrit Texts*, in five
Volumes, will be found of special value. Paul, Trench, Trübner
and Co., Publishers.

The Rev. Dr. K. S. Macdonald's *Vedic Religion*, contains
much valuable information. It may be obtained at the principal
Tract Depôts in India.

The compiler is also indebted to the following works :

Arya Samaj, Principles and Teaching of the. A Series of Lectures
by Pandit Kharak Singh and Dr. Martyn Clark. The Punjab
Religious Book Society, Lahore.

Banerjea, Rev. Dr. K. M. *The Relation of Christianity and
Hinduism.*

Barth, *Religions of India*. Trübner's Oriental Series.

Dowson, *Dictionary of Hindu Mythology*. Trübner's Oriental
Series.

Eggeling, Professor. *Translation of the Satapatha Brahmana.*
Sacred Books of the East.

Forman, Rev. H. *The Arya Samaj*. North India Tract Society,
Allahabad.

Haug, Dr. *Translation of the Aitareya Brahmanam*. Bombay.

Kunte, Mr. M. M. B.A. *Vicissitudes of Aryan Civilization in India.* Bombay.

Müller, Professor Max, *Ancient Sanskrit Literature, Hibbert Lectures,* &c., &c.

Rajendralala Mitra, Dr. *Indo-Aryans.* 2 Vols. Newman, Calcutta.

Weber, Professor, *History of Indian Literature.* Trübner.

Whitney, Professor. *Oriental and Linguistic Studies.* Scribner.

Wilson, Professor H. H. *Translation of the Rig-Veda Sanhita.* Allen.

Wilson, Rev. Dr. J. *India Three Thousand Years Ago.* Bombay.

References are given to the longer quotations, but there are numerous short extracts, generally abridged or slightly altered, which are not acknowledged.

The reader is earnestly invited to investigate the subject for himself, and consider how far the Vedic hymns and Brahmanas meet the wants of the soul. The concluding appeal of the late Rev. Dr. Krishna Mohun Banerjea deserves special attention.

J. MURDOCH.

MADRAS, *October,* 1892.

CONTENTS.

The Religious Childhood of India, 29 ; Dyaus and Prithivi, 31 ; Aditi and the Adityas 32 ; Varuna, 33 ; Indra, 34 ; Agni, 36 ; Parjanya, 38 ; Vayu, 38 ; The Maruts, 38 ; Solar Deities, 39 ; Mitra, 40 ; Surya, 40 ; Savitri, 41 ; Vishnu, 41 ; Pushan, 42 ; Ushas, 42 ; Asvins, 43 ; Tvastri, 43 ; The Ribhus, 43 ; Vishvakarman, 44 ; Prajapati, 44 ; Brihaspati *or* Brahmanaspati, 44 ; Vach, 45 ; Soma, 45 ; Rudra, 46 ; Yama and Yami, 47 ; Vesve Devas, 47 ; Ka, 48 ; Goddesses, 48 ; The Pitris, 48 ; Sacrificial Implements, &c., 51 ; The Gods not mentioned in the Vedas, 51.

Mandala I. 66 ; Mandala II. 75 ; Mandala III. 77 ; Mandala IV. 80 ; Mandala V. 82 ; Mandala VI. 85; Mandala VII. 87 ; Mandala VIII. 93 ; Mandala IX. 94 ; Mandala X. 96.

THE VEDAS

WITH

ILLUSTRATIVE EXTRACTS.

INTRODUCTION.

Object.—The following compilation is intended chiefly for thoughtful Hindus. They are sufficiently intelligent to reject the low and degrading ideas of God given in the later Hindu books; but some of them have the idea that a pure monotheism is to be found in the Vedas, the most ancient and authoritative of their sacred writings. Careful examination will show that this belief is unfounded. The inquiry should be conducted with great seriousness, and an earnest desire to know the truth. The following short prayer may fitly be offered :

O All-wise, All-merciful God and Father, pour the bright beams of Thy light into my soul, and guide me into Thy eternal truth.

Meaning of Term.—VEDA is from the Sanskrit *vid*, know, kindred with the Latin *vid*, and the English *to wit*. In its general sense it is sometimes applied by the Brahmans to the whole body of their most ancient sacred literature. More strictly, it denotes four collections of hymns which are respectively known by the names of Rig-Veda, Yajur-Veda, Sama-Veda, and Atharva-Veda. They are supposed to contain *the* science, as teaching that knowledge which, of all others, is best worth acquiring.

" The general form of the Vedas is that of lyric poetry. They contain the songs in which the first ancestors of the Hindu people, at the very dawn of their existence as a separate nation, while they were still only on the threshold of the great country which they were afterwards to fill with their civilization, praised the gods, extolled heroic deeds, and sung of other matters which kindled their poetical fervour."*

The Vedas the highest Hindu Authorities.—The Hindu sacred books are divided into two great classes, called *Sruti* and *Smriti*. *Sruti*, which means hearing, denotes direct revelation; *Smriti*, recollection, includes the sacred books which are admitted to have been composed by human authors.

Professor Max Müller thus shows the estimation in which the Vedas are held :—

" According to the orthodox views of Indian theologians, not a single line of the Veda was the work of human authors. The whole Veda is in

---

* Whitney's *Oriental and Linguistic Studies*, Vol. I., p. 5.

some way or other the work of the Deity; and even those who received the revelation, or, as they express it, those who saw it, were not supposed to be ordinary mortals, but beings raised above the level of common humanity, and less liable therefore to error in the reception of revealed truth. . . . The human element, called *paurusheyatva* in Sanskrit, is drawn out of every corner or hiding-place, and as the Veda is held to have existed in the mind of the Deity before the beginning of time, every allusion to historical events, of which there are not a few, is explained away with a zeal and ingenuity worthy of a better cause."

" The laws of Manu, according to the Brahmanic theology, are not revelation; they are not *Sruti*, but only *Smriti*. If these laws or any other work of authority can be proved on any point to be at variance with a single passage of the Veda, their authority is at once overruled."*

The inspiration of the Veda, says Monier Williams, is regarded as so self-convincing, " as to require no proof, and to be entirely beyond the province of reason or argument."

Hindu Ignorance of the Vedas.—Although the Vedas are held in the highest estimation by the Hindus, their real character is almost entirely unknown to them. Very few copies of them existed until they were printed in Europe. It has often been said that if the Vedic Aryans were to reappear and act before their descendants their former life, they would be regarded with horror as a most impure and irreligious people. They killed cows and ate their flesh !

The later books were studied by the learned in India instead of the Vedas themselves. " When Rammohun Roy was in London," says Max Müller, " he saw at the British Museum a young German scholar, Friedrich Rosen, busily engaged in copying MSS. of the Rig-Veda. The Rajah was surprised, but he told Rosen that he ought not to waste his time on the Hymns, but that he should study the text of the Upanishads."†

Publication of the Vedas.—For a long time it was very difficult for European scholars to gain a knowledge of the Veda. " All other Sanskrit MSS. were freely communicated to Englishmen resident in India, but not the MSS. of the Veda. And even in cases where such MSS. had fallen into the hands of barbarians, the Pandits declined to translate them for them. Colebrooke alone seems to have overcome all these difficulties, and his Essays ' On the Vedas, or the Sacred Writings of the Hindus,' though published in 1805, are still extremely valuable."

Rosen published a specimen of the Hymns of the Rig-Veda in 1830. He died soon after, and only the first book of the Rig-Veda, translated into Latin, was finished by him, and published after his death in 1838.

In 1845 Max Müller was in Paris, copying the text of the Rig-Veda with the commentary of Sayana Acharya. Sayana was brother of Madhavacharya, the prime minister of the Raja of

---

* *Chips from a German Workshop*, Vol. I.   † Max Müller, *Biographical Essays*, p. 39.

Vijayanagara,* in the 14th century. His commentary was, no doubt, prepared with the assistance of the most learned Brahmans of the time. Max Müller was authorised by the East India Company to bring out an edition of both at its expense. The first volume appeared in 1849. The editing occupied about 20 years. The price of the 6 quarto volumes is £15.

A new edition, in 4 volumes, at the expense of the Maharaja of Vizianagram, has just been published. The price is 2 guineas per volume.

The text of the Rig-Veda, in Roman character, was printed in Berlin in 1861.

An English translation of the Rig-Veda, based on the commentary of Sayana, was prepared by the late Professor Wilson. Part of it was published after his death. It is expensive, the price of the 6 volumes being £6-19s.

There is a new English translation by Mr. R. T. H. Griffith, formerly Principal of the Sanskrit College, Benares. A popular commentary is also given, explaining, as far as possible, difficult passages. The opinions of Sayana, Max Müller, Muir, and other oriental scholars are quoted, where they throw light on the subject, in addition to valuable original notes. The translator has had the advantage of the labours of his predecessors, and of a long residence at Benares in close connection with some of the best Pandits in India. He is also a poet, and has sought, as far as possible, to imitate the rhythm of the original. For the price, &c., see the Prefatory Note.

All students who can afford it should possess copies of this the most recent and accurate translation of the Vedas. It should be accessible in all Public and Mission Libraries in India.

Some of the Hymns have been translated by Professor Peterson of Bombay. Bengali translations of the Rig-Veda have been published.

METRES AND LANGUAGE OF THE VEDAS.

Metres.—Great importance is attached to the Metres used. Dr. Haug says:—

" The power and significance of the Hotri-priests at a sacrifice consists in their being the masters of the sacred word, which is frequently personified by *Vach*, *i. e.* Speech, who is identical with Sarasvati, the goddess of learning in the later Hindu Pantheon. Speech has, according to the opinion of the earliest divines, the power of vivifying and killing. The sacred words pronounced by the Hotar effect, by dint of the innate power of Vach, the spiritual birth of the sacrificer, form his body, raise him up to heaven, connect him with the prototypes of those things which

---

* In what is now the Bellary District of the Madras Presidency. The ruins cover 2 square miles.

he wishes to obtain (such as children, cattle, &c.,) and make him attain to his full life term, which is a hundred years; but they are at the same time a weapon by means of which the sacrificer's enemies, or he himself (if the Hotar have any evil designs against him) can be killed, and all evil consequences of sin (this is termed *papman*) be destroyed. The power and effect of Speech as regards the obtaining of any particular thing wished for, mainly lies in the form in which it is uttered. Thence the great importance of the metres, and the choice of words and terms. Each metre is the invisible master of something obtainable in this world; it is, as it were, its exponent, and ideal. This great significance of the metrical speech is derived from the number of syllables of which it consists; for each thing has (just as in the Pythagorean system) a certain numerical proportion. The Gayatri metre, which consists of three times eight syllables, is the most sacred, and is the proper metre for Agni, the god of fire, and chaplain of the gods. It expresses the idea of Brahma : therefore the sacrificer must use it when he wishes anything closely connected with Brahma, such as acquirement of sacred knowledge, and the thorough understanding of all problems of theology. The Trishtubh, which consists of four times eleven syllables, expresses the idea of strength and royal power ; thence it is the proper metre by which Indra, the king of the gods, is to be invoked. Any one wishing to obtain strength and royal power, principally a Kshattriya, must use it. A variety of it, the Ushnih metre of 28 syllables, is to be employed by a sacrificer who aspires for longevity, for 28 is the symbol of life. The Jagati, a metre of 48 syllables, expresses the idea of cattle. Any one who wishes for wealth in cattle, must use it. The same idea (or that of the sacrifice) is expressed by the Pañkti metre (five times eight syllables). The Brihati, which consists of 36 syllables, is to be used when a sacrificer is aspiring to fame and renown ; for this metre is the exponent of those ideas. The Anushtubh metre, of 32 syllables, is the symbol of the celestial world ; thence a candidate for a place in heaven has to use it. The Viraj, of 30 syllables, is food and satisfaction ; thence one who wishes for plenty of food, must employ it." *

One or two illustrative quotations are given below from the Aitareya Brahmana :

"He who wishes for long life, should use two verses in the *Ushnih* metre ; for Ushnih is life. He who having such a knowledge uses two Ushnihs arrives at his full age (*i. e.*, 100 years).

"He who desires heaven should use two *Anushtubhs*. There are 64 syllables in two Anushtubhs. Each of these three worlds (earth, air, and sky) contains 21 places, one rising above the other (just as the steps of a ladder). By 21 steps he ascends to each of these worlds severally ; by taking the sixty-fourth step he stands firm in the celestial world. He who having such a knowledge uses two Anushtubhs gains a footing (in the celestial world).

"He who desires strength should use two Trishtubhs. Trishtubh is strength, vigour, and sharpness of senses. He who knowing this, uses

---

* Introduction to the Aitareya Brahmana, pp. 75-77.

two Trishtubhs, becomes vigorous, endowed with sharp senses and strong.

"He who desires cattle should use two Jagatis. Cattle are Jagati like. He who knowing this uses two Jagatis, becomes rich in cattle."[*]

"The metres," says Max Müller, "were originally connected with dancing and music. The names for metre in general confirm this. *Chhandas,* metre, denotes stepping; *vritta,* metre from *vrit,* to turn, meant originally the last three or four steps of a dancing movement, to turn, the *versus* which determined the whole character of a dance and of a metre. *Trishtubh,* the name of a common metre in the Veda, meant three steps, because its turn, its vritta, or *versus,* consisted of three steps, one short and two long.

"The laws regulating the succession of long and short syllables within the limits of the hemistich are in general anything but strict; all that is aimed at seems to be to give the whole a kind of rhythmical flow, or general metrical movement, on which the four last syllables shall stamp the peculiar character; their quantity is much more definitely established, yet even among them exceptional irregularities are by no means rare."

Griffith thus briefly describes the metres:

"The Hymns are composed in various metres, some of which are exceedingly simple and others comparatively complex and elaborate, and two or more different metres are frequently found in the same Hymn; one Hymn, for instance, in Book I., shows nine distinct varieties in the same number of verses. The verses or stanzas consist of three or four *pádas,* semi-hemistichs[†] or lines, each of which contains 8, 11, or 12 syllables, sometimes, but rarely, 5, and still less frequently four or more than twelve. As regards quantity, the first syllables of the line are not strictly defined, but the last four are regular, the measure being iambic (short and long) in the 8 and 12 syllable verses, and trochaic (long and short) in these of 11 syllables."[‡]

Specimens of Metres.

The Gayatri.—This is a common metre. It is so called because the Gāyatrí, the most sacred text in the Vedas, is composed in it. It contains three times eight syllables. The first hymn is in this metre. The following is the first verse:

Agnimīlē purōhitam yajñasya dēva mrtvijam |
Hōtāram rātnadhātamam||

I laud Agni, the great high priest, god, minister of sacrifice,
The herald, lavishest of wealth.

Trishtubh.—This is one of the commonest metres. It consists

---

* Haug's Translation, pp. 12, 13.
† Hemistich, half line.
‡ Preface to Translation, pp. xv. xvi.

of four times eleven syllables. The name means three steps, one short and two long. The following is an example :

Anárambhane tad avírayethám anásthána agrabhane samudre | yad aśviná ūhuthur Bhujyum astam śatásitrám návam átasthiv- áṁsam | I. 116, 5.

5. Ye put forth your vigour in the ocean, which offers no stay or standing-place, or support, when ye bore Bhujyu to his home, standing on a ship propelled by a hundred oars."*

Anushtubh.—This contain 32 syllables. A candidate for a place in heaven has to use it. The following is an example :

Srushtiváno hi dáśushe deváh Agne vichetasah !
tán rohidaśva girvanas trayasttriṁśatam á vaha ! i. 45, 2.

"Agni, the wise gods lend an ear to their worshipper. God with the ruddy steeds, who lovest praise, bring hither those three and thirty." †

Jagati.—This metre of 48 syllables is said to "express the idea of cattle. Any one who wishes for wealth in cattle must use it." Example :

Na taṁ rájánáv Adite kutaś chana na aṁhah aśnoti duritaṁ nakir bhayam | Yam Aśviná suhavá rudravarttaní purora- thaṁ kṛinuthah patnyá saha | x. 39, 11.

"Neither distress, nor calamity, nor fear from any quarter as- sails the man whom ye Asvins, along with (your) wife, cause to lead the van in his car ; and as loving to ascend their chariot." ‡

Max Müller gives a list, according to Saunaka, of the metres em- ployed in the Rig-Veda. The number of verses in which the principal occur are as follows : Trishtubh, 4,253; Gayatri, 2,451 ; Jagati, 1,348 ; Anushtubh, 855 ; Ushnih, 341 ; Pankti, 312 ; various, 849 ; total, 10,409.‖

Every intelligent man knows that the above assertions regarding the influence of metres is pure nonsense. Like the curse denounced against those who read the Vedas, it was a device of the Brahmans to impose upon the simple-minded people of the time.

Language.—The language of the Vedas is an older dialect, varying very considerably, both in its grammatical and lexical character, from the classical Sanskrit. Its grammatical peculiarities run through all departments. It is untrammeled by the rules by which Sanskrit after it passed into oblivion as a vernacular dialect was forced, as it were, into a mould of regularity by long grammatical treatment, and received a development which is in some respects foreign and unnatural. The dissimilarity between the two in re- spect of the stock of words of which each is made up is not less marked. Not single words alone, but whole classes of derivatives

---

* Muir's Sanskrit Texts, Vol. V. pp. 244, 245.
† Muir's Sanskrit Texts, Vol. V. p. 10.
‡ Muir's Sanskrit Texts, Vol. V. p. 236.
‖ Ancient Sanskrit Literature, p. 222.

and roots, which the Veda exhibits in familiar use, are wholly wanting, or have left but faint traces in the classical dialect.*

All living languages change in course of time. The following is a specimen of English from Chaucer, considered the "Father of English poetry ;" written about 500 years ago :

"A Clerk ther was of Oxenforde also,
That unto logike hadde long ygo.
As lene was his hors as is a rake,
And he was not right fat I undertake ;
But looked holwe, and thereto soberly.

The hymns of the Rig-Veda were undoubtedly composed in the language of the time. As the people of Italy who once spoke Latin, now speak Italian, derived from Latin, so in India, Sanskrit merged into what are called the Prakrits. In the time of Buddha, about 500 B. C., Sanskrit had ceased to be a *spoken* language. But it became a *written* language, polished by grammarians, and during the last 2,000 years it has remained substantially the same.

Muir gives examples of the differences of Vedic from later Sanskrit, one of which is quoted. Rig-Veda I. 2, 1.

Vedic Text.

Vāyav āyāhi darśata ime somāḥ arankritāḥ |
teshām pāhi śrudhi havam ||

Modern Sanskrit.

Vāyav āyāhi darśanīya ime somāḥ alankritāḥ |
teshām piba śrinu havam ||

"Come, O Vayu, these somas are prepared. Drink of them ; hear our invocation."

Here it will be observed that four Vedic words darśata, arankritāḥ, pāhi, śrudhi, differ from the modern Sanskrit forms. The frequent diversity between the Vedic and ordinary Sanskrit is re- cognized in every page of his work by the great grammarian Pānini.†

PRINCIPAL DIVISIONS OF THE VEDAS.

RIG-VEDA.—The name means the Veda of hymns of praise. *Rich*, which before the initial soft letter of Veda, is changed into *Rig*, is derived from a root which in Sanskrit means to celebrate. When standing by itself, *rich* becomes *rik*.

The hymns are called *Mantras* or *Suktas* (praises). The entire number form the *Sanhita* (or *Samhita*) collection. They are arranged in two methods. One divides them amongst eight *Khandas* (portions), or *Astakas* (eighths), each of which is again subdivided into eight *Adhyayas*, lectures. The other plan classes

---

* Abridged from Whitney.   † Muir's *Sanskrit Texts*, Vol. II. pp. 205, 206.

the *Suktas* under ten *Mandalas*, circles, subdivided into rather more than a hundred *Anuvakas*, or sub-sections. A further subdivision of the *Suktas* into *Vargas*, or paragraphs of about five stanzas each, is common to both classifications.*

At an early period systematic indexes to various portions of Vedic literature were prepared. They are known as Anukramanis, from *anu*, along, and *kram*, to step. The most perfect is that of Katyayana on the Rig-Veda. It gives the first words of each hymn, the number of verses, the names and family of the poets, the names of the deities, and the metres of every verse. As early as about 600 B.C. every verse, every word, every syllable had been carefully counted. The number of verses varies from 10,402 to 10,622 ; that of the *padas*, or words, is 153,826 ; that of the syllables, 432,000.

The ten books form separate collections, each belonging to one of the ancient families of India. The first seven books resemble each other in character and arrangement. They begin with hymns addressed to Agni, and these hymns, with the exception of the tenth Mandala, are invariably followed by hymns addressed to Indra. After the hymns addressed to these two deities we generally meet with hymns addressed to the Visva Devas, or 'all the gods.' This shows that the Mandalas do not represent collections made independently by different families; but collections carried out simultaneously in different localities, under the supervision of one central authority.

The eighth Mandala contains 92 hymns, assigned to a great number of different authors ; hymns of the same author do not always stand together, and of any internal arrangement according to divinities there is no trace. The ninth Mandala contains 114 hymns addressed to the Soma, the intoxicating drink prepared from the Soma plant. The tenth Mandala wears the appearance of being a later appendage to the collection. The first half is arranged upon no apparent system ; the second commences with the longer hymns and diminishes their length regularly to the close. Many of the hymns do not differ from the mass of those found in the earlier books, but others are evidently of a later date and conceived in another spirit.

The Rig-Veda is an historical collection intended to preserve from further corruption those ancient songs which the Aryans had brought with them, as their most precious possession, from the earliest seats of the race.

In the eyes of the historical student the Rig-Veda is the Veda *par excellence*. The other Vedas contain chiefly extracts from the Rig-Veda, together with sacrificial formulas, charms, and incantations. The Rig-Veda contains all that had been saved of the

* Professor Wilson's Introduction, p. xiv.

ancient, sacred, and popular poetry, a collection made for its own sake, and not for the sake of any sacrificial performances.

The priests who specially recited the verses of the Rig-Veda were called Hotris.

YAJUR-VEDA.—The name comes from *Yaj*, sacrifice. It contains the formulas and verses to be muttered by the priests and their assistants who had chiefly to prepare the sacrificial ground, to dress the altar, slay the victims, and pour out the libations. The first sentences in one of the two divisions were to be uttered by the priest as he cut from a particular tree a switch with which to drive away the calves from the cows whose milk was to furnish the material of the offering.

There are two principal texts of the Yajur-Veda, called respectively the White and the Black, or the Vajasaneyi and Taittiriya Sanhitas. The Vishnu Purana gives the following explanation of their names : Vaisampayana, a pupil of the great Vyasa, was the original teacher of the Black Yajur-Veda. Yajnavalkya, one of his disciples, having displeased him, was called upon by his master to part with the knowledge which he had acquired from him. He forthwith vomited the Yajur-Veda. The other disciples of Vaisampayana, assuming the form of partridges (tittiri), picked up from the ground its several dirtied texts. From this circumstance it received the name of *Taittiriya Krishna Yajur-Veda.* A more rational explanation is that Vaisampayana taught it to Yaska, who taught it to Tittiri, who also became a teacher. Yajnavalkya afterwards, by the performance of severe penances, induced the Sun to impart to him those Yajur texts which his master had not possessed. The Sun then assumed the form of a horse (Vajin), and communicated to him the desired texts. Hence the Sanhita was called Vajasaneyi, and also White (or bright) because it was revealed by the Sun.

Another explanation of the names is that the Vajasaneyins called their collection the White on account of its clear arrangement, while they applied the term Black, for the opposite reason, to the texts of the older school.

The Black and White Yajus differ in their arrangement. In the former the sacrificial formulas are for the most part immediately followed by their explanation ; in the latter, they are entirely separated from one another.

A large portion of the materials of the Yajur-Veda is derived from the Rig-Veda, to about the half of which it is equal in both forms united. But it contains prose passages which are new.

As the manual of the priesthood, it became the great subject of study, and it has a great number of different Sukhas or Schools. The priests who used it were called *Adhwaryus,* offerers.

The text of both divisions has been printed either in India or in the West.

SAMA-VEDA.—This is wholly metrical. It contains 1549 verses, only 78 of which have not been traced to the Rig-Veda. The verses have been selected and arranged for the purpose of being chanted at the sacrifices of which the intoxicating juice of the Soma plant was the chief ingredient. Many of the invocations are addressed to Soma, some to Agni, and some to Indra. There are special song books directing the manner in which they were to be intoned. The priests who recited the Sama-Veda were called Udgatris, chanters.

The text has been printed, and there is an English translation by Dr. Stevenson.

ATHARVA-VEDA.—This Veda is of later origin than the others. Manu speaks of only the Three Vedas. One-sixth of the work is in prose, and about one-sixth of the hymns is found in the Rig-Veda.

It is sometimes called the *Cursing-Veda*, because it contains so many mantras supposed to be able to cause the destruction enemies. A further account of it, with some illustrative extracts, are given in a following chapter.

BRAHMANAS.

The BRAHMANAS, 'belonging to Brahmans,' are that part of the Veda which is intended for the guidance of Brahmans in the use of the hymns of the Mantra, and therefore of later production ; but the Brahmanas, equally with the Mantra, are held to be *Sruti*, revealed word. They contain the details of the Vedic ceremonies, with long explanations of their origin and meaning ; they give instructions as to the use of particular verses and metres ; and they abound with curious legends, human and divine, in illustration. Though their professed object is to teach the sacrifice, they allow a much larger space to dogmatical, exegetical, mystical, and philosophical speculations than to the ceremonial itself.

Each of the Sanhitas has its Brahmanas, and these generally maintain the essential character of the Veda to which they belong. Thus the Brahmanas of the Rik are specially devoted to the duties of the Hotri, who recites the verses, those of the Yajur to the performance of the sacrifices by the Adhwaryu, and those of the Saman to the chanting by the Udgatri. The Rik has the Aitareya Brahmana, which is perhaps the oldest, and may date as far back as the seventh century, B. C. It has another, called Kaushitaki. The Black Yajur Veda has the Taittiriya Brahmana, and the White Yajur Veda has the Satapatha Brahmana, one of the most important of all the Brahmanas. The Sama Veda has eight Brahmanas, of which one of the best known is the Tandya. The Atharva has only one, the Gopatha Brahmana. "The Brahmanas," says Professor Eggeling, "form our chief, if not our only, source of information regarding one of the most important periods in the social and mental development of India. They are also of the highest importance as the only genuine prose works which the Sanskrit as a popular language has produced."

THE ARANYAKAS AND UPANISHADS.

Aranyaka means 'belonging to the forest.' The Aranyakas are attached to the Brahmanas, and are intended for study in the forest by Brahmans who have retired from the world. They expound the mystical sense of the ceremonies, discuss the nature of God, &c. There are four of them extant : 1. Brihad ; 2. Taittiriya; 3. Aitareya; and 4. Kaushitaki Aranyaka. The Aranyakas are closely connected with the Upanishads, and the names are occasionally used interchangeably. Thus the Brihad is called indifferently Brihad Aranyaka or Brihad Aranyaka Upanishad : it is attached to the Satapatha Brahmana. The Aitareya Upanishad is a part of the Aitareya Brahmana.

Max Müller says :—

" We cannot hesitate for a moment to consider the Aranyaka as an enlargement upon the Brahmana. The chief interest which the Aranyakas possess at the present moment consists in their philosophy. The philosophical chapters well known under the name of Upanishads are almost the only portion of Vedic literature which is extensively read to this day. They contain, or are supposed to contain, the highest authority on which the various systems of philosophy in India rest. Not only the Vedanta philosopher, who by his very name, professes his faith in the ends and objects of the Veda, but the Sankhya, the Vaiseshika, the Nyaya, and Yoga philosophers, all pretend to find in the Upanishads some warranty for their tenets, however antagonistic in their bearing. The same applies to the numerous sects that have existed and still exist in India. Their founders, if they have any pretensions to orthodoxy, invariably appeal to some passage of the Upanishads in order to substantiate their own reasonings. Now it is true that in the Upanishads themselves there is so much freedom and breadth of thought that is not difficult to find in them some authority for almost any shade of philosophical opinion. The old Upanishads did not pretend to give more than ' guesses at truth,' and when, in course of time, they became invested with an inspired character, they allowed great latitude to those who professed to believe in them as revelation. Yet this was not sufficient for the rank growth of philosophical doctrines during the latter ages of Indian history ; and when none of the ancient Upanishads could be found to suit the purpose, the founders of new sects had no scruple and no difficulty in composing new Upanishads of their own. This accounts for the large and even growing number of these treatises. Every new collection of MSS., every new list of Upanishads given by native writers adds to the number which were known before ; and the most modern compilations seem now to enjoy the same authority as the really genuine treatises."[*]

* *Ancient Sanskrit Literature*, pp. 316, 317.

Contradictions of the Upanishads.—Max Müller has the following remarks on this point :

" The early Hindus did not find any difficulty in reconciling the most different and sometimes contradictory opinions in their search after truth ; and a most extraordinary medley of oracular sayings might be collected from the Upanishads, even from those which are genuine and comparatively ancient, all tending to elucidate the darkest points of philosophy and religion, the creation of the world, the nature of God, the relation of man to God, and similar subjects. That one statement should be contradicted by another seems never to have been felt as any serious difficulty."[*]

The same remark applies to the Rig-Veda, as will be shown in the chapter describing its gods.[†]

THE SUTRAS.

The Sutra period forms the connecting link between the Vedic and the later Sanskrit. *Sutra* means string ; and all the works written in this style, on subjects the most various, are nothing but one uninterrupted string of short sentences, twisted together into the most concise forms. Shortness is the great object of this style of composition, and it is a proverbial saying (taken from the Mahabhashya) amongst the Pandits, that an author rejoiceth in the economising of half a short vowel as much as in the birth of a son. " Every doctrine thus propounded, whether grammar, metre, law, or philosophy, is reduced to a mere skeleton." It is impossible to understand them without the commentary by which these works are usually accompanied.

" *The* Sutras" generally signify those which are connected with the Vedas, *viz.*, the Kalpa Sutras, relating to ritual ; the Grihya Sutras, to domestic rites ; and the Samayacharika Sutras, to conventional usages.

The Sutras, although based upon the Sruti, are yet avowedly composed by human authors. Whenever they appear to be in contradiction with the Sruti, their authority is at once overruled.

THE VEDAS, THE MAIN POINT OF CONSIDERATION.

Although the different divisions of Vedic literature have been briefly described, attention will be chiefly confined to the Vedas, strictly so called.

---

[*] *Ancient Sanskrit Literature*, pp. 320, 321.
[†] See *Philosophic Hinduism* for a more detailed account of the Upanishads, with illustrative extracts. Sold by Mr. A. T. Scott, Tract Depôt, Madras. Price 2½ As. Post-free, 3 As.

HINDU ACCOUNTS OF THE ORIGIN OF THE VEDAS.

The common belief in India is that the Vedas are eternal. They existed in the mind of the Deity before the beginning of time. At the commencement of each Kalpa, Brahm reveals them to Brahma, and they issue from his four mouths. They are taught by Brahma to the Rishis whose names they bear.

The different opinions entertained regarding the origin of the Vedas will now be considered. The writings of Dr. John Muir furnish a storehouse of information on the subject. He gives the passages both in Sanskrit and in English translations. The Third Volume of his *Sanskrit Texts* treats of " The Vedas, Opinions of their Authors, and of later Indian writers of their Origin, Inspiration, and Authority." Only a few quotations can be made.

Opinions may be classed under two heads.

1. Opinions expressed in the Hindu Sacred Books.

The Vedas sprung from the mystical sacrifice of Purusha.

The hymn Purusha Sukta of the Rig-Veda (x. 90) contains the following :—

तस्माद् यज्ञात् सर्वहुतः ऋचः सामानि जज्ञिरे ।

छन्दांसि जज्ञिरे तस्माद् यजुस् तस्माद् अजायत ।

" From that universal sacrifice sprung the Rich and Saman verses : the metres sprung from it : from it the Yajush arose."

2. *The Vedas were cut or scraped off from Skambha as being his hair and his mouth.*

The Atharva-Veda (x. 7, 20) says,

यस्माद् ऋचो अपातक्षन् यजुर् यस्माद् अपाकषन् ।

सामानि यस्य लोमानि अथर्वाङ्गिरसो मुखम् ।

स्कम्भं तं ब्रूहि कतमः स्विद् एव सः ।

" Declare who is that Skambha (the Supporting-Principle) from whom they cut off the Rich verses; from whom they scraped off the Yajush, of whom the Saman verses are the hairs, and the verses of Atharva and Angiras the mouth."

3. *The Vedas sprung from Indra, and he sprung from them.*

The Atharva-Veda (xiii. 4, 38) says,

स वै ऋग्भ्यो अजायत तस्माद् ऋचो अजायन्त ।

" Indra sprung from the Rich verses; the Rich verses sprung from him."

4. *The Vedas sprung from Time.*

Atharva-Veda (xix. 54, 3.)

कालाद् ऋच: समभवन् यजु: कालाद् अजायत ।

"From Time the Rich verses sprung ; the Yajush sprung from
Time."
5.   *The Vedas sprung from the leavings of Sacrifice.*
Atharva-Veda (xi. 7, 24.)

ऋच: सामानि छन्दांसि पुराणं यजुषा सह ।

उच्छिष्टाज् जज्ञिरे सर्वे दिवि देवा: दिवि श्रिता: ।

"From the leavings of the sacrifice sprung the Rich and Saman
verses, the metres, the Purana with the Yajush, and all the gods
who dwell in the sky."
6.   *The Vedas were produced from Agni, Vayu and Surya.*
The Chhandogya Upanishad contains the following :

प्रजापतिर् लोकान् अभ्यतपत् । तेषां तप्यमानानां रसान्

प्राबृहद् अग्निम् पृथिव्या: वायुम् अन्तरिक्षाद् आदित्यं

दिव: । स एतास् तिस्रो देवता: अभ्यतपत् । तासां

तप्यमानानां रसान् प्राबृहद् अग्नेर् ऋचो वायोर् यजूंषि

साम आदित्यात् । स एतां त्रयीं विद्याम् अभ्यतपत् ।

तस्यास् तप्यमानाया: रसान् प्राबृहद् भूर् इति ऋग्भ्यो

भुवर् इति यजुर्भ्य: स्वर् इति सामभ्य: ।

"Prajapati infused warmth into the worlds, and from them so
heated he drew forth their essences, *viz.* Agni (fire) from the earth,
Vayu (wind) from the air, and Surya (the sun) from the sky.   He
infused warmth into these three deities, and from them so heated
he drew forth their essences,—from Agni the Rich verses, from
Vayu the Yajush verses, and from Surya the Saman verses.   He
then infused heat into this triple science and from it so heated he
drew forth its essences,—from Rich verses the syllable *bhuh,* from
Yajush verses, *bhuvah,* and from Saman verses *svar.*"
Manu assigns to them the same origin.
7.   *The Vedas are the breathings of the Great Being.*
Satapatha Brahmana (xiv. 5, 4, 10) :

स यथा आर्द्रैधाग्नेर् अभ्याहितात् पृथग् धूमा: विनिश्चरन्ति

एवं वै अरे ऽ स्य महतो भूतस्य निश्वसितम् एतद् यद्

ऋग्वेदो यजुर्वेद: सामवेदो ऽ थर्वा ङ्गिरस: इतिहास:

पुराणं विद्या उपनिषद: श्लोका: सूत्राण्य अनुव्याख्यानानि
व्याख्यानानि अस्यैव एतानि सर्वाणि निश्वसितानि ।

"As from a fire made of moist wood various modifications of
smoke proceed, so is the breathing of this great Being the Rig-Veda,
the Yajur-Veda, the Sama-Veda, the Atharvangirases, the Itihasas,
Puranas, Science, the Upanishads, Slokas, aphorisms, comments of
different kinds—all these are his breathings."

8. *The Vedas were dug by the gods out of the Mind-Ocean.*
Satapatha Brahmana (vii. 5, 2, 52).

"समुद्रे त्वा सदने सादयामि" इति । मनो वै समुद्र: ।
मनसो वै समुद्राद् वाचा ऽ भ्या देवास् त्रयीं विद्यां निरखनन् ।

"Mind is the Ocean. From the mind-ocean, with speech for a
shovel, the gods dug out the triple Vedic science."

9. *The Vedas are the hair of Prajapati's beard.*
Taittiriya Brahmana, (iii. 39, 1).

प्रजापतेर् वै एतानि इमश्रूणि यद् वेद: ।

10. *Vach (speech) is the mother of the Vedas.*
Taittiriya Brahmana (ii. 8, 85).

वाग् अक्षरं प्रथमजा ऋतस्य वेदानां माता अमृतस्य नाभि: ।

"Vach is an imperishable thing and the first-born of the ceremonial, the mother of the Vedas, and the centre-point of immortality."

11. *The Vedas issued from the mouth of Brahma.*
The Bhagavata Purana (iii. 12, 34, and 37) says :

कदाचिद् ध्यायत: स्रष्टुर् वेदा: आसंश् चतुर्मुखात् ।
कथं स्रक्ष्याम्य अहं लोकान् समवेतान् यथापुरा ।
......ऋग् यजुस् सामाथर्वाख्यान् वेदान् पूर्वादिभिर् मुखै: ।
शस्त्रम् इज्यां स्तुतिस्तोमं प्रायश्चित्तं व्यधात् क्रमात् ।

"Once the Vedas sprung from the four-faced Creator, as he was
meditating how shall I create the aggregate worlds as before ? ...
He formed from his eastern and other mouths the Vedas called Rich,
Yajush, Saman and Atharvan, together with praise, sacrifice,
hymns, and expiation."

The Vishnu Purana gives the same explanation.

12. *The Vedas were produced from the Gayatri.*
Harivamsa, verse 11516.

ततो ऽ सृजद् वै त्रिपदां गायत्रीं वेदमातरम् ।

अकरोच् चैत्र चतुरो वेदान् गायत्रिसम्भवान् ।

After framing the world, Brahma " next created the Gayatri of
three lines, mother of the Vedas, and also the four Vedas which
sprung from the Gayatri."

13. *Sarasvati was the mother of the Vedas.*

Mahabharata, Santi-parva, verses 12, 920.

वेदानां मातरं पइय मत्स्थां देवीं सरस्तीम् ।

" Behold Sarasvati, mother of the Vedas, abiding in me."

14. *The Vedas are Vishnu.*

Vishnu Purana, iii. 3, 19 :

स ऋज्ञयः साममयः स चात्मा स यजुर्मयः ।

ऋग् यजुः साम सारात्मा स एवात्मा शरीरिणाम् ।

" He is composed of the Rich, of the Saman, of the Yajush ; he
is the soul, consisting of the essence of the Rich, Yajush and
Saman, he is the soul of embodied spirits."

**2. Opinions of the Rishis with regard to the origin of the Vedic
Hymns.**

The names of the authors of each hymn are preserved in the
Anukramani, or explanatory table of contents, which has been
handed down with the Veda itself, and of which the authority is
unquestioned. The names of the fathers of the writers are often
given as well as their own.

In later times when the Vedas were claimed to be eternal, it was
pretended that these writers were only the Rishis by whom the
hymns " were seen," or to whom they were communicated by
Brahma. Of this there is not the slightest proof.

*The Rishis claim to have written the hymns themselves, just as
a carpenter makes a car, &c.*

In some hymns they express no consciousness whatever of deriv-
ing assistance from any supernatural source.

Rig-Veda, i. 47, 2.

········कण्वासो वाम् ब्रह्म कृण्वन्ति अध्वरे तेषां सुशृणतं

हवम् ।

" The Kanvas make a prayer to you : hear well their invocation."

एवा ते हरियोजन्द् सुवृक्ति इन्द्र ब्रह्माणि गोतमासः अक्रन् ।

i. 64, 61. " Thus O Indra, yoker of steeds, have the Gotamas
made hymns for thee efficaciously."

एतानि वाम् अश्विना वर्धनानि ब्रह्मस्तोमं गृत्समदासः अक्रन् ।

ii. 39, 8.   "These magnifying prayers, [this] hymn, O Aśvins, the Gritsamadas have *made* for you."

........अथ प्रियं शूषम् इन्द्राय मन्म ब्रह्मकृतो बृहदुक्थाद् अवाचि ।

x. 54, 6.   " An acceptable and honorific hymn has been uttered to Indra by Vrihaduktha, maker of hymns."

सनायते गोतमः इन्द्र नव्यम् अतक्षद् ब्रह्महरियोजनाय इत्यादि ।

i. 62, 13.   " Nodhas, descendant of Gotama, fashioned this new hymn for [thee] Indra."

एतं ते स्तोमं तुविजातविप्रो रथं न धीरः स्वपा अतक्षम् ।

v. 2, 11.   "I, a sage, have fabricated this hymn for thee, O powerful [deity], as a skilful workman fashions a car."

अस्मै इद् उ स्तोमं संहिनोमि रथं न तष्टा इव इत्यादि ।

i. 61, 4.   " To him (Indra) I send forth a hymn, as a carpenter a car."

The above are only specimens of 57 extracts given by Dr. Muir.

Some hymns ask for or acknowledge divine assistance just as poets of all nations often do.   One poet says (Rig-Veda vi. 47, 10) :

इन्द्र मृळ महां जीवातुम् इच्छ चोदाय धियम् अयसो न धाराम् । यत् कच्चि अहं त्वायुर् इदं वदामि तज् जुषस्व कृद्धि मा देववन्तम् ।

" O god (Indra), have mercy, give me my daily bread ; sharpen my mind, like the edge of an iron instrument.   Whatever I now may utter, longing for thee, do thou accept it; give me divine protection."

. स प्रत्रथा कविवृधाः इन्द्रो वाकस्य वक्षणिः ।

viii. 52, 4.   " Indra was of old the promoter of the poet, and the augmenter of the song."

Instead of the hymns being eternal, or of infinite age, many of them are spoken of as *new*, while others are of ancient date.   The Rishis entertained the idea that the gods would be more highly gratified if their praises were celebrated in new, and perhaps more elaborate and beautiful compositions, than if older and possibly ruder, prayers had been repeated.

Dr. Muir gives 52 quotations under this head. Only a few need be given:

स न: स्तवान: आभर गायत्रेण नवीयसा रयिं वीरखतीम् इषम् ।

R. V. i. 12, 11. " Glorified by our newest hymn, do thou bring to us wealth and food with progeny."

तान् पूर्व्या निविदा हूमहे वयम् भगम् मित्रम् अदितिं दक्षम् अस्रिधम् इत्यादि ।

i. 89, 3. " We invoke with an ancient hymn Bhaga, Mitra, &c.

य: पूर्व्यामिर् उत नूतनामिर् गीर्भिर् वावृधे ग्रिणताम् ऋषीनाम् ।

vi. 44, 13. " He (Indra) who grew though the ancient and modern hymns of lauding Rishis."

आ सखाय: सुबर्दुघाम् धेनुम् अजव्वम् उपनव्य वच: ।

vi. 48, 11. " Friends, drive hither the milch cow with a new hymn."

नु नव्यसे नवीयसे सूक्ताय साधय पथ: प्रत्नवद् रोचय रुच: ।

ix. 9, 8. " Prepare (O Soma) the paths for our newest, most recent hymn ; and, as of old, cause the lights to shine."

Panini openly states the fact that there are old and new Brahmanas ; whereas, according to the doctrine of later times, the Brahmanas are neither old nor new, but eternal and of divine origin. He rests his opinion as to the difference of dates on the evidence of language.

One argument for the eternity of the Vedas is that sound is eternal. To any person of common sense the simple statement of this proof, is its refutation. The same argument would prove every book to be eternal.

3. **Internal Evidence of the Authorship of the Vedas.**—When a deed is produced in court which is affirmed to have been written many hundred years ago, there are often means of judging from the document itself as to its age. Suppose, for example, it contained the names of Warren Hastings or Hyder Ali, it could at once be known that it could not be older than last century. If it were asserted that these referred to other persons of the same name who lived long before or that they were prophecies, the conclusion would be that it was an attempt to support one falsehood by another. If the Vedas are eternal, why are the names of so many persons mentioned in them who lived in comparatively recent times ?

" The hymns of the Rig-Veda themselves supply us with numerous data by which we can judge of the circumstances to which they owed their origin, and of the manner in which they were created. They afford us very distinct indications of the locality in which they were composed. The Indus is the great river; the Ganges is only twice mentioned ; the Sarasvati was the eastern boundary.

" The hymns show us the Aryan tribes living in a state of warfare with surrounding enemies (some of them, probably, alien in race and language), and gradually, as we may infer, forcing their way onward to the east and south. They supply us with numerous specimens of the particular sorts of prayers, *viz.*, for protection and victory, which men so circumstanced would naturally address to the gods whom they worshipped, as well as of the more common supplications which men in general offer up for the various blessings which constitute the sum of human welfare."*

The following hymn to Indra, asking him to destroy the Dasyus, the aborigines, and give food and a camp with running water, bears internal evidence that it was composed at a time when the Aryans were invading India :

1. Glad thee : thy glory hath been quaffed, lord of bay steeds, as 'twere the bowl's enlivening mead.
   For thee the strong there is strong drink, mighty, with countless powers to win.
2. Let our strong drink, most excellent, exhilarating, come to thee, Victorious, Indra ! bringing gain, immortal, conquering in fight.
3. Thou, hero, winner of the spoil, urgest to speed the car of man. Burn, like a vessel with the flame, the lawless Dasyu, conqueror !
4. Empowered by thine own might, O sage, thou stolest Surya's chariot wheel.
   Thou barest Xutra with the steeds of Wind to Sushna as his death.
5. Most mighty is thy rapturous joy, most splendid is thine active power,
   Wherewith, foe-slaying, sending bliss, thou art supreme in gaining steeds.
6. As thou, O Indra, to the ancient singers wast ever joy, as water to the thirsty,
   So unto thee I sing this invocation. May we find food, a camp with running water.†

4. Conclusion as to the Authorship of the Vedas.

Quotations have been given from Hindu sacred books containing fourteen different opinions as to the origin of the Vedas. In opposition to these, the authorship of many of the hymns is distinctly claimed by persons whose names are given. The hymns themselves show that they were written when the Aryans were entering India, when they had not advanced much beyond the border, and were engaged in constant wars with the aborigines.

---

* Muir's *Sanskrit Texts*, Vol. III, 217, 218.
† Book I, Hymn 175. Translated by R. T. H. Griffith.

Victory in battle was often ascribed to the virtue of some hymn. Thus in the Rig-Veda, vii. 33, 3, " Did not Indra preserve Sudas in the battle of the ten kings through your prayer, O Vasishthas ?"

Such hymns were considered unfailing spells, and became the sacred war-songs of a whole tribe. They were handed down from father to son as the most valuable heirloom.

The legitimate conclusion is that the Vedic hymns were written by the authors whose names they bear, and that they are not eternal.

THE TIME WHEN THE VEDAS WERE COMPOSED.

The Cambridge Professor of Sanskrit says, " The very word history has no corresponding Indian expression. From the very earliest ages down to the present time, the Hindu mind seems never to have conceived such an idea as an authentic record of past facts based on evidence."

Hindu writers framed their chronology, like their geography and astronomy, out of their own heads. It was as easy to write a crore of years as a century, and the former was the more marvellous.

There is no date in India known with certainty till the time of Chandragupta, about 300 B. C., which was ascertained through the Greeks. The precise time when the Vedas were written cannot, therefore, be known with certainty. Indeed, their composition probably extended over several centuries. Max Müller estimates that they were composed, such as we now have them, about 1500 B. C.* In his *Hibbert Lectures*, (p. 340), he expresses the opinion that the Samhita (collection) was closed about 1000 B. C. The Brahmanas may date from 800 to 600 B. C. The Sutras may range from 600 to 200 B. C.

THE VEDAS AT FIRST HANDED DOWN BY TRADITION.

The oldest inscriptions in India are those of Asoka, the Buddhist king, who reigned from 259 to 222 B. C. Nearchus, the admiral of Alexander the Great, who sailed down the Indus (325 B. C.), mentions that the Indians wrote letters on cotton that had been well beaten together, " but that their laws were not written." Writing was used by merchants and others, but not for literary purposes.

Max Müller says; "There is not one single allusion in these hymns (of the Rig-Veda) to any thing connected with writing."

" Pure Brahmans never speak of their *granthas* or books. They speak of their *Veda*, which means ' knowledge.' They speak of their *Sruti*, which means what they have heard with their ears. They speak of *Smriti*, which means what their fathers have declared unto them. We meet with *Brahmanas*, i.e., the sayings of Brahmans ; with *Sutras*, i.e. the

---

* *India, What can it teach us ? p. 53.*

strings of rules; with *Vedangas, i.e.* the members of the Veda; with *Pravachanas, i.e.* preachings; with *Sastras, i.e.* teachings; with *Darsanas, i.e.* demonstrations; but we never meet with a book, or a volume, or a page."*

The Vedas, for many centuries, were handed down entirely by memory. The Guru recited a portion, and his pupils repeated it after him. There is a reference to this in the hymn about the frogs : " the one repeats the sounds of the other, as a pupil the words of his teacher."

The following account of the method of instruction is abridged from Max Müller :

" How then was the Veda learnt? It was learnt by every Brahman during 12 years of his studentship or Brahmacharya. This, according to Gautama, was the shortest period, sanctioned only for men who wanted to marry and to become Grihasthas. Brahmans who did not wish to marry were allowed to spend 48 years as students. The Prátisákhya gives us a glimpse into the lecture-rooms of the Brahmanic Colleges. 'The Guru,' it is said, ' who has himself formerly been a student, should make his pupils read. He himself takes his seat either to the east, or the north, or the north-east. If he has no more than one or two pupils, they sit at his right hand. If he has more, they place themselves according as there is room. They then embrace their master and say, ' Sir, read ! ' The master gravely says, 'Om,' *i.e.* 'Yes.' He then begins to say a *prasna* (a question), which consists of 3 verses. In order that no word may escape the attention of his pupils, he pronounces all with the high accent, and, repeats certain words twice, or he says ' so ' (*iti*) after these words.'

" It does not seem as if several pupils were allowed to recite together, for it is stated distinctly that the Guru first tells the verses to his pupil on the right, and that every pupil, after his task is finished, turns to the right, and walks round the tutor. This must occupy a long time every day, considering that a lecture consists of 60 or more *prasnas*, or of about 180 verses. The pupils are not dismissed till the lecture is finished. At the end of the lecture, the tutor, after the last half-verse is finished says, ' Sir,' the pupil replies ' Yes, sir.' He then repeats the proper verses and formulas, which have to be repeated at the end of every reading, embraces his tutor, and is allowed to withdraw." †

Years were spent in learning the books by rote. Some selected certain books; others different ones ; so that, in this way, hymns were preserved from generation to generation.

" A Brahman," says Max Müller, " is not only commanded to pass his apprenticeship in the house of his Guru, and to learn from his mouth all that a Brahman is bound to know, but the fiercest imprecations are uttered against all who would presume to acquire their knowledge from written sources. In the Mahabharata we read,

---

* *Ancient Sanskrit Literature*, pp. 497, 512.
† *Ancient Sanskrit Literature*, pp. 503, 506.

'Those who sell the Vedas, and even those who write them, those also who defile them, they shall go to hell.' Kumarila says, 'That knowledge of the truth is worthless which has been acquired from the Veda, if the Veda has not been rightly comprehended, if it has been learnt from writing, or been received from a Sudra.' "*

The Brahmans persuaded the people to regard the Vedas with such superstitious awe, that a mere error of pronunciation was supposed to mar their miraculous power.

Professor Whitney thus explains why it was forbidden to write the Vedas:

"It is not very difficult to conjecture a reason why the Brahmans may, while acquainted with letters, have rigorously ignored them, and interdicted their confessed use in connection with the sacred literature. The Brahman priesthood was originally a class only, which grew into a close hereditary caste on the strength, mainly, of their special possession of ancient hymns, and their knowledge of how these were to be employed with due effect in the various offices of religion. The hymns had unquestionably long been handed down by oral tradition from generation to generation, in the custody of certain families or branches of the caste ; each family having chiefly in charge the lyrics which its own ancestors had first sung. These were their most treasured possession, the source of their influence and authority. It might, then, naturally be feared that, if committed to the charge of written documents, when writing came to be known and practised among the more cultivated of the people—a class which could not be entirely restricted to the Brahmanic caste—and if suffered to be openly copied and circulated, passed from hand to hand, examined by profane eyes, the sacred texts would become the property of the nation at large, and the Brahmanic monopoly of them would be broken down. If, on the contrary, the old method of oral instruction alone in sacred things were rigidly kept up, if all open and general use of written texts were strictly forbidden, it is clear that the schools of Brahmanic theology would flourish, and remain the sole medium of transmission of the sacred knowledge, and that the doctrines and rites of religion would be kept under the control of the caste."†

The Druids, the ancient British priests, acted exactly in the same way. Cæsar says that some of them spent twenty years in learning a large number of verses by heart, and that they considered it wrong to commit them to writing.

The Vedas were first printed by European Scholars. Some of the editions have already been noticed.

SOCIAL LIFE IN VEDIC TIMES.

The ancestors of the Aryan nations, at a remote period, lived together, probably in the highlands of Central Asia. It was colder

---

* *Ancient Sanskrit Literature,* p. 502.
† *Oriental and Linguistic Studies,* pp. 86, 87.

than India, for they counted their years by winters. In the Vedic prayers for long life, the worshipper asks for a hundred winters (*himas*). Like the northern tribes, they laid great stress upon the *ashvamedha*, or horse-sacrifice. Compared with their neighbours, they had a white or fair complexion.

When the Aryans increased in number so that their original home was unable to support them, they emigrated in bands. Some went westward towards the setting sun, and peopled Europe. Others turned their faces eastwards, and advanced towards the valley of the Indus. They marched in a large body, with their families, their servants, their cattle. India was probably entered by the mountain passes near Peshawar. Rivers were forded at conveniently shallow places, or, if deep, they were crossed in boats.

The greater part of India was then covered with forest, with scattered villages and towns belonging to the aboriginal tribes, who were of a dark complexion, and spoke a strange language. The Aryas had the pride of race in an extravagant degree, showing great contempt and hatred of the other nations with whom they came in contact. They called the aborigines the "black skin," and as their noses were not so large as theirs, they were described as "goat-nosed" or "noseless." The aborigines were also called *Dasyus*, a word supposed to mean *enemies*. So many of them were enslaved, that the word *dasa* was afterwards applied to a servant.

Some of the Dasyus were like the Bhils or other wild tribes of India at present; others had a partial civilization. In several of the Vedic hymns the wealth of the Dasyus is mentioned, *e. g.* : "Subdue the might of the Dasa; may we through Indra divide his collected wealth." They had forts and cities. "Indra and Agni, by one effort together ye have shattered 90 forts belonging to the Dasyus." "O Indra, impetuous, thou didst shatter by thy bolt 99 cities for Puru."

The Aryans, as they advanced, gradually established themselves in the forests, fields, and villages of the aborigines. The latter contended as bravely as they could against their invaders. Their black complexion, barbarous habits, rude speech, and savage yells during their night attacks, made the Aryas, speak of them as demons.

The Aryans were the more powerful. The Dasyus were either driven before them or were reduced to slavery. The first great distinction in India was between the white and dark races, the conquerors and the conquered, the freeman and the slave. One of the earliest aboriginal tribes brought under subjection was called Sudras, and the name was extended to the whole race.

The war of invasion lasted for centuries, nor were the aborigines, as a whole, subjugated at any period.

The Indus is the great river of the Vedas. The name India was derived from Sindhu, the frontier river. The Ganges, literally the Go, Go, is only twice named in the Vedas. Several smaller rivers are mentioned. By degrees the Aryas spread eastward till they reached the Sarasvati, which was the boundary in Vedic times.

The state of society among the Aryans, as indicated by the hymns, will now be described.

Villages and Towns.—The invaders gradually settled in the Panjab. Villages were placed near watercourses, in positions favourable for pasturage and agriculture. The villages in some cases grew into towns, and these into cities. The houses in general, as at present, were built of mud. Some were of so frail a construction that they trembled as the Maruts passed, that is, when the fierce winds blew. In tracts bordering on the hills, where stone was abundant, that material was sometimes used. Indra is said to have demolished a hundred cities of stone. Iron cities or fortifications are mentioned.

Rajas and Headmen.—The country occupied by the Aryas was people by various tribes, and divided unto numerous principalities. Many names of kings occur in the Rig-Veda. Their meetings, whether friendly or hostile, are mentioned. Indra is represented as living in the society of his wives like a king. When Mitra is said to occupy a great palace with a thousand pillars and a thousand gates, we may suppose that this is but an exaggerated description of a royal residence such as the poet had seen. The kings or chiefs did not acknowledge one superior. Hence sometimes an Aryan leader fought with an Aryan leader.

Mention is made of *purpati*, lords of cities, and *gramani*, heads of villages.

Domestic Relations—In Vedic times the marriage of one wife seems to have been the rule. In some cases, from the *Svayamvara* ceremony, the bride could choose her husband. This shows that early marriage did not prevail. There was also more or less polygamy. A Rishi is said to have married in one day ten damsels. Two gods, the Ashvins, together took one wife. "Thus," says Dr. Rajendralala Mitra, "you have in the Rig-Veda, self-choice, polygamy, and polyandry." Widows were permitted to marry.

The general opinion of the female sex seems to have been that put into the mouth of Indra : "Indra himself hath said, The mind of woman brooks not discipline. Her intellect hath little weight." R. V. viii. 33, 17.

Dress.—References are made to well-dressed females and to well-made garments. From these passages and others relating to jewels, it may be gathered that considerable attention was already paid to personal decoration. The materials of the clothing were probably cotton and wool. The form of the garments was much the same as among the modern Hindus. A turban is mentioned. References to the needle and sewing suggest that made dresses were not unknown.

Food.—Foremost came the products of the cow. Butter and curds were essential at every meal. Fried grain, mixed with milk, was particularly relished. Barley and wheat were ground and baked into cakes. But *flesh* was considered *the best food*. The Satapatha Brahmana says : *Etad u ha vai paramam annádyam yan mámsam,** Indeed, the best food is flesh.

One of the most remarkable changes in Hindu customs since Vedic times is that with regard to the use of certain kinds of animal food. The late Dr. Rajendralala Mitra occupies the highest rank among Indian scholars, and he investigated the subject simply to give the real facts of the case. In his *Indo-Aryans*, he has a chapter headed, " Beef in Ancient India." It begins as follows :

The title of this paper will, doubtless, prove highly offensive to most of my countrymen; but the interest attached to the enquiry in connexion with the early social history of the Aryan race on this side of the Himalaya, will, I trust, plead my excuse. The idea of beef—the flesh of the earthly representative of the divine Bhagavati—as an article of food is so shocking to the Hindus, that thousands over thousands of the more orthodox among them never repeat the counterpart of the word in their vernaculars, and many and dire have been the sanguinary conflicts which the shedding of the blood of cows has caused in this country. And yet it would seem that there was a time when not only no compunctious visitings of conscience had a place in the mind of the people in slaughter- ing cattle—when not only the meat of that animal was actually esteemed a valuable aliment—when not only was it a mark of generous hospitality, as among the ancient Jews, to slaughter the ' fatted calf' in honor of respected guests,—but when a supply of beef was deemed an absolute necessity by pious Hindus in their journey from this to another world, and a cow was invariably killed to be burnt with the dead. To English- men, who are familiar with the present temper of the people on the sub- ject, and to a great many of the natives themselves, this remark may ap- pear startling ; but the authorities on which it is founded are so authentic and incontrovertible that they cannot, for a moment, be gainsaid."

Dr. R. Mitra quotes Colebrooke as follows : " It seems to have been anciently the custom to slay a cow on that occasion (the re- ception of a guest) and a guest was therefore called a *goghna*, or ' cow killer.' " In the " *Uttara-Rama-charitra* the venerable old poet and hermit Valmiki, when preparing to receive his brother sage Vasish- tha, the author of one of the original law books (Smritis) which regulates the religious life of the people, and a prominent character even in the Vedas, slaughtered a lot of calves expressly for the en- tertainment of his guests. Vasishtha, in his turn, likewise slaugh- tered the ' fatted calf' when entertaining Visvamitra, Janaka, Satananda, Jamadaguya, and other sages and friends."†

In the Rig-Veda, 1st Ashtaka, 4th Adhyaya, 29th Varga, the

---

* Quoted by Rev. F. Kittel on Sacrifice, p. 48.
† *Indo-Aryans*, Vol. I. pp. 356-358.

following prayer is addressed to Indra : "Hurl thy thunderbolt against this Vritra and sever his joints, as (butchers cut up) a cow, that the rains may issue from him."

The late Mr. Kunte, B. A., of Poona, author of the *Suddarshana Chintanika*, says in his Prize Essay on *The Vicissitudes of Aryan Civilization in India* : "Hospitality was the rule of life, and guests were received with great ceremony : cows were specially killed for them." (p. 196).

The ancient Aryans highly valued their cows, but they did not make gods of them and worship them like the Hindus at the present time.

The sacrifice of oxen and cows, *gomedha*, will be noticed under another head.

Intoxicating liquors are mentioned in the hymns. Nearly a whole Mandala of the Rig-Veda is devoted to the praise of the Soma juice. Wine or spirit *sura*, was also in use. "The earliest Brahman settlers," says Dr. R. Mitra, "were a spirit-drinking race, and indulged largely both in Soma beer and strong spirits. To their gods the most acceptable and grateful offering was Soma beer, and wine or spirit was publicly sold in shops for the use of the community. In the Rig-Veda Sanhita a hymn occurs which shows that wine was kept in leather bottles and freely sold to all comers. The *sura* of the *Sautramani* and the *Vajapaya* was no other than arrack, manufactured from rice meal. In the Ramayana the great sage Visvamitra is said to have been entertained with *maireya* and *sura* by his host Vasishtha. In the Mahabharata, the Yadavas are represented as extremely addicted to drinking.

Buddhism must have contributed much to check the spread of drunkenness in India, as it did in putting down the consumption of flesh meat ; but it was never equal to the task of suppressing it.*

Grades of Society.—The two great divisions of the people in Vedic times were the Aryans and the aborigines, afterwards called Sudras. The chief occupations of the Aryans were fighting and cultivating the soil. Those who fought gradually acquired influence and rank, and their leaders appear as Rajas. Those who did not share in the fighting were called Vis, Vaisyas, or householders.

At first any one might preside at a sacrifice. In the Vedas there are kings who composed their own hymns to the gods, Rajarishis, who united in their person the power both of king and priest. Visvamitra, the author of the Gayatri, was a Kshatriya. The Brahman was at first simply an assistant at sacrifices ; afterwards he became a *purohita*, or family priest, and thus acquired influence.

Fighting and cultivation were sometimes united. Mr. Kunte says : "The patriarch and his sons and perhaps grandsons quietly

---

* Abridged from the *Indo-Aryans*, Vol, I., pp.389—399.

cultivated their land, but when necessary, they mounted their horses, and, sword in hand, marched against their enemies. As yet the Brahmana was not afraid of wielding a sword, nor was the Kshatriya ashamed of tilling the land."*

Max Müller says : " The system of castes, in the ordinary sense of the word, did not exist doing the Vedic age. What we may call castes in the Veda is very different even from what we find in the laws of Manu, still more from what exists at the present day."†

Professions and Trades.—Dr. Wilson, in his *India Three Thousand Years Ago,* gives the following sketch of the Social Life of the Aryas.

" The Aryas, in the times of the Vedas, were principally a pastoral, though to a certain extent an agricultural, people. Their flocks and herds and their sheep, goats, cows, buffaloes, horses, camels, and teams of oxen, with the hump on their shoulders, are frequently mentioned, and made the subjects of supplication and thanksgiving both to gods and men. A daughter among them in the earliest times was designated *duhitri,* or milk-maid (the English word *daughter* has the same origin) ; and a *Gopa* and Gopal, or keeper of cattle, among them, came to mean a protector in general, no doubt from the owners or keepers of cows having great importance in the community."

" *Gotra,* cow-house, was applied to the fences erected to protect the herd from violenco or prevent the cattle from straying. The Brahman boasting of his sacred blood and divine generation speaks of the particular *gotra,* to which he belongs, little dreaming that the word is itself a testimony that the fathers of his race were herdsmen."‡

" That the Aryans were not, however, merely a nomadic people is very evident. As well as their enemies, they had their villages and towns as well as cattle-pens ; and many of the appliances, conveniences, luxuries, and vices, found in congregated masses of the human family. They knew the processes of spinning and weaving, on which they were doubtless principally dependent for their clothing. They were not strangers to the use of iron and to the crafts of the blacksmith, copper-smith, carpenter, and other artisans. They used hatchets in felling the trees of their forests, and they had planes for polishing the wood of their chariots. They constructed rims of iron to surround the wheels of their carts. They fabricated coats of mail, clubs, bows, arrows, javelins, swords or cleavers, and discs to carry on their warfare, to which they were sometimes called by the sound of the conch shell. They made cups, pitchers, and long and short ladles, for use, in their domestic economy and the worship of the gods. They employed professional barbers to cut off their hair. They knew how to turn the precious metals and stones to account ; for they had their golden earrings, golden bowls, and jewel necklaces. They had chariots of war from which they fought, and ordinary conveyances drawn by horses and bullocks; they had rider-bearing steeds and grooms to attend them. They had eunuchs in their community.

---

* *Vicissitudes of Aryan Civilization,* p. 191,
† *Hibbert Lectures,* p. 342.
‡ Rev. W. O. Simpson.

The daughters of vice were seen in their towns, and that, it would appear, with but a small accompaniment of shame; venders of spirits were also tolerated by them.   They constructed skiffs, boats, rafts and ships ; they engaged in traffic and merchandise in parts somewhat remote from their usual dwellings.   Occasional mention is made in their hymns of the ocean which they had probably reached by following the course of the Indus. Parties among them covetous of gain are represented as crowding the ocean in vessels on a voyage.   A naval expedition to a foreign country is alluded to as frustrated by a shipwreck." pp. 29—33, (abridged).

The caste prohibition against crossing the "black water," is not found in the Vedas, but was a later invention of the Brahmans to keep the Hindus better under their control.   While the Aryas were so far civilised, writing seems to have been unknown.   They had no books and newspapers like their descendants at present.

Amusements.—Gambling was very common among the early Indians, and numerous illustrations are derived from the practice. In one of the hymns a gambler apparently describes his own experience :

1.   The tumbling, air-born (products) of the great Vibhidaka tree (*i.e.*, the dice) delight me as they continue to roll on the dice board.   The exciting dice seem to me like a draught of the soma-plant growing on mount Mujavat.

7.   Hooking, piercing, deceitful, vexatious, delighting to torment, the dice dispense transient gifts, and again ruin the winner; they appear to the gambler covered with honey.

13.   Never play with dice : practice husbandry ; rejoice in thy pro-perty, esteeming it sufficient. x. 34.

"At a sacrifice," says Mr. Kunte, "the Kshatriya especially played at dice with his wife or wives and sons."

Dancers or actors afforded entertainment to the Aryans.   Ushas is said to display herself like a dancer who decks herself with ornaments.   Allusion is made to the living going forth to dance and laugh after a funeral.   Drums are mentioned, and a hymn in the Atharva Veda is addressed to that musical instrument.

Crime.—Thieves or robbers are mentioned in some passages as infesting the highways or stealing secretly.   The following occurs in a hymn to Pushan : "Drive away from our path the waylayer, the thief, the robber."   Another hymn says : " Men cry after him in battle as after a thief stealing clothes."   Cattle were often stolen. "The aborigines found it easy to revenge themselves on the invad-ing Aryas by driving away their cows.   But the Aryas were also prepared against the annoyance.   As soon as the herd of cows disappeared, hue and cry was raised, and sharp men who traced the track of a thief by observing foot-prints, set to work.   The thief was detected.   With shouts of thanks to Indra, the herd was recovered and driven home."

Wars.—In the Rig-Veda, wars are frequently mentioned.   Cows and horses were often the cause. Indra is thus addressed. " O mighty Indra, we call upon thee as we go fighting for cows and horses." Max Müller says, " Fighting among or for the cows (*Gosu-yudh*) is used in the Veda as a name for a warrior in general (I. 112, 122), and one of the most frequent words for battle is *gavisti*, literally ' striving for cows.' "

Mr. Kunte thus describes the mode of warfare :

" Different bands of the Aryas marched under their leaders, each having a banner of his own, singing of the prowess of their ancestors, and of the aid which Indra or Brihaspati granted them, and blowing conches. The leader drove in a war-chariot covered with cow-hides : some used the bow and arrows : others had darts. The army was divided into infantry and cavalry. Often did the leader of bands attack a town, and putting every inhabitant to the sword, occupied it. Sometimes they were content with large booty. Thus simultaneously, many Aryan leaders, independently of each other, waged war against the Dasas and Dasyus who were often able to make an impression upon the invaders."*

Disposal of the Dead.—While the Parsis and the ancestors of the Indian Aryans lived together in Central Asia, both probably exposed their dead to be devoured by vultures. After the Aryans came to India, burial was adopted. Dr. R. Mitra says : " This continued probably from their advent in India to about the 14th or 13th century B.C. Then came incremation with a subsequent burial of the ashes. This lasted from the 14th or 13th century B. C. to the early part of the Christian era, when the burial was altogether dispensed with, or substituted by consignment of the ashes to a river."†

THE GODS OF THE VEDAS.

The Religious Childhood of India.—Max Müller says :
" In the hymns of the Veda we see man left to himself to solve the riddle of this world. We see him crawling on like a creature of the earth with all the desires and weakness of his animal nature. Food, wealth, and power, a large family and a long life, are the theme of his daily prayers. But he begins to lift up his eyes. He stares at the tent of heaven, and asks who supports it ? He opens his eyes to the winds, and asks them whence and whither ? He is awakened from darkness and slumber by the light of the sun, and him whom his eyes cannot behold, and who seems to grant him the daily pittance of his existence, he calls ' his life, his breath, his brilliant Lord and Protector.' "‡

" The great majority of Vedic hymns consists in simple invocations of the fire, the water, the sky, the sun, and the stones, often under the same

---

* *Vicissitudes*, pp. 118, 119.   † *Indo-Aryans*, Vol. II, p. 120.
‡ *Chips*, Vol. I. 2nd Ed. p. 69.

names which afterwards became the proper names of Hindu deities, but
as yet nearly free from all that can be called irrational or mythological.
There is nothing irrational, nothing I mean we cannot enter into or
sympathise with, in people imploring the storms to cease, or the sky to rain,
or the sun to shine. I say there is nothing irrational in it, though perhaps it might be more accurate to say that there is nothing in it that
would surprise any body who is acquainted with the growth of human
reason, or, at all events, of childish reason. It does not matter how we
call the tendency of the childish mind to confound the manifestation with
that which manifests itself, effect with cause, act with agent....We all
know that it exists, and the youngest child who beats the chair against
which he has fallen, or who scolds his dog, or who sings, ' Rain, rain, go
to Spain,' can teach us that, however irrational all this may seem to us,
it is perfectly rational, natural, aye inevitable in the first periods, or the
childish age of the human mind.''*

The Devas.—Max Müller thus explains the origin and gradual
change in the meaning of this word :

" *Deva* meant originally bright, and nothing else. Meaning bright,
it was constantly used of the sky, the stars, the sun, the dawn, the day,
the spring, the rivers, the earth; and when a poet wished to speak of all
these by one and the same word—by what we should call a general term
—he called them all *Devas*. When that had been done, *Deva* did no
longer mean ' the Bright ones,' but the name comprehended all the
qualities which the sky and the sun and the dawn shared in common,
excluding only those that were peculiar to each.

" Here you see how, by the simplest process, the *Devas* the bright
ones, might become and did become the *Devas*, the heavenly, the kind,
the powerful, the invisible, the immortal—and in the end something very
like the *theoi* or *dii* of Greeks and Romans.''†

Origin and Immortality.—In the Vedas the gods are spoken of
as immortal, but they are not regarded in general as self-existent
beings ; in fact, their parentage, in most cases, is mentioned.

Very different accounts are given of the origin of the gods. In
many passages the gods are described as being the offspring of
Heaven and Earth. Ushas, the dawn, is characterised as the mother
of the gods ; Brahmanaspati is called their father ; Soma is said to
be the generator of Heaven, Earth, Agni, Surya, Indra, and Vishnu.
Some of the gods are spoken of as being fathers and others as being
sons. The most extraordinary feat is ascribed to Indra : " Thou
hast indeed begotten thy father and mother together from thy own
body." As Max Müller remarks, " A god who once could do that,
was no doubt capable of anything afterwards."

" The same god is sometimes represented as supreme, sometimes,
as equal, sometimes as inferior to others. There are as yet no
genealogies, no settled marriages between gods and goddesses.

---

* *India : What can it teach us?* pp. 108, 109.
† *Ibid.* pp. 218, 219.

The father is sometimes the son, the brother is the husband, and she who in one hymn is the mother, is in another the wife."

In some places Savitri and Agni are said to have conferred immortality on the gods: elsewhere it is said that the gods drink soma to obtain the same gift; but it is generally taught that they obtained their divine rank through austerities. The gods originally were all alike in power; but three of them desired to be superior to the rest; *viz.* Agni, Indra, and Surya. They continued to offer sacrifices for this purpose until it was obtained.

The immortality of the gods is only relative. They are supposed to be subject to the same law of dissolution as other beings. "Many thousands of Indras and of other gods have, through time, passed away in every mundane age." The gods both desire and are capable of *mukti*, liberation from future births.

Some of the principal gods will now be described.

Dyaus and Prithivi.

Dyaus, says Max Müller, is one of the oldest gods, not only of the Vedic Aryans, but of the whole Aryan race. He was worshipped before a word of Sanskrit was spoken in India, or a word of Greek in Greece.* He adds:

"If I were asked what I consider the most important discovery which has been made during the nineteenth century with respect to the ancient history of mankind, I should answer by the following short line:

Sanskrit DYAUSH-PITAR = Greek ΖΕΥΣΠΑΤΗΡ(ZEUS PATER) = Latin JUPITER = Old Norse TYR.

"Think what this equation implies! It implies not only that our own ancestors and the ancestors of Homer and Cicero (the Greeks and Romans) spoke the same language as the people of India—this is a discovery which, however incredible it sounded at first, has long ceased to cause any surprise—but it implies and proves that they all had once the same faith, and worshipped for a time the same supreme Deity under exactly the same name—a name which meant Heaven-Father."†

"Those simple-hearted forefathers of ours," says C. Kingsley, "looked round upon the earth and said within themselves, ' Where is the All-father, if All-father there be ? Not in this earth; for it will perish. Nor in the sun, moon, or stars; for they will perish too. Where is He who abideth for ever ?'

"Then they lifted up their eyes, and saw, as they thought, beyond sun, and moon, and stars, and all which changes and will change, the clear blue sky, the boundless firmament of heaven.

"That never changed; that was always the same. The clouds and storms rolled far below it, and all the bustle of this noisy world; but there the sky was still, as bright and calm as ever. The All-father must

---

* *Hibbert Lectures,* pp. 276, 228.
† *Nineteenth Century,* Oct. 1885.

be there, unchangeable in the unchanging heaven ; bright and pure, and boundless like the heavens ; and, like the heavens too, silent and far off."

" ' And how,' says Max Müller, " did they call that All-father ?

" Five thousand years ago, or, it may be earlier, the Aryans speaking as yet neither Sanskrit, Greek, nor Latin, called him *Dyupatar*, Heaven-father.

" Four thousand years ago, or, it may be earlier, the Aryans who had travelled southward to the rivers of the Punjab called him *Dyaush-pita*, Heaven-father.

" Three thousand years ago, or, it may be earlier, the Aryans on the shores of the Hellespont, called him Ζεὺς πατήρ, Heaven-father.

"Two thousand years ago, the Aryans of Italy looked up to that bright heaven above, and called it *Ju piter*, Heaven-father.

" And a thousand years ago the same Heaven-father and All-father was invoked in the dark forests of Germany by the Teutonic Aryans, and his old name of *Tiu* or *Zio* was then heard perhaps for the last time.

" If we want a name for the invisible, the infinite, that surrounds us on every side, the unknown, the true Self of the world, and the true self of ourselves—we, too, feeling once more like children, kneeling in a small dark room, can hardly find a better name than : ' Our Father, which art in Heaven.' "*

There are clear traces in some of the hymns of the Rig-Veda that at one time Dyaus, the sky, was the supreme deity.

At an early period, however, the earth, under the name of Prithivi, was associated with Dyaus. The Aitareya Brahmana mentions their marriage : " The gods then brought the two (Heaven and Earth) together, and when they came together, they performed a wedding of the gods."

The ancient Greeks had the same ideas. The earth is addressed as, " Mother of gods, the wife of the starry Heaven." Their marriage, too, is described.

The Hindus thought their gods were much like themselves ; so heaven and earth were called the father and mother of the gods.

In the hymns there are various speculations about the origin of Dyaus and Prithivi. A perplexed poet enquires, " Which of these two was the first, and which the last ? How have they been produced ? Sages, who knows ?"

In the Veda Dyaus is chiefly invoked in connection with the Earth. " He is invoked by himself also, but he is a vanishing god, and his place is taken in most of the Vedic poems by the younger and more active god, Indra."†

ADITI AND THE ADITYAS.

ADITI, from *a*, not, and *diti*, bound, means what is boundless, infinite, eternal. Max Müller considers it as meaning what is

---

* *Hibbert Lectures*, pp. 216, 217.
† *India : What can it teach us ?* p. 195.

beyond the earth, the sky, the sun, and the dawn. Muir says,
"Perhaps Aditi may best be regarded as a personification of universal, all-embracing Nature." In Rig-Veda, i. 89, 10, she is thus described: "Aditi is the sky; Aditi is the air; Aditi is the mother, and
father, and son; Aditi is all the gods and the five tribes; Aditi is
whatever has been born; Aditi is whatever shall be born." In
Rig-Veda, x, 72, 4. It is said, "Daksha sprang from Aditi, and
Aditi from Daksha."

Aditi is not the subject of any separate hymn, but she is supplicated for blessings in children and cattle, for protection, and for
forgiveness. Whitney says, "This personification never went far
enough to entitle her fairly to a place in the list of Vedic divinities."

The Adityas, the sons of Aditi, are more frequently mentioned
than their mother. In Rig-Veda, ii. 27, 1, six are mentioned:
Mitra, Aryaman, Bhaga, Varuna, Daksha, and Amsa. In x, 72, 8,
9, it is said that Aditi had 8 sons, of whom she presented only 7 to
the gods, casting out Marthanda, the eighth, though she is said to
have afterwards brought him forward. Varuna was considered the
chief.

In after times the Adityas were increased to 12, as representing
the sun in the twelve months of the year.

VARUNA.

Varuna, like Dyaus, is another representative of the highest
heaven, as encompassing all things. The name is derived from
var, to cover, and is identical with the Greek *Ouranos*, heaven.

"Varuna," says the Rig-Veda, "stemmed asunder the wide
firmaments; he lifted on high the bright and glorious heaven; he
stretched out apart the starry sky and the earth." In the
Atharva-Veda, illimitable knowledge is ascribed to him:

"Varuna, the great lord of these worlds, sees as if he were near. If
a man stands or walks or hides, if he goes to lie down or to get up, what
two people sitting together whisper to each other, King Varuna knows
it; he is there as the third. This earth, too, belongs to Varuna, the
King, and this wide sky with its ends far apart. The two seas (the
sky and the ocean) are Varuna's loins; he is also curtained in this small
drop of water. He who should flee far beyond the sky, even he would
not be rid of Varuna, the King. His spies proceed from heaven towards
this world; with thousand eyes they overlook this earth. King Varuna
sees all this, what is between heaven and earth, and what is beyond.
He has counted the twinklings of the eyes of men. As a player throws
down the dice, he settles all things." ix. 16.

Varuna, says Max Müller, "is one of the most interesting creations of the Hindu mind, because though we can still perceive the
physical background from which he rises, the vast, starry, brilliant
expanse above, his features more than those of any of the Vedic

gods have been completely transfigured; and he stands before us
as a god who watches over the world, punishes the evil doer, and
even forgives the sins of those who implore his pardon."*

Varuna is the only Vedic deity to whom a high moral character
is attributed. Whitney says:

" While in hymns to the other divinities long life, wealth, power are
the objects commonly prayed for, of the Adityas is craved purity, forgiveness of sin, freedom from its further commission. To them are
offered humble confessions of guilt and repentance. It is a sore grief to
the poets to know that man daily transgresses Varuna's commands;
they acknowledge that without his aid they are not masters of a single
moment; they fly to him for refuge from evil, expressing at the same
time all confidence that their prayers will be heard and granted." †

Mitra is generally associated with Varuna. He is a form of the
sun, representing day, while Varuna denotes night. They together
uphold and rule the earth and sky, guard the world, encourage
religion, and with their nooses seize the guilty.

In the Puranas, Varuna is stripped of all his majestic attributes, and represented as a mere god of the ocean.

INDRA.

" In Sanskrit," says Max Müller, " the drops of rain are called
ind-u, masculine themselves; he who sends them is called *Ind-ra*,
the rainer, the irrigator, and in the Veda the name of the principal
deity worshipped by the Aryan settlers in India.‡ The name of
Indra is peculiar to India, and must have been formed after the
separation of the great Aryan family had taken place, for we find it
neither in Greek, nor in Latin, nor in German."§

The gods of the Hindus are somewhat like kings who reign for
a time, and then give place to successors. The first struggle for
supremacy in the Hindu pantheon is between Heaven and Earth
and Indra. Max Müller says:

" When we see those two giant spectres of Heaven and Earth on the
backguard of the Vedic religion, exerting their influence for a time, and
then vanishing before the light of younger and more active gods, we learn
a lesson which it is well to learn, and which we can hardly learn anywhere else—the lesson *how gods were made and unmade*,—how the
Beyond or the Infinite was named by different names in order to bring
it near to the mind of man, to make it for a time comprehensible, until,
when name after name had proved of no avail, a nameless, God was
felt to answer best the restless cravings of the human heart."‖

Dyaus and Varuna, representing the bright blue sky or the
starry heavens, were the highest deities of the Aryans in their

---

* *India : What can it Teach us?* p. 195.
† *Oriental and Linguistic Studies*, 1st Ser. p. 43.
‡ *Hibbert Lectures*, p. 212.   § *India: What can it Teach us?* p. 182.
‖ *India: What can it Teach us?* p. 163.

original home. In India they came to a country where for months together the earth is exposed to the scorching rays of the sun, sometimes without a single shower, so that it is impossible for the fields to be ploughed or the seed to be sown. It is not surprising, therefore, that a god in whose hands are the thunder and lightning, at whose command the refreshing showers fall to render the earth fruitful, should most frequently be appealed to, and that the most laudatory songs should be addressed to him. Indra is the most popular deity of the Vedas.

"In the burning months of the hot season," says Dr. Mullens, "the ancient Aryans turn to Indra. It is Vritra (Drought) his enemy and theirs, that withholds the refreshing showers for which all eyes long. And when at length along the western horizon the vapours thicken, and the desired storm bursts in grandeur—when they see the blinding dust whirling in lofty columns on its mighty march, and the swift sand flies low along the ground—when they see the blue flashes which pierce the clouds, and hear the crashing peals of the awful thunder, it is Indra and his Maruts who are fighting the celestial battle on their behalf. And when the driving rain pours from the heavy clouds, and the earth drinks it in, all nature renews its life, fresh verdure clothes the fields, and the birds carol their joyous songs, it is to the mighty Indra, the conqueror, that their thanks are paid, and from him that fresh blessings are humbly craved."*

Sometimes the clouds are represented under the figure of herds of cows stolen by the demons, and hidden in the hollows of the mountains. Indra finds them, splits the caverns with his bolt, and they are again set at liberty, and their teats shower down rain.

Different accounts are given of his parentage. In one hymn Ekashtaka is said to be his mother; in another he is said to have sprung from the mouth of Purusha; while a third makes him to have been generated by Soma. According to the Mahabharata, Indra is one of the sons of Kasyapa.

Indra is exalted above Dyaus. "The divine Dyaus bowed before Indra, before Indra the great Earth bowed with her wide spaces." "At the birth of thy splendour, Dyaus trembled, the Earth trembled for fear of thy anger."

Indra drives a golden chariot drawn by two yellow horses; the thunderbolt is his weapon, the rainbow is his bow; the Maruts, or storm-winds, are his companions. Like other Hindu gods, he is provided with a wife, called Indrani.

In the Vedas, Indra is characterised by his fondness for war and the intoxicating soma juice.

Even as an infant, Indra is said to have manifested his warlike tendencies. "As soon as he was born, the slayer of Vritra grasped his arrow, and asked his mother, Who are they that are

---

* *Hindu Philosophy*, pp. 19, 20.

renowned as fierce warriors?" "His love of the soma juice was shown as early." "On the day that thou wast born, thou didst, from love of it, drink the mountain-grown juice of the soma plant." A frequent epithet of Indra is *somapā*, soma-drinker. In the hymns he is invited by his worshippers to drink like "a thirsty stag" or like a "bull roaming in a waterless waste"; to fill his belly by copious potations. His inebriety is said to be "most intense." The sensations of the god after drinking the soma are described: "The draughts which I have drunk impel me like violent blasts. The five tribes of men appear to me not even as a mote: I have quaffed the soma. The two worlds do not equal one half of me: I have quaffed the soma. One-half of me is in the sky, and I have drawn the other down. I have quaffed the soma." Rig-Veda, x. 119.

Thus exhilarated, Indra goes forth to war. Some of his feats are thus described in the Rig-Veda, I. 53 :

"6. These draughts inspired thee, O lord of the brave, these were vigour, these libations, in battles, when for the sake of the poet, the sacrificer, thou struckest down irresistibly ten thousands of enemies.

"7. From battle to battle thou advancest bravely, from town to town thou destroyest all this with might, when thou, Indra, with Nami as thy friend, struckest down from afar the deceiver Namuchi."

While the Aryans were engaged in fierce contests with the aborigines, Indra held the highest rank. When the latter had been reduced to subjection, Indra gave place to other deities. In the Puranas he reigns over Swarga; but is often in fear lest he should be dethroned. Many instances are recorded of his adultery. According to the Mahabharata, he seduced Ahalya, the wife of Gautama, his spiritual teacher. By the curse of the sage, Indra's body was impressed by a thousand marks, so that he was called Sa-yoni; but these marks were afterwards changed to eyes, and he is hence called 'the thousand-eyed.'

AGNI.

Agni is the god of fire, the Latin *ignis*, fire. He is one of the most prominent deities of the Rig-Veda, as far more hymns are addressed to him than to any other divinity except Indra.

Fire is very necessary for human existence. It enables food to be cooked; it gives the power of carrying on work at night; in cold climates it preserves people from being frozen to death. In early times, when lucifer matches were unknown, fire was looked upon with somewhat like religious awe. The production of fire by the friction of wood or its sudden descent from the sky in the form of lightning, seemed as marvellous as the birth of a child. In the hymns of the Vedas fire is praised and worshipped as the best and kindest of the gods, the only god who had come down from heaven

to live on earth, the friend of man, the messenger of the gods, the
mediator between gods and men, the immortal among mortals. He,
it is said, protects the settlements of the Aryans, and frightens
away the "black-skinned enemies."

Soon, however, fire was conceived by the Vedic poets under the
more general character of light and warmth, and then the presence
of Agni was perceived, not only on the hearth and the altar, but in
the Dawn, in the Sun, and in the world beyond the Sun, while at
the same time his power was recognised as ripening, or as they
called it, as cooking, the fruits of the earth, and as supporting also
the warmth and the life of the human body. From that point of
view Agni, like other powers, rose to the rank of a Supreme God.
He is said to have stretched out heaven and earth—naturally,
because without his light heaven and earth would have been invisible and undistinguishable. The next poet says that Agni held
heaven aloft by his light, that he kept the two worlds asunder ; and
in the end Agni is said to be the progenitor and father of heaven
and earth, and the maker of all that flies, or walks, or stands, or
moves on earth.*

Various accounts are given of the origin of Agni. He is said to
be a son of Dyaus and Prithivi ; he is called the eldest son of
Brahma, and is then named Abhimani ; he is reckoned amongst the
children of Kasyapa and Aditi, and hence one of the Adityas. In
the later writings he is described as a son of Angiras, king of the
Pitris. He is occasionally identified with other gods and goddesses,
as Indra, Vishnu, Varuna, Rudra, Sarasvati, &c. "All gods," it
is said, "are comprehended in him."

Agni was worshipped in the fire kindled in the morning. The
whole family gathered around it, regarding it with love and awe, as
at once a friend and a priest. It was a visible god conveying the
oblation of mortals to all gods. His nobleness was extolled, as
though a god he deigned to sit in the very dwellings of men. At
sunset, Agni is the only divinity left on earth to protect mortals
till the following dawn ; his beams then shine abroad, and dispel
the demons of darkness.

Agni's proper offering is ghee. When this is sprinkled into the
flame, it mounts higher and glows more fiercely ; the god has
devoured the gift, and thus testifies his satisfaction and pleasure.
Several of his epithets describe his fondness for butter. He is
butter-fed, butter-formed, butter-haired, butter-backed, &c. He
himself exclaims, "butter is my eye." The poor man who cannot
offer ghee, brings a few pieces of wood to feed the fire.

As destroyer of the Rakshas, Agni assumes a different character. He is represented in a form as hideous as the beings he is invoked to devour. He sharpens his two iron tusks, puts his enemies

---

* *India : What can it Teach us ?* pp. 176, 177.

into his mouth, and swallows them. He heats the edges of his shafts and sends them into the hearts of the Rakshas.

The first hymn of the Rig-Veda is addressed to Agni, and all the other books, except two, begin with hymns to him.

PARJANYA.

Parjanya was an older Aryan god than Indra. The latter, as already mentioned, as peculiar to India. Two Aryan languages have carried the name of Parjanya to the shores of the Baltic. His functions were somewhat similar to those of India. He is the god of thunder-storms and rain, the generator and nourisher of plants and living creatures.

Three hymns are addressed to Parjanya in the Rig-Veda. In some passages he appears as a supreme god. He is called father, like Dyaus, the sky. He is called *asura*, the living or life-giving god, a name peculiar to the oldest and greatest gods. One poet says, " He rules as god over the whole world ; all creatures rest in him ; he is the life (âtmâ) of all that moves and rests (vii. 101. 6). In other hymns he is represented as performing his office, namely that of sending rain upon the earth, under the control of Mitra and Varuna, who are then considered as the highest lords, the mightiest rulers of heaven and earth." In other verses Parjanya appears simply as a name of cloud or rain.* In later times the name is applied to Indra.

VAYU.

The second hymn of the Rig-Veda is addressed to *Vayu*, the blower. He is also called *Vata*, the blast. There are not many hymns belonging to him. In the Purusha sukta, Vayu is said to have sprung from the breath of Purusha, and in another hymn he is called the son-in-law of Tvastri. He is often associated with Indra, and rides in the same chariot with him, Indra being the charioteer. One hymn, referring to both, says: "Drink of the soma, for to you twain belongs the right to take the first draught." He is called the king of the whole world, the first born, the breath of the gods, the germ of the whole world, whose voices we hear, though we can never see him. Rig-Veda, x, 168.

In later books Hanuman is said to be his son.

THE MARUTS, OR STORM GODS.

" The Maruts, literally the Smashers, are clearly the representatives of such storms as are known in India when the air is darkened by dust and clouds, when in a moment the trees are

---

* *India : What can it Teach us ?* pp. 184, 185.

SOLAR DEITIES.

39

stripped of their foliage, their branches shivered, their stems
snapped, when the earth seems to reel and the mountains to shake,
and the rivers are lashed into foam and fury. Then the poet sees
the Maruts approaching with golden helmets, with spotted skins on
their shoulders, brandishing golden spears, whirling their axes,
shooting fiery arrows, and cracking their whips amidst thunder
and lightning. They are the comrades of India, sometimes like
Indra, the sons of Dyaus, or the sky, but also the sons of another
terrible god, called Rudra, or the Howler, a fighting god, to
whom many hymns are addressed. In him a new character is
evolved, that of a healer and saviour,—a very natural transition in
India, where nothing is so powerful for dispelling miasmas, restoring
health, and imparting fresh vigour to man and beast, as a thunder-
storm, following after weeks of heat and drought."*

The number of them in one place is said to be thrice sixty, and
in another only twenty-seven. Different parentage is also assigned
to them. They are sons of Rudra, sons and brothers of Indra,
sons of the ocean, sons of heaven, sons of earth.

The Hymns to the Maruts, with copious notes, have been
translated by Max Müller.

SOLAR DEITIES.

With reference to light, Whitney says :

"The very prominent part which this element has played in giving
form to the earliest religions of all nations is well known ; that of the
Indian forms no exception ; he even manifests a peculiar sensitiveness to
the blessings of the light, and a peculiar abhorrence of darkness. The
former is to him life, motion, happiness, breath ; the latter death, helpless-
ness, evil, the time and abode of demons. Accordingly, the phenomena
of the night, moon and stars, he almost ignores ; the one makes no figure
at all in his religion, the others are but rarely even alluded to."†

Max Müller thus shows how the sun was gradually developed
into a supreme being :

"The first step leads us from the mere light of the sun to that light
which in the morning wakes man from sleep, and seems to give new life,
not only to man, but to the whole of nature. He who wakes us in
the morning, who recalls the whole of nature to new life, is soon called
' the giver of daily life.'

"Secondly, by another and bolder step, the giver of daily light and life,
becomes the giver of light and life in general. He who brings light and
life to-day, is the same who brought life and light in the first of days.
As light is the beginning of the day, so light was the beginning of crea-

---

* *India : What can it Teach us ?* pp. 180, 181.
† *Oriental and Linguistic Studies,* 1st Ser p. 37.

tion, and the sun, from being a mere light-bringer or life-giver, becomes a creator, then soon also a ruler of the world.

"Thirdly, as driving away the dreaded darkness of the night, and like-wise as fertilizing the earth, the sun is conceived as a defender and kind protector of all living things.

"Fourthly as the sun sees everything and knows everything, he is asked to forget and forgive what he alone knows."[*]

MITRA.

In the Vedas Mitra is generally associated with Varuna: he is seldom mentioned alone. Sayana says, " Mitra is the god who presides over the day, and Varuna is the god who rules over the night." Mitra is the same as the Persian Mithra. He must have been worshipped before the Persian and Indian branches of the Aryans separated. He is a form of the sun. Mitra and Varuna have the same attributes. In hymn iii. 59, Mitra is addressed alone. The following are a few quotations : " Mitra uttering his voice calls men to activity. Mitra sustains the earth and the sky. Mitra with unwinking eye beholds (all) creatures. Mitra, son of Aditi, may the mortal who worships thee with sacred rites have food. He who is protected by thee is neither slain nor conquered."

SURYA.

Surya, the sun god, is in one hymn styled the son of Dyaus ; in another he is called the son of Aditi. Ushas is in one place said to be his wife, while in another she is described as his mother. He moves in a car which is sometimes said to be drawn by one and sometimes by seven fleet and ruddy horses. Pushan goes as his messenger with his golden ships, which sail in the aërial ocean. Surya is the preserver and soul of all things stationary and moving ; enlivened by him men perform their work; he is far-seeing, all-seeing, beholds all creatures, and the good and bad deeds of mortals. By his greatness he is the divine leader of the gods. The epithets archi-tect of the universe and possessed of all divine attributes, are applied to him.

In many passages, however, the dependent position of Surya is asserted. He is said to have been caused to shine by Indra, who also once carried off one of the wheels of his chariot. Mitra and Varuna sometimes conceal him by clouds and rain.[†]

In the Ramayana, Sanjna, the daughter of Visvakarma, is the wife of Surya. As his brightness was too great for his wife, Visvakarma cut part of him away. The fragments fell blazing to the earth, and from them Visvakarma formed the discus of Vishnu, the trident of Siva, and the weapons of the other gods !

---

[*] *Hibbert Lectures*, pp. 265, 266.
[†] Abridged from Muir's *Sanskrit Texts*, Vol. V. pp. 156-159.

SAVITRI.

Savitri is sometimes distinguished from Surya, sometimes identified with him. The two names are sometimes employed indiscriminately to devote the same deity. Sayana says that the sun before his rising is called Savitri, and Surya from his rising to his setting. The name is supposed to mean *Generator*.

Savitri is pre-eminently the golden deity, being golden-eyed, golden-handed, golden-tongued, the yellow-haired. Luminous in his aspect, he ascends a golden car, drawn by radiant, brown, white-footed horses, and beholding all creatures, he pursues an ascending and descending path. He is lord of all desirable things and sends blessings from the sky, from the atmosphere, and the earth.*

The worship of Savitri has continued to present time. It is to him that the Gayatri is addressed at his rising by every devout Brahman. This short verse is supposed to exert magical powers. It is as follows:

Tat Savitur varenyam bhargo devasya dhímohi |
    dhiyo yo nah prachodayát | iii. 62, 10.

It has been variously translated. Griffith renders it thus :

" May we attain that excellent glory of Savitar the god :
    So may he stimulate our prayers."

Wilson says that it was " in its original use, a simple invocation of the sun to shed a benignant influence upon the customary offices of worship." The Skanda Purana thus extols it :

" Nothing in the Vedas is superior to the Gayatri. No invocation is equal to the Gayatri, as no city is equal to Kasi. The Gayatri is the mother of the Vedas and of Brahmans. By repeating it a man is saved. What is there indeed that cannot be effected by the Gayatri? For the Gayatri is Vishnu, Brahma, and Siva and the three Vedas."

VISHNU.

Vishnu is the only one of the great gods of the Hindu triad who makes his appearance under the same name in the Veda. In the Veda, however, he is not in the first rank of gods. He is the sun in his three stations of rise, zenith, and setting. This the Vedic poets conceive of as striding through heaven at three steps. This is Vishnu's great deed, which in all his hymns is sung to his praise. It constitutes the only peculiar trait belonging to him. Concerning these steps it is said that two of them are near the habitation of men. The third none can attain, not even the bird in its flight. He took them for the benefit of mortals, that all might live safe and happy under them. The middle station, the zenith, is called Vishnu's place.†

---

* Abridged from Muir's *Sanskrit Texts*, Vol. V. pp. 162-170.
† Whitney's *Oriental and Linguistic Studies* 1st Ser. pp. 41, 42.

In Manu the name Vishnu is mentioned, but not as that of a great deity. In the Mahabharata and Puranas, he becomes the second member of the triad, the preserving power, the all-pervading spirit.

Pushan.

The word Pushan comes from the root *push* ; the primary idea is that of nourisher. He is the protector and nourisher of cattle (*pashupā*). He was originally the sun as viewed by shepherds. As a cowherd he carries an ox goad, and he is drawn by goats. He is a guide on roads and journeys. He is called the lover of his sister Suryā, conceived as a female deity.

"Though in one place" says Max Müller, "he is spoken of as only higher than mortals and equal to the gods, he is in other places called the lord of all that rests and moves. Like all solar deities, he sees everything, and like Savitri he is also supposed to conduct the souls of the departed to the regions of the blessed."[*]

In later books he is represented as toothless. He feeds upon a kind of conjee, and the offerings made to him are of ground materials. The cause of his being toothless is variously explained. One account is that at the Daksha sacrifice Rudra knocked out his teeth while he was eating the purodasa offering.

Ushas.

This goddess corresponds to the eos of the Greeks, and to the Aurora of the Romans. The hymns specially addressed to her are about in 20 in number :

"The worship of the Indian," says Whitney, " commenced at day-break ; Ushas, the dawn, is the earliest object of his morning songs. The promise of the day is hailed with overflowing and inspiring joy ; the feeling of relief as the burden of darkness is lifted off the world, and the freedom and cheerfulness of the day commence again, prompts to truly poetic strains, and the songs to Ushas are among the finest in the Veda. She is addressed as a virgin in glittering robes, who chases away the darkness, or to whom her sister might willingly yields her domain ; who prepares a path for the sun; is the signal of the sacrifice, rouses all beings from slumber, gives sight to the darkened ; and power of motion to the prostrate and helpless. In the midst of such gladsome greetings, however, the poet is reminded, by the thought of the many dawns that have thus shown upon the earth, and the many that are to follow them, of those, who, having witnessed the former ones are now passed away, and of those who shall welcome them who he is no more. So he is led to mournful reflections on the wasting away of life, as one day after another is subtracted from the time allotted to each mortal."[†]

Hibbert Lectures, pp. 263, 269.
† *Oriental and Linguistic Studies*. 1st Series. pp. 37, 38.

Ushas is represented as the daughter of heaven and loved by the sun, but vanishing before him at the very moment when he tries to embrace her with his golden rays. Agni and the gods generally are described as waking from sleep with Ushas.

ASVINS.

The name of these deities has long been a riddle. Max Müller says, " Why they were called Asvinau (dual) horsemen has never been explained; but we are probably not very far wrong if we interpret horsemen as the riders or representatives of the heavenly horse or the sun."* Roth says, " They are the earliest bringers of light in the morning sky, who in their chariot hasten onwards before the Dawn, and prepare the way for her."

They are ever young and handsome, bright, swift as falcons, and possessed of many forms. They ride in a golden car drawn by horses or birds. As personifications of the morning twilight, they are said to be children of the sun by a nymph who concealed herself in the form of a mare; hence she was called *Asvini*, and her sons Asvins. But inasmuch as they precede the rise of the sun, they are called his parents in his form Pushan. Their attributes are numerous, but relate mostly to youth and beauty, light and speed, duality, the curative power and active benevolence. They were the physicians of Swarga.†

TVASHTRI.

Tvashtri is the Vulcan of the Romans. He is the most skilful of workmen, who is versed in all wonderful contrivances. He sharpens and carries the great iron axe, and forges the thunderbolts of Indra. He forms husband and wife for each other. He has given to the heaven and earth and to all things their form. He is master of the universe, the first-born protector and leader. He is the bestower of blessings, and is possessed of abundant wealth, and grants prosperity.

In later times Tvashtri is regarded as one of the Adityas. He is said to have had twin children. One was a daughter, Saranya, who married Vivasvat. The other was a son, Trisiras, who had 3 heads, 6 eyes, and 3 mouths, and was slain by Indra.

THE RIBHUS.

The Ribhus are said to be three sons of Sudhanwan, a descendant of Angiras. They are celebrated in the Rig-Vedas as skilful workmen, who fashioned Indra's chariot and horses, and made their parents young again. By command of the gods, and with

---

* *The Academy*, August, 13, 1892.
† Dowson's *Dictionary of Hindu Mythology*, pp. 29, 30.

a promise of exaltation to divine honours, they made a single sacrificial cup fashioned by Tvashtri into four. They are also spoken of as supporters of the sky.*

VISHVAKARMAN.

Vishvakarman, all-creating, was originally an epithet of any powerful god; but in course of time it came to designate a personification of the creative power. In this character Vishvakarman was the great architect of the universe. As such, two hymns are addressed to him.

In later books he is identified with Tvashtri. In the Ramayana he is represented as having built the city of Lanka for the Rakshasas.

PRAJAPATI.

"Prajapati, the lord of creatures," says Max Müller, is "in many respects identical with Visvakarman, the maker of all things, yet enjoying a greater individuality than Visvakarman, particularly in the Brahmanas. In some of the hymns of the Veda, Prajapati occurs still as a mere epithet of Savitri, the sun.

"He is also invoked as bestowing progeny, and there is one hymn (Rig-Veda x. 121) where he is celebrated as the creator of the universe, as the first of all gods, also called Hiranyagarbha, the golden germ, or the golden egg.†"

"Now and then, in reading certain chapters of the Brahmanas, one imagines that the craving after one supreme personal God has at last found its satisfaction in Prajapati, the lord of all living things, and that all the other gods would vanish before this new radiance. Thus we read:

"Prajapati alone was all this in the beginning. Prajapati is Bharata, the supporter, for he supports all this. Prajapati created living creatures. From his higher vital breath he created the gods ; from his lower vital breath he created men. Afterwards he created death as one who should be a devourer for all living creatures. Of that Prajapati one half was mortal, the other immortal, and with that half which was mortal he was afraid of death." Satapatha Brahmana, x, 1, 3, 1, ‡

BRIHASPATI AND BRAHMANASPATI.

In the Rig-Veda the two names are equivalent. He is a deity in whom the action of the worshipper upon the gods is personified. He is the suppliant, the sacrificer, the priest who intercedes with the gods on behalf of men, and protects them from the wicked. He represents the priests and the priestly order. He is also desig-

---

* Dowson's *Dictionary of Hindu Mythology*. p. 267.
† This hymn is quoted in the selections.
‡ *Hibbert Lectures*, pp. 294, 297.

nated as the purohita of the gods. He is the lord and protector of prayer.

In the Rig-Veda he is described as the father of the gods; to have blown forth the births of the gods like a blacksmith. In some passages he is identified with Agni, but this is opposed by others.

In later times he is a Rishi, and regent of the planet Jupiter.

VACH.

VACH, "speech," is the personification of speech by whom knowledge was communicated to man. She was 'generated by the gods,' and is called "the divine Vach," "queen of the gods." In the Taittireya Brahmana she is called "the mother of the Vedas," and "the wife of Indra who contains within herself all worlds." She is celebrated in two hymns of the Tenth Book.

SOMA.

Hindus, at present, differ in their habits in two remarkable respects from their forefathers in Vedic times. One has already been noticed. The ancient Aryans delighted in eating beef, which is an utter abomination to their descendants. The other change is with regard to the use of intoxicants. Nearly a whole book of the Rig-Veda, containing 114 hymns, is devoted to the praise of Soma, and there are constant references to it in a large proportion of the other hymns. The ancient Aryans rejoiced in drinking; respectable Hindus now wisely abstain from what inebriates.

Not only were the people themselves fond of drinking the Soma juice, but the gods were represented as eager to partake of the beverage. Professor Whitney thus explains how it came to be worshipped:

" The simple-minded Aryan people, whose whole religion was a worship of the wonderful powers and phenomena of nature, had no sooner perceived that this liquid had the power to elevate the spirits, and produce a temporary frenzy, under the influence of which the individual was prompted to, and capable of, deeds beyond his natural powers, than they found in it something divine : it was to their apprehension a god, endowing those into whom it entered with godlike powers ; the plant which afforded it became to them the king of plants; the process of preparing it was a holy sacrifice ; the instruments used therefore were sacred."*

The Soma is a creeping plant, with small white fragrant flowers. It yields a milky juice, which, when fermented, is intoxicating. The hymns addressed to Soma were intended to be sung while the juice of the plant was being pressed out and purified.

Various accounts are given of the way in which the Soma plant was obtained. In some passages the plant is said to have been

* Oriental and Linguistic Studies. 1st Series. pp. 10, 11.

brought from a mountain and given to Indra; in others King Soma is said to have dwelt among the Gandharvas. A third account is that Soma existed in the sky, and that Gayatri became a bird, and brought it.

When Soma was brought to the gods, there was a dispute as to who should have the first draught. It was decided that a race should be run; the winner to have the first taste. Vayu first reached the goal, Indra being second.

The juice of the plant is said to be an immortal draught which the gods love. Soma, the god in the juice, is said to clothe the naked and heal the sick, through him the blind see, and the lame walk. Many divine attributes are ascribed to him. He is addressed as a god in the highest strains of veneration. All powers belong to him; all blessings are besought of him as his to bestow. He is said to be divine, immortal, and also to confer immortality on gods and men. Future happiness is asked from him: "Place me, O Pavamana, in that everlasting and imperishable world where there is eternal light and glory." IX. 113. 7.

In later times Soma was a name given to the moon. When the Vishnu Purana was written, intoxicants were strictly forbidden; hence Soma, as the god of the soma juice, was no longer known and praised. According to that Purana, Soma was the son of Atri, the son of Brahma.

The ancient Greeks had also a god of wine, called Bacchus.

RUDRA.

Rudra means 'howler' or 'roarer.' In the Vedas he has many attributes and names. He is the howling terrible god, the god of storms, the father of the Rudras or Maruts. He is described as armed with a strong bow and fleet arrows. He is called the slayer of men. His anger, ill-will, and destructive shafts are deprecated. He is the cause of health and prosperity to man and beast. He is frequently characterised as the possessor of healing remedies. As already mentioned, this may have its explanation in tempests clearing the air, and making it healthier.

"Rudra's chief interest," says Whitney, "consists in the circumstance that he forms the point of connection between the Vedic religion and the late Siva-worship. Siva is a god unknown to the Vedas; his name is a word of not unfrequent occurrence in the hymns, indeed, but means simply 'propitious.' As given to him whose title it has since become, it seems one of these euphemisms* so frequent in the Indian religion, applied as a soothing and flattering address to the most terrible god in the whole Pantheon. The precise relation between Siva and Rudra is not yet satisfactorily traced out."†

---

* Pleasing terms to express what is disagreeable
† *Oriental and Linguistic Studies*, 1st Series, p. 34

YAMA AND YAMI.

Yama and Yami are represented as the twin son and daughter of Visvavat, the Sun. By some they are looked upon as the originators of the human race. In Rig-veda X. 10, there is a dialogue between Yama and her brother, when she begs her brother to make her his wife. He declines her offer, because it is a sin that a brother should marry a sister. In the Atharva Veda Yama is said to be the first of men who died, the first that departed to the celestial world.

"Yama," says Muir, "is nowhere represented in the Rig-Veda as having anything to do with the punishment of the wicked. The hymns of that Veda contain no prominent mention of any such penal retribution. Yama is still to some extent an object of terror. He is represented as having two insatiable dogs, with four eyes and wide nostrils, which guard the road to his abode, and which the departed are advised to hurry past with all speed."

In the epic poems Yama is the god of departed spirits, and judge of the dead. Pluto, the Yama of the Romans, is represented as having Cerberus, a savage dog with three heads.

PLUTO.

VISVE DEVAS.

In the Rig-Veda a number of hymns are addressed to two deities, as Mitra and Varuna, Indra and Agni, Indra and Varuna. "The names of two gods who shared certain functions in common were formed into a compound with a dual termination, and this compound became the name of a new deity. Thus we have hymns not only to Mitra and Varuna, but to Mitrâvarunau as one. ...A

third expedient was to comprehend all the gods by one common
name ; to call them Visve Devas, the All-gods, and to address prayers and sacrifices to them in their collective capacity."*

KA, WHO?

"New gods," says Max Müller, "were actually created out of
words which were intended as names of divine beings. There
are several hymns in the Rig-Veda containing questions as to who
is the true or the most powerful god. A rule had been laid down,
that in every sacrificial hymn there must be a deity addressed
by the poet. In order to discover a deity where no deity existed
the most extraordinary objects, such as a present, a drum, stones,
plants, were raised to the artificial rank of deities. In accordance
with the same system we find the authors of the Brahmanas had so
completely broken with the past that, forgetful of the poetical
character of the hymns and the yearning of the poets after the unknown God, they exalted the interrogative pronoun itself into a
deity, and acknowledged a god Ka or Who?"† In some places it
is said that Ka is Prajapati. In the later Sanskrit literature of the
Puranas, Ka appears as a recognised god, as a supreme god, with
a genealogy of his own, perhaps even with a wife. The Mahabharata identifies Ka with Daksha, and the Bhagavata Purana applies
the term to Kasyapa.

GODDESSES.

Several goddesses are mentioned in the Vedas ; but with the
exception of Prithivi, Aditi, and Ushas, little importance is attached
to them. Sarasvati is celebrated both as a river and as a deity.
The wives of Agni, Varuna, the Ashvins, &c. are mentioned, but
no distinct functions are assigned to them. Their insignificance is
in striking contrast the prominent place assumed by the wife of
Siva in the later mythology.

THE PITRIS.

The following account of the Pitris is abridged from Max
Müller's *India, What can it Teach us?*—

"There was in India, as elsewhere, another very early faith, springing up naturally in the hearts of the people, that their fathers and
mothers, when they departed this life, departed to a Beyond, wherever
it might be, either in the East from whence all the bright Devas seemed
to come, or more commonly in the West, the land to which they seemed to
go, called in the Veda the realms of Yama or the setting sun. The idea
that beings which once had been, could ever cease to be, had not yet
entered their minds ; and from the belief that their fathers existed some-

---

* *Hibbert Lectures*, p. 291.
† *Ancient Sanskrit Literature*, p. 433.

where, though they could see them no more, there arose the belief in another Beyond, and the germs of another religion.

Nor was the actual power of the fathers quite imperceptible or extinct even after their death. Their presence continued to be felt in the ancient laws and customs of the family, most of which rested on their will and their authority. While the fathers were alive and strong, their will was law; and when, after their death, doubts or disputes arose on points of law or custom, it was but natural that the memory and the authority of the fathers should be appealed to settle such points—that the law should still be their will.

Thus Manu says (IV. 178), 'On the path on which his fathers and grandfathers have walked, on that path of good men let him walk, and he will not go wrong.'

In the same manner then in which, out of the bright powers of nature, the Devas or gods had arisen, there arose out of predicates shared in common by the departed, such as pitris, fathers, preta, gone away, another general concept, what we should call *Manes*, the kind ones, *Ancestors*, *Shades*, *Spirits*, or *Ghosts*, whose worship was nowhere more fully developed than in India. That common name, Pitris, Fathers, gradually attracted to itself all that the fathers shared in common. It came to mean not only fathers, but invisible, kind, powerful, immortal, heavenly beings, and we can watch in the Veda, better perhaps than anywhere else, the inevitable, yet most touching metamorphosis of ancient thought,—the love of the child for father and mother becoming transfigured into an instinctive belief in the immortality of the soul.

In the Veda the Pitris are invoked together with the Devas, but they are not confounded with them. The Devas never become Pitris, and though such adjectives as *deva* are sometimes applied to the Pitris, and they are raised to the rank of the older classes of Devas, it is easy to see that the Pitris and Devas had each their independent origin, and that they represent two totally distinct phases of the human mind in the creation of its objects of worship.

We read in the Rig-Veda, VI. 52, 4: 'May the rising Dawns protect me, may the flowing Rivers protect me, may the firm Mountains protect me, may the Fathers protect me at this invocation of the gods.' Here nothing can be clearer than the separate existence of the Fathers, apart from the Dawns, the Rivers, and the Mountains, though they are included in one common Devahûti, or invocation of the gods.

We must distinguish, however, from the very first, between two classes, or rather between two concepts of Fathers, the one comprising the distant, half-forgotten, and almost mythical ancestors of certain families, or of what would have been to the poets of the Veda, the whole human race, the other consisting of the fathers who had but lately departed, and who were still, as it were, personally remembered and revered.

The old ancestors in general approach more nearly to the gods. They are often represented as having gone to the abode of Yama, the ruler of the departed, and to live there in company with some of the Devas.

We sometimes read of the great-grandfathers being in heaven, the grandfathers in the sky, the fathers on the earth, the first in company with the Adityas, the second with the Rudras, the last with the Vasus. All these are individual poetical conceptions.

Yama himself is sometimes invoked as if he were one of the Fathers, the first of mortals that died or that trod the path of the Fathers leading to the common sunset in the West. Still his real Deva-like nature is never completely lost, and, as the god of the setting sun, he is indeed the leader of the Fathers, but not one of the Fathers himself.

The following is from one of the hymns of the Rig-Veda by which those ancient Fathers were invited to come to their sacrifice :

1. May the Soma-loving Fathers, the lowest, the highest, and the middle, arise. May the gentle and righteous Fathers who have come to life (again) protect us in these invocations !

4. Come hither to us with your help, you Fathers who sit on the grass ! We have prepared these oblations for you, accept them ! Come hither with your most blessed protection, and give us health and wealth without fail !

5. The Soma-loving Fathers have been called hither to their dear viands which are placed on the grass. Let them approach, let them listen, let them bless, let them protect us ! X. 15.

The daily Pitriyagna, or ancestor worship, is one of the five sacrifices, sometimes called the great sacrifices, which every married man ought to perform day by day.*

There are full descriptions of the worship due to the Fathers in the Brahmanas and Sutras. The epic poems, the law books, the Puranas, all are brimful of allusions to ancestral worship. The whole social fabric of India, with its laws of inheritance and marriage, rests on a belief in the Manes.

To the mind of a Hindu, says Professor Bhattacharyya, in his *Tagore Law Lectures* (p. 130), "Ancestor worship, in some form or other, is the beginning, the middle, and the end of what is known as the Hindu religion."

The word Sraddha does not occur in the Vedas or in the ancient Brahmanas. It is, therefore, a word of more modern origin. It is explained as that which is given in faith to Brahmans for the sake of the Fathers.†

Chinese Ancestral Worship.—The dead are supposed, by the Chinese, to be dependent upon the living for food, clothing, and money. These are presented at certain times, especially in the third month of the year. The Hindus offer to the dead pindas, or balls of rice. The Chinese give them the food which they themselves like best,—boiled pork, fowls, ducks, tea, &c., which they afterwards consume themselves or give to the poor. Clothing, chairs, tables, horses, &c. are made of paper and burnt. Round pieces of papers, of the size of dollars, are thinly covered with tin or some other metal, and burnt. Paper man-servants and maid-servants are similarly supplied. The Chinese are foolish enough to believe that their ancestors will get these things in reality in another world.

---

* *India, What can it Teach us?* pp. 219—229.   † *Ibid.* p. 235.

Sacrificial Implements, etc.

Divine powers are ascribed in the hymns to various objects. A hymn to the Yupa, or sacrificial post, is quoted in the selections. The weapons of war form the subject of hymn 75, Book VI. The arrow is thus addressed :

16. " Loosed from the bow string fly away, thou arrow, sharpened by our prayer,
Go to the foemen, strike them home, and let not one be left alive."

The ladle, a kind of large spoon, likewise receives great honour. " We revile not the ladle, which is of exalted race; verily we assert the dignity of the wooden implement. The ladle has established the sky."

The mortar is thus addressed : " O sovran of the forest, as the wind blows soft in front of thee, Mortar, for Indra press thou forth the Soma-juice that he may drink." I. 28, 6. The sacrificial grass is said to support heaven and earth, and wonderful attributes are predicated of Vasa, the cow. There is a hymn professedly addressed to frogs, which is quoted in the selections. It concludes with thanks for riches bestowed, and prayer for prolongation of life. VII. 103.

The Gods not mentioned in the Vedas.

Many of the principal gods now worshipped by the Hindus, says Professor Wilson, are either wholly unnamed in the Veda, or are noticed in an inferior and different capacity. The names of Siva, of Mahadeva, of Durga, of Kali, of Rama, of Krishna, never occur, as far as we are yet aware ; we have a Rudra, who, in after times, is identified with Siva, but who, even in the *Puranas,* is of very doubtful origin and identification, whilst in the *Veda* he is described as the father of the winds, and is evidently a form of either Agni or Indra. There is not the slightest allusion to the form in which for the last ten centuries at least, he (Siva) seems to have been almost exclusively worshipped in India—that of the *Linga :* neither is there the slightest hint of another important feature of later Hinduism, the *Trimurthi,* or Tri-une combination of Brahma, Vishnu, and Siva, as typified by the mystical syllable *Om.**

The gods now chiefly worshipped by the Hindus were the inventions of later times. Sir A. C. Lyall explains, in his *Asiatic Studies,* how the worship of new gods sprang up. A man, looked upon as holy, when he died, had a shrine set up in his honour. If he was supposed to make a few good cures at the outset, especially among women and valuable cattle, his reputation spread through the country. " This," says he, " is the kind of success which has made

---

* *Introduction to the Translation of the Rig-Veda,* pp. xxvi, xxvii.

the fortune of some of the most popular, the richest, and the most widely known gods in Berar, who do all the leading business." One of the richest temples in South India, Tirupati, near Madras, was set up in honour of a man named Balaji. When any local god acquired high repute, the Brahmans made him an incarnation of Vishnu or Siva.

The gods of the Hindus were, like their kings, one dynasty succeeding another.

THE OFFERINGS AND SACRIFICES OF THE VEDAS.

Importance of Sacrifice in Vedic Times.—Mr. Kunte says :

" It is impossible to understand and appreciate the spirit of the civilization of the ancient Aryas as it is revealed in the collection of hymns called the Rik-Sanhita, without studying their sacrificial system, the soul of their civilization. No matter what hymn is read, it directly or indirectly cannot but refer to a sacrifice. Either the musical modes of the Udgata singer are mentioned, or the name of a sacrifice such as *Yajna* or *Makha*, or some prayer asking a god to partake of their sacrificial portion (*Yajniya Bhaga*) occurs. The main ground of the picture of society drawn in the Rik-Sanhita is a sacrifice."*

Dr. Haug has the following remarks on the supposed influence attached to sacrifice :

" The sacrifice is regarded as the means for obtaining power over this and the other world, over visible as well as invisible beings, animate as well as inanimate creatures. Who knows its proper application, and has it duly performed, is in fact looked upon as the real master of the world ; for any desire he may entertain, if it be even the most ambitious, can be gratified, any object in view can be obtained by means of it. The *Yajna* (sacrifice) taken as a whole is conceived to be a kind of machinery, in which every piece must tally with the other, or a sort of large chain in which no link is allowed to be wanting, or a staircase, by which one may ascend to heaven, or as a personage endowed with all the characteristics of a human body. It exists from eternity, and proceeded from the Supreme Being (Prajapati or Brahma) along with the *Traividya, i. e.,* the threefold sacred science (the Rik verses, the Samans or chants, and the Yajus or sacrificial formulas). The creation of the world itself was even regarded as the fruit of a sacrifice performed by the Supreme Being."†

Kinds of Offerings and Sacrifices.—The products of the cow were offered—milk, curds, and butter. Grain was offered in different forms—fried, boiled, or as flour-balls (pinda). Sacrifices included goats, sheep, cows, buffaloes, horses, men—the last two being considered of the greatest value. Somayajna was the most frequent kind of offering. Incense was burnt, but tufts of wool and horse dung were also used.

---

* *Vicissitudes of Aryan Civilization*, pp. 21, 22.
† *Introduction to Aitareya Brahmana*, pp. 73, 74.

Times of Offering, &c.—The central part of a house was dedicated to the gods. When a new house was entered upon, the fire was kindled for the first time by rubbing together pieces of wood, after which it was not allowed to go out. Morning and evening devout Aryas assembled around the sacred fire. The master of the house, as *agnihotri,* made offerings to it of wood and ghee, hymns were chanted, the children joining in the chorus and the words *svaha* and *vausat* were reiterated till the roof resounded.

The new and full moons were seasons of sacrifice. The house was decorated ; grass was tied over the door and about its sides.

Every four months, at the beginning of spring, the rainy season, and autumn, sacrifices were offered.

The first ripe fruits were offered generally twice a year.

A he-goat was sacrificed once a year at the beginning of the rainy season in the house of the sacrificer.

If addition, offerings and sacrifices were made on many other occasions, some of which will be mentioned hereafter.

Sacrificial Implements.—Among these were the following : *Yúpa,* a post to which the animal to be sacrificed was tied ; pots of various kinds for holding water, for boiling milk and flesh ; a wooden tub in which to keep the filtered soma juice ; a knife to cut up the body of the slain animal ; an axe to divide the bones ; a spit to roast parts of the flesh ; several kinds of wooden spoons ; a cup for drinking and offering soma, &c. The *Sphya* was a piece of wood, shaped like a wooden sword, with which lines were drawn round the sacrificial ground. One of the priests had to hold it up high so long as the chief ceremonies lasted, to keep off rakshas, evil spirits.

Sacrificers and Priests.—In early times any one might preside at a sacrifice. The Brahman was at first simply an assistant. King Janaka asserted his right of performing sacrifices without the intervention of priests.

As great importance was attached to the hymns sung at sacrifices, Brahmans who committed them to memory acquired more and more power. As time advanced also, the ceremonies became more and more complicated, till at some sacrifices 16 priests were required, each performing his own peculiar office.

One priest watched over the whole in a sitting posture. The duties of the different classes of priests are thus described by Max Müller :

" The Adhvaryus were the priests who were intrusted with the material performance of the sacrifice. They had to measure the ground, to build the altar (Vedi), to prepare the sacrificial vessels, to fetch wood and water, to light the fire, to bring the animal and immolate it. They formed, as it would seem, the lowest class of priests, and their acquirements were more of a practical than an intellectual character. Some of the offices which would naturally fall to the lot of the Adhvaryus, were considered so degrading, that other persons besides the priests were frequently employed in them. The Samitri, for instance, who had to slay the animal, was not a priest, he need not even be a Brahman, and the same remark applies to the Vaikartas, the butchers, and the so-called Chamasadhvaryus. The number of hymns and invocations which they had to use at the sacrifices were smaller than that of the other priests. These, however, they had to learn by heart., But as the chief difficulty consisted in the exact recitation of hymns and in the close observance of all the euphonic rules, as taught in the Pratisakhyas, the Adhvaryus were allowed to mutter their hymns, so that no one at a distance could either hear or understand them. Only in cases where the Adhvaryu had to speak to other officiating priests, commanding them to perform certain duties, he was of course obliged to speak with a loud and distinct voice. All their verses and all the invocations which the Adhvaryus had to use, were collected in the ancient liturgy of the Adhvaryus together with the rules of the sacrifice. In this mixed form they exert in the Taittiriyaka. Afterwards the hymns were collected by themselves, separated from the ceremonial rules, and this collection is what we called the *Yajur-Veda-Sanhita*, or the prayer-book of the Adhvaryus priests.

"There were some parts of the sacrifice, which according to ancient custom, had to be accompanied by songs, and hence another class of priests arose whose particular office it was to act as the chorus. This naturally took place at the most solemn sacrifices only. Though as yet we have no key as to the character of the music which the Udgatris performed. we can see from the numerous and elaborate rules, however unintelligible, that their music was more than mere chanting. The words of their songs were collected in the order of the sacrifice, and this is what we possess under the name of *Sama-Veda-Sanhita*, or the prayer book of the Udgatri priests.

"Distinct from these two classes we have a third class of priests, the Hotris, whose duty it was to recite certain hymns during the sacrifice in praise of the Deities to whom any particular act of the sacrifice was addressed. Their recitation was loud and distinct, and required the most accurate knowledge of the rules of euphony or Siksha. The Hotris, as a class, were the most highly educated order of priests. They were supposed to know both the proper pronunciation and the meaning of their hymns, the order and employment of which was taught in the Brahmanas of the Bahvrichas. But while both the Adhvaryus and Udgatris were confessedly unable to perform their duties without the help of their prayer books, the Hotris were supposed to be so well versed in the ancient sacred poetry, as contained in the ten Mandalas of the Rig-Veda, that no separate prayer-book or Sanhita was ever arranged for their special benefit.

"The Hotri learnt, from the Brahmana, or in later times, from the Sutra, what special duties he had to perform. He knew from these sources the beginnings or the names of the hymns which he had to recite at every part of the service.

"The most ancient name for a priest by profession was *Purohita*, which only means one placed before. The original occupation of the Purohita may simply have been to perform the usual sacrifices; but, with the ambitious policy of the Brahmans, it soon become a stepping-stone to political power. Thus we read in the Aitariya-Brahmana : "Breath does not leave him before time ; he lives to an old age ; he goes to his full time, and does not die again, who has a Brahman as guardian of his land, as Purohita. He conquers power by power; obtains strength by strength ; the people obey him, peaceful and of one mind."*

A few of the principal offerings and sacrifices will now be described.

Soma.

Soma juice was an essential part of every offering of importance. Dr. Rajendralala Mitra says that it was made with the expressed juice of a creeper, diluted with water, mixed with barley meal, clarified butter, and the meal of wild paddy, and fermented in a jar for nine days. It may be concluded that a beverage prepared by the vinous fermentation of barley meal, should have strong intoxicating effects, and it is not remarkable, therefore, that the Vedas should frequently refer to the exhilaration produced by its use on men and gods.†

The Aryans were fond of the Soma themselves. It is thus described : "O Soma, poured out for Indra to drink, flow on purely in a most sweet and most exhilarating current." IX. 1, 1.

"We have drunk the Soma, we have become immortal, we have entered into light, we have known the gods. What can an enemy now do to us ?" VIII. 48, 3.

All the gods are supposed to delight in the soma juice. The following are some extracts from the hymns :

O Soma, gladden Varuna and Mitra ; cheer Indra Pavamana ! Indra Vishnu.

Cheer thou the gods, the company of Maruts : Indru, cheer mighty Indra to rejoicing. IX. 90, 5.

"Make Vayu glad, for furtherance and bounty ; cheer Varuna and Mitra as they cleanse thee.

Gladden the gods, gladden the host of Maruts ; make Heaven and Earth rejoice, O God, O Soma." IX. 97, 42.

Indra hath drunk, Agni hath drunk ; all deities have drunk their fill. VII. 58, 11.

But Indra is the deity especially addicted to love of the Soma. "Even as a thirsty steer who roams the deserts may he drink eagerly the milked-out Soma." (V. 36. 1.). "Then Indra at a single draught drank the contents of thirty pails, Pails that were filled with Soma-juice." (VIII. 66, 4). "His belly, drinking deepest draughts of Soma, like an ocean swells." (I. 8, 7). After Indra has had his fill of soma, he is asked to grant cattle

* Ancient Sanskrit Literature, pp. 471—487 (abridged).
† Indo-Aryans, Vol. I, p. 419.

and horses : "Impetuous god, when thou hast drunk the Soma, enraptured send us cattle in abundance. With kine and horses satisfy this longing." (III. 50. 3, 4). Another effect was to strengthen Indra to conquer Vritra :

3. " Impetuous as a bull, he chose the Soma, and quaffed in three-fold sacrifice the juices."

5. Indra with his own great and deadly thunder smote unto pieces Vritra, worst of Vritras. I. 32.

The soma juice offered to the gods was apparently poured on the bundles of kusa grass provided for them as seats. "These dripping soma juices are offered upon the sacred grass : drink them, Indra, (to recruit thy) vigour."

ANIMAL SACRIFICES.

The animals chiefly sacrificed were goats, sheep, cows, bullocks, buffaloes, deer, and occasionally horses. Large numbers were sometimes sacrificed. Three hundred buffaloes are mentioned as having been offered to Indra.

Modern Hindus, who now worship the cow, can scarcely believe that their Aryan forefathers sacrificed her and ate her flesh. But times without number the Vedas refer to ceremonies, called *gomedha*, in which the cow was sacrificed. Minute directions are given as to the character of the animal to be chosen. The Taittiriya Brahmana of the Yajur Veda gives the following rules :

" A thick-legged cow to Indra ; a barren cow to Vishnu and Varuna ; a black cow to Pushan ; a cow that has brought forth only once to Vayu ; a cow having two colours to Mitra and Varuna ; a red cow to Rudra ; a white barren cow to Surya, &c."

One great sacrifice, called the *Panchasaradiya sava*, was celebrated every five years. At this seventeen young cows were immolated. " Whoever wishes to be great," says the Taittiriya Brahmana, " let him worship through the Panchasaradiya. Thereby, verily, he will be great."

" In the Asvalayana Sutra," says Dr. Mitra, " mention is made of several sacrifices of which the slaughter of cattle formed a part. One of them, in the Grihya Sutra, is worthy of special notice. It is called *Sulagava*, or 'spitted cow,' *i e.,* Roast Beef."*

Oxen were sacrificed as well as cows. The Taittiriya Brahmana prescribes : " A dwarf ox to Vishnu ; a drooping horned bull to Indra ; a piebald ox to Savitri ; a white ox to Mitra, &c."

Ignorant Hindus now allege that the animals were not really killed, but that after the form of sacrificing had been performed, they were allowed to go free. This statement is a pure fabrica-

---

* *Indo-Aryans*, Vol. I, p. 363.

tion. "Nothing," says Dr. Clark, "is more conclusive than the evidence on this point that the animal sacrificed was really killed and subsequently eaten. It was first tied to the sacrificial post after the recital of appropriate mantras and the performance of certain special rites; some kusa grass was then spread, and the animal was laid on it with its head to the west and its feet to the north." After it was killed, the Adhvaryu said, 'It is immolated (sanjnapta).'"

"That the animal slaughtered was intended for food," says Dr. R. Mitra, "is evident from the directions given in the Asvalayana Sutra to eat of the remains of the offering; but to remove all doubt on the subject I shall quote here a passage from the Taittiriya Brahmana in which the mode of cutting up the victim after immolation is described in detail: it is scarcely to be supposed that the animal would be so divided if there was no necessity for distribution."

Only a few extracts need be given:

"Separate its hide so that it may remain entire. Cut open its breast so as to make it appear like an eagle (with spread wings). Separate the forearms; divide the arms into spokes; separate successively in order the 26 ribs. Dig a trench for burying the excrements. Throw away the blood to the Rakshasas. O slayer of cattle, O Adhrigu, accomplish your task; accomplish it according to rules."

The Gopatha Brahmana of the Atharva-Veda gives in detail the names of the different individuals who are to receive shares of the meat for the parts they take in the ceremony. The following are a few of them:

"The Prastata is to receive the two jaws along with the tongue; the Pratiharta, the neck and the hump; the Udgata, the eagle-like wings; the Neshta, the right arm; the Sadasya, the left arm; the householder who ordains the sacrifice the two right feet: his wife, the two left feet, &c."

Diverse imprecations are hurled against those who venture to depart from this order of distribution.

Some had poor shares, but all were allowed plentiful libations of the soma beer.

Ashvamedha.—This rite was probably borrowed from the Scythians in Central Asia, who often sacrificed horses. The same importance was not attached to it in Vedic times as it acquired in after ages.

A year's preparation was needed for the horse sacrifice. According to the Taittiriya Brahmana, "ten times eighteen" domestic animals were to be sacrificed with it. Two hundred and sixty wild animals were also brought and tied to the sacrificial posts, but they were let loose after the fire had been carried round them.

The first animal sacrificed was a goat to Pushan. That the

horse was killed and cooked is evident from the following extract from the Rig-Veda, I. 162 :

11 "What from thy body which with fire is roasted, when thou art set upon the spit, distilleth,—
Let not that lie on earth or grass neglected, but to the longing gods let all be offered.

12 They who observing that the horse is ready call out and say, The smell is good ; remove it,
And, craving meat, await the distribution,—may their approving help promote our labour.

13 The trial-fork of the flesh-cooking caldron, the vessels out of which the broth is sprinkled,
The warming-pots, the covers of the dishes, hooks, carving-boards,—all these attend the charger.

18 The four-and-thirty ribs of the swift charger, kin to the gods, the slayer's hatchet pierces.
Cut ye with skill, so that the parts be flawless, and piece by piece declaring them dissect them."

This hymn would be nonsense if the horse was not really killed and cooked. Professor Wilson says :

" That the horse is to be actually immolated admits of no question ; that the body was cut up into fragments is also clear ; that these fragments were dressed, partly boiled, and partly roasted, is also undisputable ; and although the expressions may be differently understood, yet there is little reason to doubt that part of the flesh was eaten by the assistants, part presented as a burnt offering to the gods."[*]

The horse, however, was comforted by the thought that it was going to the gods :—

20 " Let not thy dear soul burn thee as thou comest, let not the hatchet linger in thy body.
Let not a greedy clumsy immolator, missing the joints, mangle thy limbs unduly.

21 No, here thou diest not, thou art not injured ; by easy paths unto the gods thou goest.
The bays, the splendid deer are now thy fellows ; and to the ass's pole is yoked the charger."

In the Rig-Veda the object of the *Ashvamedha* is no more than, as usual with other rites, the acquiring of wealth and posterity :

22 " May this good steed bring us all-sustaining riches, wealth in good kine, good horses, manly offspring.
Freedom from sin may Aditi vouchsafe us : the steed with our oblations gain us lordship."

The Yajur Veda and the Satapatha Brahmana contain full directions for the performance of the sacrifice.

---

[*] Introduction to Translation of Rig-Veda, Vol. II, pp. xiii, xiv.

In the Ramayana the horse sacrifice is employed by the childless Dasaratha as the means of obtaining sons. In the Balakandam it is said that his principal queen Kausalya, " with three strokes slew that horse, experiencing great glee. And with the view of reaping merit, Kausalya, with an undisturbed heart, passed one night with that horse."*

Wilson says :—

" In the morning, when the queen is released from this disgusting and, in fact, impossible, contiguity, a dialogue, as given in the Yajush, and in the Ashvamedha section of the Satapatha Brahmana, and as explained in the Sutras, takes place between the queen and the females accompanying or attendant upon her, and the principal priests, which, though brief, is in the highest degree both silly and obscene. We find no vestige, however, of these revolting impurities in the Rig-Veda, although it is authority for practices sufficiently coarse, and such as respectable Hindus of the present generation will find it difficult to credit as forming a part of the uncreated revelations of Brahma."†

According to the Ramayana, Kausalya acquired so much merit by killing the horse and embracing it all night, that she bore Rama. Any person of intelligence can judge of the truth of this.

Not long ago, the Arya Samajists of Lahore, ignorant of its origin, printed an Urdu translation of part of Mahidhari's commentary on the Yajur Veda. They were convicted in the Appellate Court of having published obscene literature, and were fined.

A later idea was that the Ashvamedha was celebrated by a monarch desirous of universal dominion. Another fiction was that a hundred celebrations deposed Indra from the throne of Swarga, and elevated the sacrificer to his place.

PURUSHAMEDHA, HUMAN SACRIFICES.

Human sacrifices, though now regarded with horror, were practised in ancient times by nearly all nations. The Aryan Hindus, the Greeks, Romans, Germans and Britons, once lived together, speaking the same language, and following the same customs. We know that human sacrifices were offered by the Western Aryans at an early period. In England, large numbers of human beings were burnt alive in images made of wicker work. At Athens, a man and a woman were annually sacrificed to expiate the sins of the nation. The Germans sometimes immolated hundreds at a time. It is therefore very probable that the practice prevailed also among the Eastern Aryans.

---

* English Translation, p. 38.
† Introduction to Translation of the Rig-Veda, Vol. II. p. xiii.

The subject has been carefully investigated by Dr. Rajendralala Mitra, the most distinguished Indian scholar of modern times, in a paper originally published in the *Journal of the Asiatic Society of Bengal*. Some maintain that human sacrifices are not authorised in the Vedas, but were introduced in later times. Dr. R. Mitra says : " As a Hindu writing on the actions of my forefathers—remote as they are—it would have been a source of great satisfaction to me if I could adopt this conclusion as true ; but I regret I cannot do so consistently with my allegiance to the cause of history."

His paper on the subject occupies 84 pages in his *Indo-Aryans*, giving numerous quotations both in Sanskrit and English. The following is only a brief summary. Dr. R. Mitra first describes the prevalence of human sacrifices in all parts of the world, both in ancient and modern times. He adds : " Benign and humane as was the spirit of the ancient Hindu religion, it was not all opposed to animal sacrifice ; on the contrary, most of the principal rites required the immolation of large numbers of various kinds of beasts and birds. One of the rites enjoined required the performer to walk deliberately into the depth of the ocean to drown himself to death. This was called *Mahaprasthana*, and is forbidden in the present age. Another, an expiatory one, required the sinner to burn himself to death, on a blazing pyre—the *Tushanala*. This has not yet been forbidden. The gentlest of beings, the simple-minded women of Bengal, were for a long time in the habit of consigning their first-born babes to the sacred river Ganges at Sagar Island, and this was preceded by a religious ceremony, though it was not authorised by any of the ancient rituals. If the spirit of the Hindu religion has tolerated, countenanced or promoted such acts, it would not be by any means unreasonable or inconsistent, to suppose that it should have, in primitive times, recognised the slaughter of human beings as calculated to appease, gratify, and secure the grace of the gods."

But to turn from presumptive evidence to the facts recorded in the Vedas. The earliest reference to human sacrifice occurs in the first book of the Rig-Veda. It contains seven hymns supposed to have been recited by one Sunahsepa when he was bound to a stake preparatory to being immolated. The story is given in the Aitareya Brahmana of the Rig-Veda.

Harischandra had made a vow to sacrifice his first-born to Varuna, if that deity would bless him with children. A child was born, named Rohita, and Varuna claimed it ; but the father evaded fulfilling his promise under various pretexts until Rohita, grown up to man's estate, ran away from home, when Varuna afflicted the father with dropsy. At last Rohita purchased one Sunahsepa from his father Ajigarta for a hundred cows. When Sunahsepa had been prepared, they found nobody to bind him to the sacrificial post. Then Ajigarta said, " Give me another hundred, and I shall bind him." They gave him another hundred cows, and he bound him. When Sunahsepa had been prepared and bound, when the Apri hymns had been sung, and he had been led round the fire, they found nobody to kill him. Next Ajigarta said, " Give me another hundred, and I shall kill him." They gave him another hundred cows, and he came whetting the knife. Sunah-sepa then recited the hymns praising Agni, Indra, Mitra, Varuna, and other gods. He says :—

> 13 " Bound to three pillars captured Sunahsepa thus to the ·Aditya made his supplication.
> Him may the sovran Varuna deliver, wise, ne'er deceived, loosen the bonds that bind him." I. 24.

Varuna, pleased with the hymns of Sunahsepa, set him free. Disgusted with his father, he forsook him, and became the adopted son of Visvamitra, his maternal uncle.

This story shows that human sacrifices were really offered. If Harischandra had simply to tie his son to a post and after repeat-ing a few mantras over him, let him off perfectly sound, he could easily have done so. "The running away of the son from his father would also be unmeaning; the purchase of a substitute stupid ; the payment of a fee of a hundred head of cattle to under-take the butcher's work quite supererogatory ; and the sharpening of the knife by Ajigarta a vain preliminary." Dr. R. Mitra adds : " Seeing that, until the beginning of this century, the practice of offering the first-born to the river Ganges was common, and the story simply says that Sunahsepas was offered to the water-god Varuna as a substitute for the first-born Rohita, he can perceive nothing in it inconsistent or unworthy of belief."

This view is supported by Max Müller. He says that the story in the Aitareya Brahmana " shows that, at that early time, the Brahmans were familiar with the idea of human sacrifices, and that men who were supposed to belong to the caste of the Brahmans were ready to sell their sons for that purpose."

The *Purushamedha* was celebrated for the attainment of suprem-acy over all created beings. Its performance was limited to Brah-mans and Kshatriyas. It could be commenced only on the tenth of the waxing moon in the month of Chaitra, and altogether it re-quired 40 days for its performance, though only 5 out of the 40 days were specially called the days of the Purushamedha, whence it got the name of *panchaha*. Eleven sacrificial posts were required for it, and to each of them was tied an animal fit for Agni and Soma (a barren cow), the human victims being placed between the posts.

The earliest indication of this rite occurs in the Vajasaneyi San-hita of the White Yajur Veda. The passage in it bearing on the subject is supposed to describe the different kinds of human victims appropriate for particular gods and goddesses. The section, in which it occurs, opens with three verses which, the commentator says, were intended to serve as mantras for offerings of human victims. Then follows a series of 179 names of gods in the dative case, each followed by the name of one or more persons in the objective case ; thus : " to Brahma, a Brahmana, to the Maruts, a Vaisya," &c. The copula is nowhere given, and it is quite optional with the reader to supply whatever verb he chooses. The whole of their names occurs also in the Taittiriya Brahmana of the Black Yajur Veda, with only a few slight variations, and in some cases having the verb *alabhate* after them. This verb is formed of the root *labh*, " to kill" with the prefix *á*, and commentators have generally accepted the term to mean slaughter, though in some cases it means consecration before slaughter.

Dr. R. Mitra quotes the 179 names in full, and gives long explanatory extracts from the Brahmanas and Apastambha. He arrives at the following conclusion : " Probably the number originally sacrificed was few, and that when the rite became emblematic, the number was increased in confirmation of some liturgical theory, particularly as it did not involve any trouble or difficulty. But whether so or not, certain it is that at one time or other men were immolated for the gratification of some divinity or other in this rite or its prototype."

The presumption is strong that the real sacrifice belonged to the Sanhita, and the Brahmana divested it of its hideousness and cruelty and made it emblematic, even as the Vaishnavas have, within the last five or six hundred years, replaced the sacrifice of goats and buffaloes to Chandika by that of pumpkins and sugar-cane.

Nor is the Purushamedha the only sacrifice at which human sacrifices were ordained. The Ashvamedha, or horse sacrifice, required the immolation of a human being just as much as the former, and hence it is that the horse sacrifice was prohibited in the Kali Yuga along with it.

The Satapatha Brahmana, in another passage, has a verse which is remarkable for the manner in which the human victim is therein referred to. It says, " Let a fire offering be made with the head of a man. The offering is the rite itself (*yajna*) ; therefore does it make a man part of the sacrificial animals ; and hence it is that among animals man is included in sacrifice."

Passing from the Brahmanas to the Itihasas, we have ample evidence to show that the rite of Purushamedha was not unknown to their authors. The Institutes of Manu affords the same evidence, but it would seem that when it came into currency, the rite was looked upon with horror, and so it was prohibited as unfit to be performed in the present age.

But while the Puranas suppressed the Purushamedha they afford abundant indications of another rite requiring the immolation of a human victim having come into vogue. This was *narabali*, or human sacrifice to the goddess Chamunda, or Chandika,—a dark, fierce sanguinary divinity.

The Kalika Purana says : " By a human sacrifice attended by the forms laid down, Devi remains gratified for a thousand years, and by a sacrifice of three men one hundred thousand years." A human sacrifice is described as *atibali* (highest sacrifice.) " The fact is well known," says Dr. R. Mitra, " that for a long time the rite was common all over Hindustan ; and persons are not wanting who suspect that there are still nooks and corners in India where human victims are occasionally slaughtered for the gratification of the Devi."

" Apart from the sacrifices enjoined in the Sastras, there used, in former times, to be offered human victims to several *dii minores* (inferior gods) by way of expiations or good-will offerings whenever a newly excavated tank failed to produce sufficient water, or a temple or building cracked, accidents which were attributed to malevolent divinities, who generally yielded to the seductive influence of sanguinary offerings."

" The offering of one's own blood to the goddess is a mediæval and modern rite. It is made by women, and there is scarcely a respectable house in all Bengal, the mistress of which has not, at one time or other, shed her blood under the notion of satisfying the goddess by the operation. Whenever her husband or a son is dangerously ill, a vow is made that, on the recovery of the patient, the goddess would be regaled with human blood, and in the first Durga Puja following, or at the temple at Kalighat, or at some other sacred fane, the lady performs certain ceremonies, and then bares her breast in the presence of the goddess, and with a nail-cutter (*naruna*) draws a few drops of blood from between her busts, and offers them to the divinity."

Dr. R. Mitra gives the following summary of the conclusions which may be fairly drawn from the facts cited above :

1*st*. That looking to the history of human civilization and the rituals of the Hindus, there is nothing to justify the belief that in ancient times the Hindus were incapable of sacrificing human beings to their gods.

2*nd*. That the Sunahsepa hymns of the Rik Sanhita most probably refer to a human sacrifice.

3*rd*. That the Aitareya Brahmana refers to an actual and not a typical human sacrifice.

4*th*. That the Purushamedha originally required the actual sacrifice of men.

5*th*. That the Satapatha Brahmana sanctions human sacrifice in some cases, but makes the Purushamedha emblematic.

6*th*. That the Taittiriya Brahmana enjoins the sacrifice of a man at the Horse Sacrifice.

7*th*. That the Puranas recognise human sacrifices to Chandika, but prohibit the Purushamedha rite.

8th. That the Tantras enjoin human sacrifices to Chandika, and require that when human victims are not available, the effigy of a human being should be sacrificed to her.

REACTION AGAINST SACRIFICES.

There have been many changes in the religious beliefs and practices of the Hindus. They have changed their gods again and again, as has been already shown ; Dyaus, Varuna, Agni, Indra, now being superseded by Vishnu, Siva, Rama, and Krishna.

Their practices have also changed. When the Aryans entered the Punjab, they were largely a pastoral people, their flocks and herds affording a large proportion of their food. It has been shown that the Aryans in Vedic times ate beef and drank freely the intoxicating soma beer. Much of their time was spent in fighting with the aborigines, whose fields and cattle they sought to take. Indra, supposed to be strong in battle, was therefore the principal god.

By degrees the Aryans were settled in peaceful possession of the country, the aborigines having either retired to the mountains or been reduced to slavery. The Aryans became milder than their forefathers. Instead of considering beef the best of food and delighting in soma beer, they began to think that no life should be taken, and that no intoxicating liquors should be tasted.

The new doctrine of transmigration arose, unknown to the Vedic Aryans, who did not believe that at death they passed from one body to another. This was a strong reason against the use of meat. A man's grandmother might become a sheep, and, if killed, he might eat her.

Animal worship, which sprang up, was another influence. The old Aryans worshipped chiefly the heavenly bodies ; they did not look upon cows as sacred, but killed and ate them freely. For a people to eat their gods, seemed as wicked as to eat their parents.

The chief leader in the movement against sacrifices and the use of soma beer, was Gautama Buddha, the son of an Indian Raja, who lived about 2,400 years ago. His first command was, " Thou shalt not take any life." This referred to life of any kind. His priests were forbidden even to pluck up any vegetable, which was supposed to have life like animals, and into which a person might pass in another birth. The following was one argument used by the Buddhists against sacrifices. The Vedic hymns say that animals sacrificed went to heaven. A man should therefore sacrifice his father, because he would go to heaven !

Another command of Buddha was, " Thou shalt not taste any intoxicating drink." The evils of drunkenness began to be felt, and though the Rig-Veda has 114 hymns in praise of the soma beer, its use was given up by the great body of the Hindus, though some tribes have retained their drinking habits.

The changes which Buddha advocated were largely carried out by the influence of Asoka, the powerful king of Magadha, whose empire extended from Bengal to the borders of Afghanistan. He reigned from about B. C. 260 to 220. There are rock inscriptions which he caused to be made in different parts of India. One of them is as follows : " This is the edict of the beloved of the gods, the Raja Piyadasi. The putting to death of animals is to be entirely discontinued."

The reaction can be gradually traced. Panini, the grammarian, says that there are old and new Brahmanas. The Aitareya Brahmana of the Rig-Veda, supposed to be the oldest, refers to sacrifices as really offered. The Satapatha Brahmana in some cases attempts to spiritualize them away. Animals and men were let loose after being tied to the sacrificial posts. Some of the leading doctrines of Buddha were adopted by the Brahmans, and the slaying of animals, even in sacrifice, became revolting to them. When Manu's Code was compiled, things were partly in a transition stage, and it is inconsistent. It says :

" 22. The prescribed beasts and birds are to be slain by Brahmans for the sacrifice, and also for the support of dependents ; for Agastya did (so) formerly.

" 23. There were, indeed, offerings of eatable beasts and birds in the ancient sacrifices and in the oblations of Brahmans and Kshatriyas." Bk. V.

On the other hand it says :

" 46. He who desires not to cause confinement, death, and pain to living beings, (but is) desirous of the good of all, gets endless happiness." V.

The superiority of not eating flesh to sacrifices is thus shown :—

" 53. He who for a hundred years sacrifices every year with a horse-sacrifice, and he who eats not flesh, the fruit of the virtue of both is equal." V.

Animal sacrifices are declared to have passed away, and others are substituted :

" 84. All the Vedic rites, oblational (an) sacrificial, pass away ; but this imperishable syllable Om is to be known to be Brahma and also Prajapati."

" 85. The sacrifice of muttering (this word, &c.) is said to be better by tenfold than the regular sacrifice ; if inaudible, it is a hundredfold (better) ; and a thousandfold, if mental." II.

The " five great sacrifices ordered for householders every day by the great seers" were :

" 70. Teaching the Veda, the Veda sacrifice ; offering cakes and water, the sacrifice to the manes ; an offering to fire, the sacrifice to the gods; offering of food, to all beings; honour to guests, the sacrifice to men." III.

The Vaishnava worship has had a considerable influence in putting a stop to animal sacrifices. It has been mentioned that within the last five or six centuries has been replaced the sacrifice of goats and buffaloes, even to Chandika, by pumpkins and sugar-cane.

Goats and buffaloes are still offered to Kali, but the image of a man, after the ceremony of *pranpratishta,* is substituted for a human being.

SUMMARY OF THE BOOKS.

Max Müller gives the following taken from Saunaka's Anu-kramanis:

	Mandalas.		Anuvákas.		Hymns.
The	1st	contains	24	and	191
„	2nd	„	4	„	43
„	3rd	„	5	„	62
„	4th	„	5	„	58
„	5th	„	6	„	87
„	6th	„	6	„	75
„	7th	„	6	„	104
„	8th	„	10	„	92 (+11 Valakhalyas.)
„	9th	„	7	„	114
„	10th	„	12	„	191
The	10 have		85	and	1017+11=1028.

The Bashkala-sakha had 8 hymns more=1025 hymns.[*]

Each Mandala will be noticed separately, and some of the most remarkable passages and hymns will be quoted in full.

MANDALA I.

This is called the book of the Satarchins, that is of a hundred or a large indefinite number of authors of verses.

Of the hymns 44 are specially addressed to Indra, 43 to Agni, 15 to the Asvins, 11 to the Maruts, 9 to the Visvedevas, 4 each to Ushas and the Ribhus, 3 to Heaven and Earth, &c. Other hymns are addressed to gods conjointly, as Indra and Agni, Mita and Varuna. Two hymns are addressed to the Horse, one is in praise of Food.

The first hymn, addressed to Agni, is given in full in Nagri, Roman, and in the English translation by Griffith. The author of it and the following hymn was Madhuchchhandas Vaisvamitra, a son or descendant of Visvamitra.

---

[*] *Ancient Sanskrit Literature*, p. 220.

॥ ओम् ॥

1. अग्निमीळे पुरोहितं यज्ञस्य देवमृत्विजम् ।
Agnimīḻe purōhitaṁ yajñasya dēvamṛtvijaṁ |
होतारं रत्नधातमम् ॥
Hōtāraṁ ratnadhātamaṁ||

2. अग्निः पूर्वेभि ऋषिभिरीड्यो नूतनैरुत ।
Agniḥ pūrvēbhi rrṣibhirīḍyō nūtanairuta |
स देवां एह वक्षति ॥
Sa dēvāṁ ēha vakṣati||

3. अग्निना रयिमश्नवत्पोषमेव दिवेदिवे ।
Agninā rayimaśnavatpōṣamēva divēdivē |
यशसं वीरवत्तमम् ॥
Yaśasaṁ vīravattamaṁ||

4. अग्ने यं यज्ञमध्वरं विश्वतः परिभूरसि ।
Agnē yaṁ yajñamadhvaraṁ viśvataḥ paribhūrasi |
स इद्देवेषु गच्छति ॥
Sa iddēvēsu gacchati||

5. अग्निर्होता कविक्रतुः सत्यश्चित्रश्रवस्तमः ।
Agnirhōtā kavikratuḥ satyaścitra śravastamaḥ |
देवो देवेभिरागमत् ॥
Dēvō dēvēbhi rāgamat||

6. यदङ्ग दाशुषे त्वमग्ने भद्रं करिष्यसि ।
Yadaṅga dāśuṣē tvamagnē bhadraṁ kariṣyasi |
तवेत्तत्सत्यमङ्गिरः ॥
Tavēttatsatyamaṅgiraḥ||

7. उपत्वाग्ने दिवेदिवे दोषावस्तर्धिया वयम् ।
Upatvāgnē divē divē dōṣāvastardhiyā vayaṁ |
नमो भरन्त एमसि ॥
Namō bharanta ēmasi||

8. राजन्तमध्वराणां गोपामृतस्य दीदिविम् ।
Rājantamadhvarāṇāṁ gōpāmṛtasya dīdiviṁ |
वर्धमानं स्वे दमे ॥
Vardhamānaṁ svē damē||

9. स नः पितेव सूनवेऽग्ने सूपायनो भव ।

Sa naḥ pitēva sūnavē'gnē sūpāyanō bhava |

स च स्वानः स्वस्तये ॥

Sa ca svānaḥ svastayē||

1. I laud Agni, the great high priest, god, minister of sacrifice,
   The herald, lavishest of wealth.
2. Worthy is Agni to be praised by living as by ancient seers :
   He shall bring hitherward the gods.
3. Though Agni man obtaineth wealth, yea, plenty waxing day by day,
   Most rich in heroes, glorious.
4. Agni, the flawless sacrifice, which thou encompassed about
   Verily goeth to the gods.
5. May Agni, sapient-minded priest, truthful, most gloriously great,
   The god, come hither with the gods.
6. Whatever blessing, Agni, thou wilt grant unto thy worshipper,
   That, Angiras,* is thy true gift.
7. To thee, dispeller of the night, O Agni, day by day with prayer,
   Bringing thee reverence, we come ;
8. Ruler of sacrifices, guard of Law eternal, radiant one,
   Increasing in thine own abode.
9. Be to us easy of approach, even as a father to his son :
   Agni, be with us for our weal.

2. Hymn to Vayu.

1. Beautiful Vayu come, for thee these Soma-drops have been prepared :
   Drink of them, hearken to our call.
2. Knowing the days, with Soma-juice poured forth, the singers call to thee,
   O Vayu, with their hymns of praise.
3. Vayu, thy penetrating voice goes forth unto the worshipper,
   Far-spreading for the Soma draught.
4. Here, Indra-Vayu, is the juice ; come for our offered dainties' sake :
   The drops are yearning for you both.
5. Vayu and Indra, well ye know libations, rich in sacred rites !
   So come ye hither rapidly.
6. Vayu and Indra, come to what the Soma-presser hath prepared :
   Soon, heroes, even with resolve.
7. Mitra, of holy strength, I call, and for destroying Varuna,
   Who make the oil-fed rite complete.
8. Mitra and Varuna, through Law, lovers and cherishers of Law,
   Have ye obtained your mighty power.
9. Our sages, Mitra-Varuna, of wide dominion, strong by birth,
   Vouchsafe us strength that worketh well.

---

*A name of Agni.

Hymn 20. RIBHUS.

1. For the celestial race this song of praise which gives wealth
   lavishly
   Was made by singers with their lips.
2. They who for Indra, with their mind, formed horses harnessed by
   a word,
   Attained by works to sacrifice.
3. They for the two Nasatyas* wrought a light car moving every
   way :
   They formed a nectar-yielding cow.
4. The Ribhus with effectual prayers, honest, with constant labour
   made
   Their sire and mother young again.
5. Together came your gladdening drops with Indra by the Maruts
   girt,
   With the Adityas, with the kings.
6. The sacrificial ladle, wrought newly by the god Twashtar's hand—
   Four ladles have ye made thereof.
7. Vouchsafe us wealth, to him who pours thrice seven libations,
   yea, to each
   Give wealth, pleased with our eulogies.
8. As ministering priests they held, by pious acts they won themselves,
   A share in sacrifice with gods.

Hymn 22. GODDESSES.

[This hymn is addressed to the Asvins and others. The verses referring to
the goddesses are quoted.]

9. O Agni, hither bring to us the willing spouses of the gods,
   And Twashtar, to the Soma-draught.
10. Most youthful Agni, hither bring their spouses, Hotra, Bharati,
    Varutri, Dhishana, for aid.
11. Spouses of heroes, goddesses, with whole wings may they come
    to us.
    With great protection and with aid.
12. Indrani, Varunani, and Agnayi hither I invite,
    For weal to drink the Soma-juice.

Hymn 25. VARUNA.

[This is one of the hymns addressed by Sunahsepa to Varuna, when bound
to the sacrificial post. (See page 61).]

1. Whatever law of thine, O god, O Varuna, as we are men,
   Day after day we violate.
2. Give us not a prey to death, to be destroyed by thee in wrath,
   To thy fierce anger when displeased.

The Asvins.

3. To gain thy mercy, Varuna, with hymns we bind thy heart, as
    binds
    The charioteer his tethered horse.
4. They flee from me dispirited, bent only on obtaining wealth,
    As to their nests the birds of air.
5. When shall we bring, to be appeased, the hero, lord of warrior
    might,
    How, the far-seeing Varuna?
6. This, this with joy, they both accept in common : never do they fail
    The ever-faithful worshipper.
7. He knows the path of birds that fly through heaven, and, sovran
    of the sea,
    He knows the ships that are thereon.
8. True to his holy law, he knows the twelve moons with their
    progeny* :
    He knows the moon of later birth.
9. He knows the pathway of the wind, the spreading, high, and
    mighty wind :
    He knows the gods who dwell above.
10. Varuna, true to holy law, sits down among his people ; he,
    Most wise, sits there to govern all.
11. From thence perceiving he beholds all wondrous things, both
    what hath been,
    And what hereafter will be done.
12. May that Aditya, very wise, make fair paths for us all our days :
    May he prolong our lives for us.
13. Varuna, wearing golden mail, hath clad him in a shining robe :
    His spies are seated round about.
14. The god whom enemies threaten out, nor those who tyrannise
    o'er men,
    Nor those whose minds are bent on wrong.
15. He who gives glory to mankind, not glory that is incomplete,
    To our own bodies giving it.
16. Yearning for the wide-seeing one, my thoughts move onward
    unto him,
    As kine unto their pastures move.
17. Once more together let us speak, because my meath† is brought :
    priest-like,
    Thou eatest what is dear to thee.
18. Now saw I him whom all may see, I saw his car above the earth :
    He hath accepted these my songs.
19. Varuna, hear this call of mine : be gracious unto us this day :
    Longing for help I cried to thee.
20. Thou, O wise god, art lord of all, thou art the king of earth and
    heaven :
    Hear, as thou goest in thy way.
21. Release us from the upper bond, untie the bond between, and
    loose
    The bonds below, that I may live.

---

* The days.   † Usually *mead*, a sweet liquor.

Hymn 42. PUSHAN.

1. Shorten our ways, O Pushan, move aside obstruction in the path :
   Go close before us, cloud-born god.
2. Drive Pushan, from our road the wolf, the wicked inauspicious wolf, *
   Who lies in wait to injure us.
3. Who lurks about the path we take, the robber with a guileful heart :
   Far from the road chase him away.
4. Tread with thy foot and trample out the firebrand of the wicked one,
   The double-tongued, whoe'er he be.
5. Wise Pushan, wonder-worker, we claim of thee now the aid wherewith
   Thou furtheredst our sires of old.
6. So, lord of all prosperity, best wielder of the golden sword,
   Make riches easy to be won.
7. Past all pursuers lead us, make pleasant our path and fair to tread :
   O Pushan, find thou power for this.
8. Lead us to meadows rich in grass : send on our way no early heat :
   O Pushan, find thou power for this.
9. Be gracious to us, fill us full, give, feed us, and invigorate :
   O Pushan, find thou power for this.
10. No blame have we for Pushan ; him we magnify with songs of praise :
    We seek the mighty one for wealth.

Hymn 90. VISVEDEVAS.

1. May Varuna with guidance straight, and Mitra lead us, he who knows,
   And Aryaman in accord with gods.
2. For they are dealers forth of wealth, and, not deluded, with their might
   Guard evermore the holy laws.
3. Shelter may they vouchsafe to us, immortal gods to mortal men,
   Chasing our enemies away.
4. May they mark out our paths to bliss, Indra, the Maruts, Pushan, and Bhaga, the gods to be adored.
5. Yea, Pushan, Vishnu, ye who run your course, enrich our hymns with kine ;
   Bless us with all prosperity.
6. The winds waft sweets, the rivers pour sweets for the man who keeps the Law :
   So may the plants be sweet for us.
7. Sweet be the night and sweet the dawns, sweet the terrestrial atmosphere ;
   Sweet be our father Heaven to us.

---

* It signifies also any godless wicked man.

8. Vanaspati* be full of sweets for us, and full of sweets the Sun:
May our milch-kine be sweet for us.

9. Be Mitra gracious unto us, and Varuna, and Aryaman:
Indra, Brihaspati, be kind, and Vishnu of the mighty stride.

Hymn 103. Indra.†

1. That highest Indra-power of thine is distant; that which is here
sages possessed aforetime.
This one is on the earth, in heaven the other, and both unite as
flag and flag in battle.

2. He spread the wide earth out and firmly fixed it, smote with his
thunderbolt and loosed the waters.
Maghavan with his puissance struck down Ahi, rent Rauhina‡
to death, and slaughtered Vyansa.

3. Armed with his bolt and trusting in his prowess he wandered
shattering the Dasas' cities.§
Cast thy dart, knowing, thunderer, at the Dasyu; increase the
Aryas might and glory, Indra.

4. For him who thus hath taught these human races, Maghavan,
bearing a fame-worthy title,
Thunderer, drawing nigh to slay the Dasyus, hath given himself the name of son for glory.

5. See this abundant wealth that he possesses, and put your trust in
Indra's hero vigour.
He found the cattle, and he found the horses, he found the plants,
the forests, and the waters.

6. To him the truly strong, whose deeds are many, to him the strong
bull let us pour the Soma.
The hero watching like a thief in ambush goes parting the possessions of the godless.

7. Well didst thou do that hero deed, O Indra, in waking with thy
bolt the slumbering Ahi.
In thee, delighted, dames divine rejoiced them, the flying Maruts
and all gods were joyful.

8. As thou hast smitten Sushna, Pipru, Vritra and Kuyava,
and Sambara's forts, O Indra.
This prayer of ours may Varuna grant, and Mitra, and Aditi and
Sindhu, Earth and Heaven.

Hymn 115. Surya.

1. The brilliant presence of the gods hath risen, the eye of Mitra,
Varuna, and Agni.
The soul of all that moveth not or moveth, the Sun hath filled the
air and earth and heaven.

---

* "The lord of the forest," here perhaps the deified sacrificial post.
† See the account of Indra page 34.
‡ Said to be a demon of drought: a dark cloud that withholds the rain.
§ The forts of the Dasyus, the aborigines.

2. Like as a young man followeth a maiden, so doth the Sun the
    Dawn, refulgent goddess :
    When pious men extend their generations, before the auspicious
    one for happy fortune.
3. Auspicious are the Sun's bay-coloured horses, bright, changing
    hues, meet for our shouts of triumph.
    Bearing our prayers, the sky's ridge have they mounted, and in
    a moment speed round earth and heaven.
4. This is the godhead, this the might of Surya; he hath with-
    drawn what spread o'er work unfinished.
    When he hath loosed his horses from their station, straight over
    all Night spreadeth out her garment.
5. In the sky's lap the Sun this form assumeth for Mitra and for
    Varuna to look on.
    His bay steeds well maintain his power eternal, at one time
    bright and darksome at another.
6. This day, O gods, while Surya is ascending, deliver us from trouble
    and dishonour.
    This prayer of ours may Varuna grant, and Mitra, and Aditi and
    Sindhu, Earth and Heaven.

Hymn 126. THE PRAISES OF BHAVAYAVYA.

[The hymn writer, Kakshivan, fell asleep on a journey. He was aroused
in the morning by Raja Svanaya who took him home and gave him at once
his ten daughters in marriage, presenting him at the same time with the
gifts mentioned in the hymn. The poet praises the liberality of Svanaya,
here called Bhavayavya, from his father Bhava.]

1. With wisdom I present these lively praises of Bhavaya dweller
    on the bank of Sindhu ;
    For he, unconquered king, desiring glory, hath furnished me a
    thousand sacrifices.
2. A hundred necklets from the king, beseeching, a hundred gift-
    steeds I at once accepted ;
    Of the lords cows a thousand, I Kakshivan. His deathless glory
    hath he spread to heaven.
3. Horses of dusky colour stood beside me, ten chariots, Svanaya's
    gift, with mares to draw them.
    Kine numbering sixty thousand followed after. Kakshivan gained
    them when the days were closing.
4. Forty bay horses of the ten cars' master before a thousand lead
    the long procession.
    Reeling in joy Rakshivan sons and Pajra's have groomed the
    coursers decked with pearly trappings.
5. An earlier gift for you have I accepted eight cows, good milkers,
    and three harnessed horses,
    Pajras, who with your wains with your great kinsman like troops
    of subjects have been fain for glory.*

---

* The hymn ends with two verses, supposed to be part of a love song. They are
omitted as indecent. Hymn 179 is omitted for the same reason.

Hymn 138. Pushan.

1. Strong Pushan's majesty is lauded evermore, the glory of his lordly might is never faint, his song of praise is never faint.
Seeking felicity I laud him nigh to help, the source of bliss,
Who, vigorous one, hath drawn to him the hearts of all, drawn them, the vigorous one, the god.

2. Thee, then O Pushan, like a swift one on his way, I urge with lauds that thou mayst make the foemen flee, drive, camel-like, our foes afar.
As I, a man, call thee, a god, giver of bless, to be my friend,
So make our loudly-chanted praises glorious, in battles make them glorious.

3. Thou, Pushan, in whose friendship they who sing forth praise enjoy advantage, even in wisdom, through thy grace, in wisdom even they are advanced.
So, after this most recent course, we come to thee with prayers for wealth.
Not stirred to anger, O wide-ruler come to us, come thou to us in every fight.

4. Not stirred to anger, come, free-giver, nigh to us, to take this gift of ours, thou who hast goats for steeds, goat-borne! their gift who long for fame,
So, wonder-worker! may we turn thee hither with our effectual lauds.
I slight thee not, O Pushan, thou resplendent one: thy friendship may not be despised.

Hymn 156. Vishnu.

1. Far shining, widely famed, going thy wonted way, fed with the oil, be helpful, Mitra-like, to us.
So, Vishnu, e'en the wise must swell thy song of praise, and he who hath oblations pay thee solemn rites.

2. He who brings gifts to him the ancient and the last, to Vishnu who ordains, together with his spouse,
Who tells the lofty birth of him the lofty one, shall verily surpass in glory e'en his peer.

3. Him have ye satisfied, singers, as well ye know, primeval germ of Order even from his birth,
Ye, knowing e'en his name have told it forth; may we, Vishnu, enjoy the grace of thee the mighty one.

4. The sovran Varuna and both the Asvins wait on this the will of him who guides the Marut host.
Vishnu hath power supreme and might that finds the day, and with his friend unbars the stable of the kine.

5. Even he the heavenly one who came for fellowship, Vishnu to Indra, godly to the godlier,
Who, maker, throned in three worlds, helps the Aryan man, and gives the worshipper his share of holy law.

Hymn 187. ANNASTUTI, PRAISE OF FOOD.

["According to Saunaka, this hymn should be recited by a person about to eat, when his food will never disagree with him; its repetition also, accompanied with oblations and worship, will secure him against want of food, and if he should have taken poison, its silent repetition will act as an antidote."—WILSON.]

1. Now will I glorify Food that upholds great strength,
   By whose invigorating power Trita (Indra) rent Vritra limb from limb.
2. O pleasant Food, O Food of meath, thee have we chosen for our own,
   So be our kind protector thou.
3. Come hitherward to us, O Food, auspicious with auspicious help,
   Health, bringing, not unkind, a dear and guileless friend.
4. These juices which, O Food, are thine throughout the regions are diffused.
   Like winds they have their place in heaven.
5. These gifts of thine, O Food, O Food most sweet to taste,
   These savours of thy juices work like creatures that have mighty necks.
6. In thee, O Food, is set the spirit of great gods.
   Under thy flag brave deeds were done; he slew the dragon with thy help.
7. If thou be gone unto the splendour of the clouds,
   Even from thence, O Food of meath, prepared for our enjoyment, come,
8. Whatever morsel we consume from waters or from plants of earth, O Soma, wax thou fat thereby,
9. What, soma, we enjoy from thee in milky-food or barley-brew, vatapi (the body) grow thou fat thereby.
10. O vegetable, cake of meal, be wholesome, firm, and strengthening: Vatapi, grow thou fat thereby.
11. O Food, from thee as such have we drawn forth with lauds, like cows, our sacrificial gifts,
    From thee who banquetest with gods, from thee who banquetest with us.

MANDALA II.

This book contains only 43 hymns. It is commonly called the Book of Gritsamada, as nearly all the hymns are ascribed to that Rishi.

Fourteen of the hymns are addressed to Indra, two of them in the form of the Kapinjula, a kind of partridge, and nine to Agni.

Hymn 6. AGNI.

1. Agni, accept these logs of wood, this waiting with my prayer on thee:
   Hear graciously these songs of praise.
2. With this hymn let us honour thee, seeker of horses, son of strength,
   With this fair hymn, thou nobly born.

3. As such, lover of song, with songs, wealth-lover, giver of our wealth!
With reverence let us worship thee.

4. Be thou for us a liberal prince, giver and lord of precious things,
Drive those who hate us far away.

5. Such as thou art, give rain from heaven, give strength which no man may resist:
Give food exceeding plentiful.

6. To him who lauds thee, craving help, most youthful envoy! through our song,
Most holy herald! come thou nigh.

7. Between both races, Agni, sage, well-skilled thou passest to and fro,
As envoy friendly to mankind.

8. Befriend us thou as knowing all. Sage, duly worship thou the gods,
And seat thee on this sacred grass.

Hymn 28. VARUNA.

1. This land of the self-radiant wise Aditya shall be supreme o'er all that is in greatness.
I beg renown of Varuna the mighty, the god exceeding kind to him who worships.

2. Having extolled thee, Varuna, with thoughtful care may we have high fortune in thy service,
Singing thy praises like the fires at coming, day after day, of mornings rich in cattle.

3. May we be in thy keeping, O thou leader, wide-ruling Varuna, lord of many heroes.
O sons of Aditi, for ever faithful, pardon us, gods, admit us to your friendship.

4. He made them flow, the Aditya, the sustainer: the rivers run by Varuna's commandment.
These feel no weariness, nor cease from flowing: swift have they flown like birds in air around us.

5. Loose me from sin as from a bond that binds me : may we swell, Varuna, thy spring of Order.
Let not my thread, while I weave song, be severed, nor my work's sum, before the time, be shattered.

6. Far from me, Varuna, remove all danger : accept me graciously, thou holy sovran.
Cast off, like cords that hold a calf, my troubles : I am not even mine eyelid's lord without thee.

7. Strike us not, Varuna with those dread weapons which, Asura, at thy bidding wound the sinner.
Let us not pass away from light to excile. Scatter, that we may live, the men who hate us.

8. O mighty Varuna, now and hereafter, even as of old, will we speak forth our worship.

For in thyself, infallible god, thy statutes ne'er to be moved are fixed as on a mountain.

9. Wipe out what debts I have myself contracted ; let me not profit, king, by gain of others.
   Full many a morn remains to dawn upon us : in these, O Varuna, while we live direct us.

10. O king, whoever, be he friend or kinsman, hath threatened me affrighted in my slumber—
    If any wolf or robber fain would harm us, therefrom, O Varuna, give thou us protection.

11. May I not live O Varuna, to witness my wealthy liberal, dear friend's destitution.
    King, may I never lack well-ordered riches. Loud may we speak, with heroes, in assembly.

Hymn 42. INDRA IN THE FORM OF A KAPINJALA.

1. Filling his race aloud with cries repeated, he (Kapinjala) sends his voice out as his boat a steerman.
   O bird, be ominous of happy fortune : from no side my calamity befall thee.

2. Let not the falcon kill thee, nor the eagle ; let not the arrow-bearing archer reach thee.
   Still crying in the region of the Fathers, speak here auspicious, bearing joyful tidings.

3. Bringing good tidings, bird of happy omen, call thou out loudly southward of our dwellings,*
   So that no thief, no sinner may oppress us. Loud may we speak, with heroes, in assembly.

MANDALA III.

This Mandala contains 62 hymns, ascribed to the Rishi Visvamitra, or to members of his family. It is said that he was born a Kshatriya, but by virtue of his intense austerities he raised himself to the Brahman caste.

The Rishis who wrote the hymns were not always friendly with one another. "Especially prominent," says Weber, "is the enmity between the families of Vasishtha and Visvamitra, which runs through all Vedic antiquity, continues to play an important part in the epic, and is kept up to the latest times ; so that, for example, a commentator of the Veda who claims to be descended from Vasishtha, leaves passages unexpounded in which the latter is stated to have had a curse imprecated upon him. This implacable hatred owes its origin to the trifling circumstance of Vasishtha having been

---

* The Pitris are supposed to dwell in the south. The cry of birds from that quarter was regarded as auspicious.

once appointed chief sacrificial priest instead of Visvamitra by one of the petty kings of those early times."*

In the Markandeya Purana, Vasishtha curses Visvamitra and turns him into a crane, while Vasishtha is changed into a starling. The two fought so furiously that the course of the universe was disturbed, and many creatures perished.

Of the hymns 22 are addressed to Indra, and 21 to Agni. This Mandala is noted as containing the Gayatri.

Hymn 8. Sacrificial Post.

[The post, to which animals to be sacrificed were tied, was regarded as a deified object when consecrated, and considered to be a form of Agni.]

1. God-serving men, O sovran of the forest, with heavenly meath (ghee) at sacrifice anoint thee.
   Grant wealth to us when thou art standing upright as when reposing on thy mother's bosom.

2. Set up to eastward of the fire enkindled, accepting prayer that wastes not, rich in heroes,
   Driving far from us poverty and famine, lift thyself up to bring us great good fortune.

3. Lord of the forest, raise thyself up on the loftiest spot of earth.
   Give splendour, fixt and measured well, to him who brings the sacrifice.

4. Well-robed, enveloped, he is come, the youthful: springing to life his glory waxeth greater.
   Contemplative in mind and god-adoring, sages of. high intelligence upraise him.

5. Sprung up he rises in the days' fair weather, increasing in the men-frequented synodn.
   With song the wise and skilful consecrate him: his voice the god-adoring singer utters.

6. Ye whom religious men have firmly planted; thou forest-sovran whom the axe hath fashioned,—
   Let those the stakes divine which here are standing be fain to grant us wealth with store of children.

7. O men who lift the ladles up, these hewn and planted in the ground,
   Bringing a blessing to the field shall bear our precious gift to gods.

8. Adityas, Rudras, Vasus, careful leaders, Earth, Heaven, and Prithivi and air's mid region,
   Accordant deities, shall bless our worship and make our sacrifice's ensign lofty.

9. Like swans that flee in lengthened line, the pillars have come to us arrayed in brilliant colour.
   They, lifted up on high, by sages, eastward, go forth as gods to the gods' dwelling-places.

---

* *History of Indian Literature*, pp. 37, 38.

10. Those stakes upon the earth with rings that deck them seem to
the eye like horns of hornèd creatures ;
Or as upraised by priests in invocation, let them assist us in the
rush to battle.
11. Lord of the wood, rise with a hundred branches : with thousand
branches may we rise to greatness,
Thou whom this hatchet, with an edge well whetted for great
felicity hath brought before us.

Hymn 48. INDRA.

1. Soon as the young Bull (Indra) sprang into existence he longed
to taste the pressed-out Soma's liquor.
Drink thou thy fill, according to thy longing, first, of the noble
mixture blent with Soma.
2. That day when thou wast born thou, fain to taste it, drankest the
plant's milk which the mountains nourish.
That milk thy mother* first, the dame who bare thee poured for
thee in thy mighty father's† dwelling.
3. Desiring food he came unto his mother, and on her breast beheld
the pungent Soma.
Wise, he moved on, keeping aloof the others, and wrought great
exploits in his varied aspects.
4. Fierce, quickly conquering, of surpassing vigour, he framed his
body even as he listed.
E'en from his birth-time Indra conquered Twashter, bore off the
Soma and in beakers drank it.
5. Call we on Maghavan, auspicious Indra, best hero in the fight
where spoil is gathered ;
The strong, who listens, who gives aid in battles, who slays the
Vritras,.wins and gathers riches.

Hymn 62. INDRA AND OTHERS.

[The tenth verse of this hymn is the Gayatri.]
1. Your well-known prompt activities aforetime needed no impulse
from your faithful servant.
Where, Indra, Varuna, is now that glory wherewith ye brought
support to those who loved you ?
2. This man, most diligent, seeking after riches, incessantly invokes
you for your favour.
Accordant, Indra, Varuna, with the Maruts, with Heaven and
Earth, hear ye mine invocation.
3. O Indra, Varuna, ours be this treasure, ours be wealth, Maruts,
with full store of heroes.
May the Varutris with their shelter aid us, and Bharati‡ and
Hotra with the mornings.
4. Be pleased with our oblations thou loved of all gods, Brihaspati :§
Give wealth to him who brings thee gifts.
5. At sacrifices, with your hymns worship the pure Brihaspati—
I pray for power which none may bend—

---

* Aditi.   † Kasyapa or Twashtar.   ‡ Wives of the gods.   § Lord of Prayer.

6. The Bull of men, whom none deceive, the wearer of each shape at will,
   Brihaspati most excellent.
7. Divine, resplendest Pushan, this our newest hymn of eulogy.
   By us is chanted forth to thee.
8. Accept with favour this my song, be gracious to the earnest thought,
   Even as a bridegroom to his bride.
9. May he who sees all living things, sees them together at a glance,—
   May he, may Pushan be our help.
10. May we attain that excellent glory of Savitar the god :
    So may he stimulate our prayers.
11. With understanding, earnestly, of Savitar the god we crave
    Our portion of prosperity.
12. Men, singers worship Savitar the god with hymn and holy rites,
    Urged by the impulse of their thoughts.
13. Soma who gives success goes forth, goes to the gathering-place of gods.
    To seat him at the seat of Law.
14. To us and to our cattle may Soma give salutary food,
    To biped and to quadruped.
15. May Soma, strengthening our power of life, and conquering our foes,
    In our assembly take his seat.
16. May Mitra, Varuna, sapient pair, bedew our pasturage with oil,
    With meath the regions of the air.
17. Far-ruling, joyful when adored, ye reign through majesty of might,
    With pure laws everlastingly.
18. Lauded by Jamadagni's song, sit in the place of holy Law :*
    Drink Soma, ye who strengthen Law.

MANDALA IV.

This book contains 58 hymns. The first forty-one are ascribed to the Rishi Vamadeva, son of Gotama; so also are the last fourteen. Twelve are addressed specially to Indra, and eleven to Agni.

Hymn 12. AGNI.

[This is one of the few hymns addressed to Agni in which sin is prominently mentioned. But the invariable reference to wealth is also introduced.]

1. Whoso enkindles thee, with lifted ladle, and thrice this day offers thee food, O Agni,
   May he excel, triumphant, through thy splendours, wise through thy mental power, O Jatavedas.†

---

*The place where sacrifice ordained by eternal Law is performed.
† An epithet of Agni. Its meaning is uncertain.

2. Whoso, with toil and trouble, brings thee fuel, serving the majesty of mighty Agni,
   He kindling thee at evening and at morning, prospers, and comes to wealth, and slays his foemen.
3. Agni is master of sublime dominion, Agni is lord of strength and lofty riches.
   Straightway the self-reliant god, most youthful, gives treasures to the mortal who adores him.
4. Most youthful god, whatever sin, through folly, here in the world of men we have committed,
   Before great Aditi* make thou us sinless : remit entirely, Agni, our offences.
5. Even in the presence of great sin, O Agni, free us from prison of the gods or mortals.
   Never may we who are thy friends be injured : grant health and wealth unto our seed and offspring.
6. Even as ye here, gods excellent and holy, have loosed the cow that by the foot was tethered,
   So also set us free from this affliction : long let our life, O Agni, be extended.

Hymn 44. ASVINS.

[Numerous hymns are addressed to the Asvins. One is quoted as a specimen.]

1. May we invoke this day your car, far-spreading, O Asvins, even the gathering of the sunlight,—
   Car praised in hymns, most ample, rich in treasure, fitted with seats, the car that beareth Surya.
2. Asvins, ye gained that glory by your godhead, ye sons of heaven, by your own might and power.
   Food followeth closely upon your bright appearing when stately horses in your chariot draw you.
3. Who bringeth you to-day for help with offered oblations, or with hymns to drink the juices ?
   Who, for the sacrifice's ancient lover, turneth you hither, Asvins, offering homage ?
4. Borne on your golden car, ye omnipresent ! come to this sacrifice of ours, Nasatyas.
   Drink of the pleasant liquor of the Soma : give riches to the people who adore you.
5. Come hitherward to us from earth, from heaven, borne on your golden chariot rolling lightly.
   Suffer not other worshippers to stay you : here are ye bound by earlier bonds of friendship.
6. Now for us both mete out, O wonder-workers, riches exceeding great with store of heroes.
   Because the men have sent you praise, O Asvins, and Ajamilhas† come to the laudation.

---

* " Apparently the great omnipresent Power which controls the forces of the universe, and from which no sins are hidden."—Griffith.　　† Men of the Rishi's family.

7. Whene'er I gratified you here together, your grace was given us,
   O ye rich in booty.
   Protect, ye twain, the singer of your praises : to you, Nasatyas, is
   my wish directed.

MANDALA V.

This Book contains 87 hymns. Of these 21 are addressed to
Agni, 11 to Mitra and Varuna, 9 each to Indra, the Maruts and
Visvedevas, and 6 to the Asvins.

Hymn 26. AGNI.

[Agni is specially addressed as the inviter of the gods to sacrifices.]

1. O Agni, holy and divine, with splendour and thy pleasant
   tongue
   Bring hither and adore the gods.
2. We pray thee, thou who droppest oil, bright-rayed ! who lookest
   on the Sun,
   Bring the gods hither to the feast.
3. We have enkindled thee, O sage, bright caller of the gods to
   feast,
   O Agni, great in sacrifice.
4. O Agni, come with all the gods, come to our sacrificial gift :
   We choose thee as invoking priest.
5. Bring, Agni, to the worshipper who pours the juice heroic
   strength :
   Sit with the gods upon the grass.
6. Victor of thousands, Agni, thou, enkindled, cherishest the laws,
   Laud-worthy, envoy of the gods.
7. Sit Agni Jatavedas down, the bearer of our sacred gifts,
   Most youthful, god and minister.
8. Duly proceed our sacrifice, comprising all the gods, to-day :
   Strew holy grass to be their seat.
9. So may the Maruts sit thereon, the Asvins, Mitra, Varuna :
   The gods with all their company.

Hymn 40. INDRA, SURYA, ATRI.

[The Hindu explanation of eclipses is that they are caused by the Asura
Rahu seeking to seize the sun and moon. In the Vedas he is called Svarbhanu. The sun is supposed to be delivered by this hymn, chanted by Atri,
and expresses his gratitude. The verses referring to the eclipse alone are
quoted.

5. O Surya, when the Asura's descendant, Svarbhanu, pierced
   thee through and through with darkness,
   All creatures looked like one who is bewildered, who knoweth not
   the place where he is standing.

6. What time thou smotest down Svarbhanu's magic that spread
itself beneath the sky, O Indra,
By his fourth sacred prayer Atri discovered Surya concealed in
gloom that stayed his function.

7. Let not the oppressor with this dread, through anger swallow
me up, for I am thine, O Atri.
Mitra art thou, the sender of true blessings : thou and king
Varuna be both my helpers.

8. The Brahman Atri, as he set the press-storms, serving the gods
with praise and adoration,
Established in the heaven the eye of Surya, and caused Svarbhanu's magic arts to vanish.

9. The Atris found the Sun again, him whom Svarbhanu of the
brood
Of Asuras had pierced with gloom. This none beside had power
to do.

Hymn 57. MARUTS.

1. Of one accord, with Indra, O ye Rudras, come borne on your
golden car for our prosperity.
An offering from us, this hymn is brought to you, as, unto one
who thirsts for water, heavenly springs.

2. Armed with your daggers, full of wisdom, armed with spears,
armed with your quivers, armed with arrows, with good bows,
Good horses and good cars have ye, O Prisni's sons : ye, Maruts,
with good weapons go to victory.

3. From hills and heaven ye shake wealth for the worshipper : in
terror at your coming low the woods bow down.
· Ye make the earth to tremble, sons of Prisni, when for victory
ye have yoked, fierce ones ! your spotted deer.

4. Impetuous as the wind, wrapped in their robes of rain, like twins
of noble aspect and of lovely form.
The Maruts, spotless, with steeds tawny-hued and red, strong in
their mightiness and spreading wide like heaven.

5. Rich in adornment, rich in drops, munificent, bright in their
aspect, yielding bounties that endure.
Noble by birth, adorned with gold upon their breasts, the singers
of the sky have won immortal fame.

6. Borne on both shoulders, O ye Maruts, are your spears : within
your arms is laid your energy and strength.
Your manliness on your heads, your weapons in your cars, all
glorious majesty is moulded on your forms.

7. Vouchsafe to us, O Maruts, splendid bounty in cattle and in
steeds, in cars and heroes.
Children of Rudra, give us high distinction : may I enjoy your
godlike help and favour.

8. Ho ! Maruts, heroes, skilled in Law, immortal, be gracious unto
us, ye rich in treasures,
Ye hearers of the truth, ye sage and youthful, mightily waxing
with loud-resonant voices.

Hymn 83. PARJANYA.

[Max Müller says the following is a very fair specimen of Vedic hymns.]

1. Song with these songs thy welcome to the mighty, with adoration
    praise and call Parjanya.
    The Bull, loud roaring, swift to send his bounty, lays in the
    plants the seed for germination.
2. He smites the trees apart, he slays the demons : all life fears him
    who wields the mighty weapon.
    From him exceeding strong flees e'en the guiltless when thunder-
    ing Parjanya smites the wicked.
3. Like a car-driver whipping on his horses, he makes the messengers
    of rain spring forward.
    Far off resounds the roaring of the lion what time Parjanya fills
    the sky with rain-cloud.
4. Forth burst the winds, down come the lightning-flashes ; the
    plants shoot up, the realm of light is streaming.
    Food springs abundant for all living creatures what time Parjanya
    quickens earth with moisture.
5. Thou at whose bedding earth bows low before thee, at whose com-
    mand hoofed cattle fly in terror,
    At whose behest the plants assume all colours, even thou Par-
    janya, yield us great protection.
6. Send down for us the rain of heaven, ye Maruts, and let the stal-
    lion's streams descend in torrents.
    Come hither with this thunder while thou pourest the waters
    down, our heavenly lord and father.
7. Thunder and roar : the germ of life deposit. Fly round us. on
    thy chariot water-laden.
    Thine opened water-skin draw with thee downward, and let the
    hollows and the heights be level.
8. Lift up the mighty vessel, pour down water, and let the liberated
    streams rush forward.
    Saturate both the earth and heaven with fatness, and for the
    cows let there be drink abundant.
9. When thou, with thunder and with roar, Parjanya, smitest sin-
    ners down,
    This universe exults thereat, yea, all that is upon the earth.
10. Thou hast poured down the rain-flood : now withhold it. Thou
    hast made desert places fit for travel.
    Thou hast made herbs to grow for our enjoyment : yea, thou hast
    won thee praise from living creatures.

Hymn 85. VARUNA.

1. Sing forth a hymn sublime and solemn, grateful to glorious
    Varuna, imperial ruler,
    Who hath struck out, like one who slays the victim, earth as a
    skin to spread in front of Surya.

2. In the tree-tops the air he hath extended, put milk in kine and vigorous speed in horses,
Sit intellect in hearts, fire in the waters, Surya in heaven, and Soma on the mountain.
3. Varuna lets the big cask, opening downward, flow through the heaven and earth and air's mid-region.
Therewith the universe's sovran waters earth as the shower of rain bedews the barley.
4. When Varuna is fain for milk he moistens the sky, the land, and earth to her foundation.
Then straight the mountains clothe them in the rain-cloud : the heroes, putting forth their vigour, loose them.
5. I will declare this mighty deed of magic, of glorious Varuna the lord immortal ;
Who standing in the firmament hath meted the earth out with the sun as with a measure.
6. None, verily, hath ever let or hindered this the most wise god's mighty deed of magic,*
Whereby, with all their flood, the lucid rivers fill not one sea wherein they pour their water.
7. If we have sinned against the man who loves us, have ever wronged a brother, friend, or comrade,
The neighbour ever with us, or a stranger, O Varuna, remove from us the trespass.
8. If we, as gamesters cheat at play, have cheated, done wrong unwittingly or sinned of purpose,
Cast all these sins away like loosened fetters, and Varuna, let us be thine own beloved.

MANDALA VI.

The Rishi of this Book is Bharadvaja, to whom, with few exceptions, all the hymns are attributed. It contains 75 hymns. To Indra 21 hymns are addressed ; to Agni, 13 ; to Pushan, 5 ; to the Visvadevas, 4.

Hymn 28. Cows.†

1. The kine have come and brought good fortune: let them rest in the cow-pen and be happy near us.
Here let them stay prolific, many-coloured, and yield through many morns their milk for Indra.
2. Indra aids him who offers sacrifice and gifts : he takes not what is his, and gives him more thereto.
Increasing ever more and more his wealth, he makes the pious dwell within unbroken bounds.

---

* *Máyâm.* The word may be rendered design.
† The cows are the deified object of the hymn, except in stanza 2 and part of 8, where the deity is Indra.

3. These are ne'er lost, no robber ever injures them : no evil-minded foe attempts to harass them.

The master of the kine lives many year with these, the cows whereby he pours his gifts and serves the gods.

4. The charger with his dusty brow o'ertakes them not, and never to the shambles do they take their way.

These cows, the cattle of the pious worshipper, roam over widespread pasture where no danger is.

5. To me the cows seem Bhaga, they seem Indra,* they seem a portion of the first-poured Soma.

These present cows, they, O ye men, are Indra. I long for Indra with my heart and spirit.

6. O cows, ye fatten e'en the worn and wasted, and make the unlovely beautiful to look on.

Prosper my house, ye with suspicious voices. Your power is glorified in our assemblies.

7. Crop good pasturage and be prolific; drink pure sweet water at good drinking-places.

Never be thief or sinful man your master, and may the dart of Rudra still avoid you.

8. Now let this close admixture be close intermingled with these cows,

Mixt with the steer's prolific flow, and, Indra, with thy hero might.

Hymn 53. PUSHAN.

[Niggardliness is condemned].

1. Lord of the path, O Pushan, we have yoked and bound thee to our hymn,

Even as a car, to win the prize.

2. Bring us the wealth that men require, a manly master of a house,

Free handed with the liberal meed.

3. Even him who would not give, do thou, O glorious Pushan, urge to give,

And make the niggard's soul grow soft.

4. Clear paths that we may win the prize; scatter our enemies afar.

Strong god, be all our thoughts fulfilled.

5. Penetrate with an awl (or goad). O sage, the hearts of avaricious churls,

And make them subject to our will.

6. Thrust with thine awl, O Pushan: seek that which the niggard's heart holds dear,

And make him subject to our will.

7. Tear up and rend in pieces, sage, the hearts of avaricious churls,

And make them subject to our will.

---

* " The worshipper regards the cows as the deities, Bhaga and Indra, who bring him happiness."—Griffith.

8. Thou, glowing, Pushan, carriest an awl that urges men to prayer;
Therewith do thou tear up and rend to shreds the heart of every
one.
9. Thou bearest, glowing, lord ! a goad with horny point that guides
the cows :
Thence do we seek thy gift of bliss.
10. And make this hymn of ours produce kine, horses, and a store of
wealth
For our delight and use as men.

Hymn 75. WEAPONS OF WAR.

["The deified objects are the armour and warlike weapons, charioteer,
chariot, horses, etc., and tutelary deities, addressed, mentioned or invoked in
the hymn."—Griffith.]
The hymn is too long for quotation. The following are some of the verses
referring to the bow and arrow, the principal offensive weapon.

2. With bow let us win kine, with bow the battle, with bow be
victors in our hot encounters.
The bow brings grief and sorrow to the foeman : armed with the
bow may we subdue all regions.
16. Loosed from the bowstring fly away, thou arrow, sharpened by our
prayer.
Go to the foemen, strike them home, and let not one be left alive.

Charioteer and chariot are thus noticed. .

6. Upstanding in the car the skilful charioteer guides his strong
horses on whithersoe'er he will.
See and admire the strength of those controlling reins which from
behind declare the will of him who drives.
7. Horses whose hoof rain dust are weighing loudly, yoked to the
chariots, showing forth their vigour.
With their forefeet descending on the foemen, they, never flinching,
trample and destroy them.

The hymn concludes thus :

19. Whoso would kill us, whether he be a strange foe or one of us,
May all the gods discomfit him. My nearest, closest mail is
prayer.

MANDALA VII.

All the hymns of this Book are ascribed to the Rishi Vasishtha,
with whom his sons are associated as the seers of parts of two
hymns. There are 104 hymns ; of which 14 are addressed to Indra,
13 to Agni, 8 to the Asvins, 7 each to Ushas and the Visvedevas,
4 to Varuna, and one to frogs. The prevailing metre is Trishtub.

Hymn 45. SAVITAR.

1. May the god Savitar, rich in goodly treasures, filling the region,
borne by steeds, come hither,
In his hand holding much that makes people happy, lulling to
slumber and arousing creatures.

2. Golden, sublime, and easy in their motion, his arms extend unto the bounds of heaven.
Now shall that mightiness of his be lauded : even Sura * yields to him in active vigour.
3. May this god Savitar, the strong and mighty, the lord of precious wealth, vouchsafe us treasures.
May he, advancing his far-spreading lustre, bestow on us the food that feedeth mortals.
4. These songs praise Savitar whose tongue is pleasant, praise him whose arms are full, whose hands are lovely.
High vital strength, and manifold, may he grant us. Preserve us evermore, ye gods, with blessings.

Hymn 46. RUDRA.

1. To Rudra bring these songs, whose bow is firm and strong, the god of heavenly nature, with swift-flying shafts.
Disposer, conqueror whom none may overcome, armed with sharp-pointed weapons : may he hear our call.
2. He through his lordship thinks in beings of the earth, on heavenly beings through his high imperial sway.
Come willingly to our doors that gladly welcome thee, and heal all sickness, Rudra, in our families.
3. May thy bright arrow which, shot down by thee from heaven, flieth upon the earth, pass us uninjured by.
Thou, very gracious god, hast thousand medicines : inflict no evil on our sons or progeny.
4. Slay us not, nor abandon us, O Rudra : let not thy noose, when thou art angry, seize us.
Give us trimmed grass and rule over the living. Preserve us evermore, ye gods, with blessings.

Hymn 49. WATERS.

1. Forth from the middle of the flood the Waters—their chief the Sea—flow cleansing, never sleeping.
Indra, the Bull, the thunderer, dug their channels ; here let those Waters, goddesses, protect me.
2. Waters which come from heaven, or those that wander dug from the earth, or flowing free by nature,
Bright, purifying, speeding to the Ocean, here let those Waters, goddesses, protect me.
3. Those amid whom goes Varuna the sovran, he who discriminates men's truth and falsehood—
Distilling meath the bright, the purifying, here let those Waters, goddesses, protect me.
4. They from whom Varuna the king, and Soma, and all the deities drink strength and vigour,
They into whom Vaisvanara Agni entered, here let these Waters, goddesses, protect me.

---

* The Sun is distinguished from Savitar.

Hymn 51. ADITYAS.

1. Through the Adityas' most auspicious shelter, through their most recent succour may we conquer.
   May they, the mighty, giving ear, establish this sacrifice, to make us free and sinless.
2. Let Aditi rejoice and the Adityas, Varuna, Mitra, Aryaman, most righteous.
   May they, the guardians of the world, protect us, and, to show favour, drink this day our Soma.
3. All universal deities, the Maruts, all the Adityas, yea, and all the Ribhus,
   Indra and Agni, and the Asvins, lauded, preserve us evermore, ye gods, with blessings.

Hymn 53. HEAVEN AND EARTH.

1. As priest with solemn rites and adorations I worship Heaven and Earth, the high and holy.
   To them, great parents of the gods, have sages of ancient time, singing, assigned precedence.
2. With newest hymns set in the seat of Order those the two parents, born before all others.
   Come, Heaven and Earth, with the celestial people, hither to us, for strong is your protection.
3. Yea, Heaven and Earth, ye hold in your profession full many a treasure for the liberal giver.
   Grant us the wealth which comes in free abundance.
   Preserve us evermore, ye gods, with blessings.

Hymn 55. VASTOSHPATI AND INDRA.

[The hymn appears to be made up of three unconnected pieces. The first verse is addressed to Vastoshpati, the guardian god of the house. Verses 2-4 are addressed by the spirits of Indra's worshippers to one of Yama's dogs who would prevent their entering the home of the pious dead. Sarama, the hound of Indra, was the mother of the two spotted watch-dogs of Yama. Verses 5-8 form a sleep song. It was recited by thieves and house-breakers to put people to sleep.—Abridged from Griffith.]

1. Vastoshpati, who killest all disease, and wearest every form, Be an auspicious friend to us.
2. When, O bright son of Sarama, thou showest, tawny-hued! thy teeth,
   They gleam like lances' points within thy mouth when thou wouldest bite: go thou to sleep.
3. Sarama's son, retrace thy way: bark at the robber and the thief.
   At Indra's singers barkest thou? Why dost thou seek to terrify us? Go to sleep.
4. Be on thy guard against the boar, and let the boar beware of thee.
   At Indra's singers barkest thou? Why dost thou seek to terrify us? Go to sleep.

5. Sleep mother, let the father sleep, sleep dog and master of the house.
   Let all the kinsmen sleep, sleep all the people who are round about.
6. The man who sits, the man who walks, and whosoever looks on us,
   Of these we closely shut the eyes, even as we closely shut this house.
7. The Bull who hath a thousand horns, who rises up from out of the sea,—
   By him the strong and mighty one we lull and make the people sleep.
8. The women sleeping in the court, lying without, or stretched on beds,
   The nations with their odorous sweets—these, one and all, we lull to sleep.

Hymn 77.   Ushas.

1. She hath shone brightly like a youthful woman stirring to motion every living creature.
   Agni hath come to feed on mortals' fuel.   She hath made light and chased away the darkness.
2. Turned to this All, far-spreading, she hath risen and shone in brightness with white robes about her.
   She hath beamed forth lovely with golden colours, mother of kine, guide of the days she bringeth.
3. Bearing the gods' own eye, auspicious lady, leading her courser white and fair to look on,
   Distinguished by her beams Dawn shines apparent, come forth to all the world with wondrous treasure.
4. Draw nigh with wealth and dawn away the foeman : prepare for us wide pasture free from danger.
   Drive away those who hate us, bring us riches : pour bounty, opulent lady, on the singer.
5. Send thy most excellent beams to shine and light us, giving us lengthened days, O Dawn, O goddess.
   Granting us food, thou who hast all things precious, and bounty rich in chariots, kine, and horses.
6. O Ushas, nobly-born, daughter of Heaven, whom the Vasishthas with their hymns make mighty,
   Bestow thou on us vast and glorious riches.   Preserve us evermore, ye gods, with blessings.

Hymn 86.   Varuna.

1. The tribes of men have wisdom through his greatness who stayed even spacious heaven and earth asunder ;
   Who urged the high and mighty sky to motion, and stars of old, and spread the earth before him.

2. With mine own heart I commune on the question how Varuna
and I may be united.
What gift of mine will he accept unangered ? When may I
calmly look and find him gracious ?
3. Fain to know this my sin I question others : I seek the wise, O
Varuna, and ask them.
This one same answer even the sages gave me, Surely this Varuna
is angry with thee.
4. What, Varuna, hath been my chief transgression, that thou
shouldest slay the friend who sings thy praises ?
Tell me, unconquerable lord, and quickly sinless will I approach
thee with mine homage.
5. Loose us from sins committed by our fathers, from those wherein we have ourselves offended.
O king, loose, like a thief who feeds the cattle, as from the cord
a calf, set free Vasishtha.
6. Not our own will betrayed us, but seduction, thoughtlessness,
Varuna ! wine, dice, or anger.
The old is near to lead astray the younger ; even slumber leadeth
men to evil-doing.
7. Slavelike may I do service to the bounteous, sarve, free from sin,
the god inclined to anger.
This gentle lord gives wisdom to the simple ; the wiser god leads
on the wise to riches.
8. O lord, O Varuna, may this laudation come close to thee, and lie
within thy spirit.
May it be well with us in rest and labour. Preserve us evermore,
ye gods, with blessings.

Hymn 103. FROGS.

[The hymn, says Max Müller, " which is called a panegyric of the frogs, is
clearly a satire on the priests." It evidently belongs to a late period of
Vedic poetry.]

1. They who lay quiet for a year, the Brahmans who fulfil their vows,
The frogs have lifted up their voice, the voice Parjanya hath
inspired.
2. What time on these, as on a dry skin lying in the pool's bed, the
floods of heaven descended,
The music of the frogs comes forth in concert like the cows'
lowing with their calves beside them.
3. When at the coming of the Rains the water has poured upon
them as they yearned and thirsted,
One seeks another as he talks and greets him with cries of
pleasure as a son his father.
4. Each of these twain receives the other kindly, while they are
revelling in the flow of waters,
When the frog moistened by the rain springs forward, and Green
and Spotty both combine their voices.
5. When one of these repeats the other's language, as he who learns
the lesson of the teacher,

Your every limb seems to be growing larger as ye converse with eloquence on the waters.

6. One as Cow-billow and Goat-bleat the other, one frog is Green and one of them is Spotty.

They bear one common name, and yet they vary, and, talking, modulate the voice diversely.

7. As Brahmans, sitting round the brimful vessel, talk at the Soma-rite of Atiratra,

So, frogs, ye gather round the pool to honour this day of all the year, the first of Rain-time.

8. These Brahmans with the Soma-juice, performing their year-long rite, have lifted up their voices ;

And these Adhvaryus, sweating with their kettles, come forth and show themselves, and none are hidden.

9. They keep the twelvemonth's god-appointed order, and never do the men neglect the season.

Soon as the Rain-time in the year returneth, these who were heated kettles gain their freedom.

10. Cow-bellow and Goat-bleat have granted riches, and Green and Spotty have vouchsafed us treasure.

The frogs who give us cows in hundreds lengthen our lives in this most fertilizing season.

Hymn 104. INDRA-SOMA.

[The hymn consists chiefly of imprecations directed against demons and evil spirits, Rakshasas and Yatudhanas, a kind of goblins. The demon foes are supposed to go about at night, disturbing sacrifices and pious men, ensnaring and even devouring human beings, and generally hostile to the human race.—Griffith. The hymn is too long to be quoted in full.]

1. Indra and Soma, burn, destroy the demon foe, send downward, O ye Bulls, those who add gloom to gloom.

Annihilate the fools, slay them and burn them up ; chase them away from us, pierce the voracious ones.

2. Indra and Soma, let sin round the wicked boil like as a caldron set amid the flames of fire.

Against the foe of prayer, devourer of raw flesh, the vile fiend fierce of eye, keep ye perpetual hate.

3. Indra and Soma, plunge the wicked in the depth, yea, cast them into darkness that hath no support,

So that not one of them may ever thence return ; so may your wrathful might prevail and conquer them.

4. Indra and Soma, hurl your deadly crushing bolt down on the wicked fiend from heaven and from the earth.

Yea, forge out of the mountains your celestial dart wherewith ye burn to death the waxing demon race.

5. Indra and Soma, cast ye downward out of heaven your deadly darts of stone burning with fiery flame,

Eternal, scorching darts; plunge the voracious ones within the depth, and let them sink without a sound.

24. Indra destroy the demon, male and female, joying and triumphing in arts of magic.
Let the fools' gods with bent necks fall and perish, and see no more the sun when he arises.
25. Look each one hither, look around: Indra and Soma, watch ye well.
Cast forth your weapon at the fiends; against the sorcerers hurl your bolt.

MANDALA VIII.

This Book is by a variety of authors. It contains 92 hymns, with 11 called Valakhilya Hymns. Of the hymns 36 are addressed to Indra, 11 to Agni, 5 to the Visvedevas, and 3 to the Maruts.

Hymn 30. VISVEDEVAS.

1. Not one of you, ye gods, is small, none of you is a feeble child : All of you, verily, are great.
2. Thus be ye lauded, ye destroyers of the foe, ye three and thirty deities,
The gods of man, the holy ones.
3. As such defend and succour us, with benedictions speak to us : Lead us not from our fathers' and from Manu's path into the distance far away.
4. Ye deities who stay with us, and all ye gods of all mankind, Give us your wide protection, give shelter for cattle and for steed.

Hymn 69. INDRA.

[This hymn is for success in a coming chariot race.]

1. O Satakratu, truly I have made none else my comforter.
Indra, be gracious unto us.
2. Thou who hast ever aided us kindly of old to win the spoil,
As such, O Indra, favour us.
3. What now? As prompter of the poor thou helpest him who sheds the juice.
Wilt thou not, Indra, strengthen us?
4. O Indra, help our chariot on, yea, thunderer, though it lag behind :
Give this my car the foremost place.
5. Ho there ! why sittest thou at ease ? Make thou my chariot to be first :
And bring the fame of victory near.
6. Assist our car that seeks the prize. What can be easier for thee ?
So make thou us victorious.

Hymn 85. INDRA.

[In this hymn, of which only a few verses are quoted, Indra is styled the " holiest of the holy" (v. 4) and maker of the world and creatures, (v. 6).]

1. For him the Mornings made their courses longer, and Nights with pleasant voices spake to Indra.

For him the floods stood still, the seven mothers, streams easy for the heroes to pass over.

2. The darter penetrated, though in trouble, thrice-seven close-pressed ridges of the mountains.
   Neither might god nor mortal man accomplish what the strong hero wrought in full-grown vigour.

3. The mightest force is Indra's bolt of iron when firmly grasped in both the arms of Indra.
   His head and mouth have powers that pass all others, and all his people hasten near to listen.

4. I count thee as the holiest of the holy, the caster-down of what hath ne'er been shaken.
   I count thee as the banner of the heroes, I count thee as the chief of all men living.

5. What time, O Indra, in thine arms thou tookest thy wildly-rushing bolt to slay the Dragon,
   The mountains roared, the cattle loudly bellowed, the Brahmans with their hymns drew nigh to Indra.

6. Let us praise him who made these worlds and creatures, all things that after him sprang into being.
   Fain would we win by song a friend in Indra, and wait upon our lord with adoration.

7. Flying in terror from the snort of Vritra, all deities who were thy friends forsook thee.
   So, Indra, be thy friendship with the Maruts : in all these battles thou shalt be the victor.

MANDALA IX.

[This Book contains 114 Hymns. With the exception of one to the Apris and two in which Soma is invoked conjointly, all the hymns are addressed to Soma. Even in the hymn to the Apris, the attributes of Agni are transferred to Soma. He is addressed as Pavamana, representing the juice as it flows through the wool which is used as a strainer, and thus undergoing purification. The hymns were intended to be sung while this process was going on. The Book contains endless repetitions.]

Hymn 1. SOMA PAVAMANA.

1. In sweetest and most gladdening stream flow pure, O Soma, on thy way,
   Pressed out for Indra, for his drink.

2. Fiend-queller, friend of all men, he hath with the plank attained unto
   His place, his iron-fashioned home.

3. Be thou best Vritra-slayer, best granter of bliss, most liberal :
   Promote our wealthy princes' gifts.

4. Flow onward with thy juice unto the banquet of the mighty gods :
   Flow hither for our strength and fame.

5. O Indu,* we draw nigh to thee, with this one object day by day :
To thee alone our prayers are said.
6. The daughter of the Sun by means of this eternal fleece makes
pure
Thy Soma that is gushing forth,
7. Ten sister maids† of slender form seize him amid the press and
hold
Him firmly on the final day.
8. The virgins send him forth : they blow the skin musician-like,
and fuse
The triple foe-repelling meath.
9. The inviolable milch-kine round about him blend, for Indra's
drink,
The fresh young Soma with their milk.
10. In the wild raptures of this draught, Indra slays all the Vritras :
he,
The hero pours his wealth on us.

Hymn 96. Soma Pavamana.

[In this hymn Soma is described as the father of the principal gods and
his hymns are characterised as " holy." Only a few verses can be quoted.]

5. Father of holy hymns, Soma flows onward, the father of the
earth, father of heaven ;
Father of Agni, Surya's generator, the father who begat Indra
and Vishnu.
6. Brahman of gods, the leader of the poets, Rishi of sages, bull
of savage creatures,
Falcon amid the vultures, axe of forests, over the cleansing
sieve goes Soma singing.
. . . .
15. Purified with our holy hymns, this Soma o'ertakes malignities
like some strong charger,
Like fresh milk poured by Aditi, like passage in ample room, or
like a docile car-horse.

Hymn 113. Soma Pavamana.

[In this hymn, where the joys of heaven are more fervently implored than
in other parts of the Rig-Veda, Soma is addressed as the god from whom the
gift of future happiness is expected.]

7. O Pavamana, place me in that deathless, undecaying world
Wherein the light of heaven is set, and everlasting lustre
shines. Flow, Indu, flow for Indra's sake.
8. Make me immortal in that realm where dwells the king, Vivasvan's son.‡
Where is the secret shrine of heaven, where are those waters
young and fresh. Flow, Indu, flow for Indra's sake.

---

* " O dropping (Soma)." † The priest's fingers.
‡ Yama, son of Vivasvan.

9. Make me immortal in that realm where they move even as they list,
In the third sphere of inmost heaven where lucid worlds are full of light. Flow, Indu, flow for Indra's sake.
10. Make me immortal in that realm of eager wish and strong desire,
The region of the golden Sun, where food and full delight are found. Flow, Indu, flow for Indra's sake.
11. Make me immortal in that land where happiness and transports, where
Joys and felicities combine, and longing wishes are fulfilled. Flow, Indu, flow for Indra's sake.

MANDALA X.

This Book contains 191 hymns. To Indra 34 are addressed, to Agni 25, to the Visvedevas 22. There are hymns on creation and several to be used as charms for the cure of sickness, the removal of rivals, against miscarriage, &c. The Book includes some of the latest hymns in the Rig-Veda. Several of the hymns are ascribed to gods, as if the real authors wished by this device to conceal their late origin.

Hymn 14. YAMA.

[Hymn 10 contains a dialogue between Yama and Yami, in which the sister asks the brother to have children by him. This has already been noticed. Hymn 14 is a funeral address, partly to Yama, the god of the dead, and partly to the soul of the departed whose body is being consumed on the pile. Yama was originally the first man who died and so showed the souls of his successors the way to the home of the departed.—Griffith. Only part is quoted.]

1. Honour the king with thine oblations, Yama, Vivasvan's son, who gathers men together,
Who travelled to the lofty heights above us, who searches out and shows the path to many.
2. Yama first found for us the road to travel: this pasture never can be taken from us.
Men born on earth tread their own paths that lead then whither our ancient Fathers have departed.

[The following verses are addressed to the spirit of the dead man whose funeral rites are being celebrated.]

7. Go forth, go forth upon the ancient pathways whereon our sires of old have gone before us.
There shalt thou look on both the kings enjoying their sacredfood, god Varuna and Yama.
8. Meet Yama, meet the Fathers (Pitris,) meet the merit of free or ordered acts in highest heaven.
Leave sin and evil, seek anew thy dwelling, and bright with glory wear another body.

9.* Go hence, depart ye, fly in all directions: this place for him the Fathers have provided.
Yama bestows on him a place to rest in adorned with days and beams of light and waters.

10. Run and outspeed the two dogs, Sarama's offspring, brindled, four-eyed, upon thy happy pathway.
Draw nigh, then to the gracious-minded Fathers where they rejoice in company with Yama.

11. And those two dogs of Thine, Yama, the watchers, four-eyed, who look on men and guard the pathway,—
Entrust this man, O king, to their protection, and with prosperity and health endow him.

12. Dark-hued, insatiate, with distended nostrils, Yama's two envoys roam among the people;
May they restore to us a fair existence here and to-day, that we may see the sunlight.

Hymn 15. FATHERS.

[This hymn is claimed to be written by Sankha son of Yama. It is the only one specially addressed to the Pitris. Offerings are made to them, which they are invited to partake, and blessings are solicited: Only verses 1—7 are quoted, but they are the principal.]

1. May they ascend, the lowest, highest, midmost, the Fathers who deserve a share of Soma,
May they who have attained the life of spirits, skilled in Law, harmless, aid us when we call them.

2. Now let us pay this homage to the Fathers, to those who passed of old, and those who followed,
Those who have rested in the earthly region, and those who dwell among the mighty races.

3. I have attained the gracious-minded Fathers, I have gained son and progeny from Vishnu.
They who enjoy pressed juices with oblation, seated on sacred grass, come oftenest hither.

4. Fathers who sit on sacred grass, come, help us: these offerings have we made for you; accept them.
So come to us with most auspicious favour, and give us health and wealth without a trouble.

5. May they, the Fathers, worthy of the Soma, invited to their favourite oblations
Laid on the sacred grass, come nigh and listen; may they be gracious unto us and bless us.

6. Bowing your bended knees and seated southward, accept this sacrifice of ours with favour.

---

* This verse is addressed to the Pisachas and other evil spirits that haunt the place of cremation.—Griffith.

Punish us not for any sin, O Fathers, which we through human
frailty have committed.

7. Lapped in the bosom of the purple Mornings, give riches to the
man who brings oblations.
Grant to your sons a portion of that treasure, and, present, give
them energy, ye Fathers.

Hymn 18.   VARIOUS DEITIES.

[This hymn, claimed to be written by a son of Yama, is important, as sanc-
tioning widow marriage.   Verse 8.   The barbarous practice of widow burning
was based upon a mistranslation of verse 7. The word *Agre* was altered into
Agne. Max Müller says : " This is, perhaps, the most flagrant instance of what
can be done by an unscrupulous priesthood. Here have thousands of lives
been sacrificed and a practical rebellion been threatened on the authority of a
passage which was mangled, mistranslated and misapplied." Mritya, the god
of death, is distinct from Yama.   Only some verses are quoted.]

1. Go hence, O Death, pursue thy special pathway apart from
which gods are wont to travel.
To thee I say it who hast eyes and hearest : touch not our
offspring, injure not our heroes.

[Verse 2 is addressed to the kinsman of the deceased. *Effacing Mrityu's
footstep*, means avoiding the path of death.]

2. As ye have come effacing Mrityu's footstep, to farther times pro-
longing your existence,
May ye be rich in children and possessions, cleansed, purified, and
meet for sacrificing.

7. Let these unwidowed dames with noble husbands adorn themselves with fragrant balm and unguent.
Decked with fair jewels, tearless, free from sorrow, first let the
matrons pass unto their houses.

[Verse 8 is spoken by the husband's brother, etc., to the wife of the dead
man, who makes her leave her husband's body.]

8. Rise, come unto the world of life, O women : come he is lifeless
by whose side thou liest.
Wifehood with this thy husband was thy portion, who took thy
hand and wooed thee as a lover.

[Verse 10 is addressed to the body. The urn containing the ashes was
buried. The earth is asked not to press heavily upon it.]

10. Betake thee to the lap of earth the mother, of earth far-spreading, very kind and gracious.
Young dame, wool-soft unto the guerdon-giver, may she preserve thee from Destruction's bosom.

11. Heave thyself, Earth, nor press thee downward heavily : afford
him easy access, gently tending him.
Earth, as a mother wraps her skirt about her child, so cover him.

Hymn 34. DICE, ETC.

[In this hymn a gambler apparently describes his own experience. The principal verses are quoted.]

1. Sprung from tall trees on windy heights, these rollers transport me as they turn upon the table.
   Dearer to me the die that never slumbers than the deep draught of Mujavan's own Soma.
2. She never vexed me nor was angry with me, but to my friends and me was ever gracious.
   For the die's sake whose single point is final mine own devoted wife I alienated.
3. My wife holds me aloof, her mother hates me: the wretched man finds none to give him comfort.
   As of a costly horse grown old and feeble, I find not any profit of the gamester.
4. Others caress the wife of him whose riches the die hath coveted, that rapid courser:
   Of him speak father, mother, brothers, saying, We know him not: bind him and take him with you.
5. When I resolve to play with these no longer, my friends depart from me and leave me lonely,
   When the brown dice, thrown on the board, have rattled, like a fond girl I seek the place of meeting.
6. The gamester seeks the gambling-house, and wonders, his body all afire, Shall I be lucky?
   Still do the dice extend his eager longing, staking his gains against his adversary.
7. Dice, verily, are armed with goads and driving-hooks, deceiving and tormenting, causing grievous woe.
   They give frail gifts and then destroy the man who wins, thickly anointed with the player's fairest good.
10. The gambler's wife is left forlorn and wretched: the mother mourns the son who wanders homeless,
    In constant fear, in debt, and seeking riches, he goes by night unto the home of others.
11. Sad is the gambler when he sees a matron, another's wife, and his well-ordered dwelling.
    He yokes the brown steeds* in the early morning, and when the fire is cold sinks down an outcast.
13. Play not with dice: no, cultivate thy corn-land. Enjoy the gain, and deem that wealth sufficient,
    There are thy cattle, there thy wife, O gambler. So this good Savitar himself hath told me.
14. Make me your friend: show us some little mercy. Assail us not with your terrific fierceness,
    Appeased be your malignity and anger, and let the brown dice snare some other captive.

---

*Begins throwing the brown dice.

Hymn 39. Asvins.

[The Rishi of this hymn and the following is Ghoshâ, daughter of Kakshivan. Being a leper, she was incapable of marriage. When she was grown
old in her father's house, the Asvins gave her health, youth, and beauty, so
that she obtained a husband. Only the opening verses are quoted.]

1. As 'twere the name of father, easy to invoke, we all assembled
   here invoke this car of yours,
   Asvins, your swiftly-rolling circumambient car which he who
   worships must invoke at eve and dawn.
2. Awake all pleasant strains, and let the hymns flow forth : raise up
   abundant fulness : this is our desire.
   Asvins, bestow on us a glorious heritage, and give our princes
   treasure fair as Soma is.
3. Ye are the bliss of her who groweth old at home, and helpers
   of the slow although he linger last.
   Man call you too, Nasatyas, healers of the blind, the thin and
   feeble, and the man with broken bones.
4. Ye made Chyavana, weak and worn with length of days, young
   again, like a car, that he had power to move.
   Ye lifted up the son of Tugra from the floods. At our libations
   must all these your acts be praised.
5. We will declare among the folk your ancient deeds heroic ; yea,
   ye were physicians bringing health.
   You, you who must be lauded, will we bring for aid, so that
   this foe of ours, O Asvins, may believe.

Hymn 72. Gods.

[The poet attempts to describe the origin of the gods and the universe.]

1. Let us with tuneful skill proclaim these generations of the gods,
   That one may see them when these hymns are chanted in a
   future age.
2. These Brahmanaspati produced with blast and smelting, like
   a smith.
   Existence, in an earlier age of gods, from non-existence sprang.
3. Existence, in the earliest age of gods, from non-existence, sprang.
   Thereafter were the regions* born. This sprang from the
   Productive Power.
4. Earth sprang from the Productive Power; the regions from the
   earth were born.
   Daksha was born of Aditi, and Aditi was Daksha's child.
5. For Aditi, O Daksha, she who is thy daughter, was brought
   forth.
   After her were the blessèd gods, born of immortal parentage.
6. When ye, O gods, in yonder deep close-clasping one another
   stood,
   Thence, as of dancers, from your feet a thickening cloud of dust
   arose.

---

* Regions, the quarters of the horizon.

7. When, O ye gods, like Yatis,* ye caused all existing things to grow,
   Then ye brought Surya forward who was lying hidden in the sea.
8. Eight are the sons of Aditi who from her body sprang to life.
   With seven she went to meet the gods : she cast Martanda † far away.
9. So with her seven sons Aditi went forth to meet the earlier age.
   She brought Martanda thitherward to spring to life and die again.

Hymn 81. VISVAKARMAN.

[Visvakarman is represented as the Creator of all things and architect of the world.]

1. He who sate down as Hotar-priest, the Rishi, our father, offering up all things existing,—
   He, seeking through his wish a great possession, came among men on earth as archetypal.
2. What was the place whereon he took his station ? What was it that supported him ? How was it ?
   Whence Visvakarman, seeing all, producing the earth, with mighty power disclosed the heavens.
3. He who hath eyes on all sides round about him, a mouth on all sides, arms and feet on all sides.
   He, the sole god, producing earth and heaven, weldeth them, with his arms as wings, together.
4. What was the tree, what wood in sooth produced it, from which they fashioned out the earth and heaven ?
   Ye thoughtful men inquire within your spirit whereon he stood when he established all things.
5. Thine highest, lowest, sacrificial natures, and these thy mid-most hero, O Visvakarman ;
   Teach thou thy friends at sacrifice, O blessèd, and come thyself, exalted to our worship.
6. Bring thou thyself, exalted with oblation, O Visvakarman, Earth and Heaven to worship,
   Let other men around us live in folly : here let us have a rich and liberal patron.
7. Let us invoke to-day, to aid our labour, the lord of speech, the thought-swift Visvakarman.
   May he hear kindly all our invocations who gives all bliss for aid, whose works are righteous.

Hymn 87. AGNI.

[This hymn is addressed to Agni Rakshoha, the slayer of the Rakshasas. The aborigines are often compared to them. Only some verses are quoted.]

1. I balm with oil the mighty Rakshas-slayer; to the most famous friend I come for shelter,
   Enkindled, sharpened by our rites, may Agni protect us in the day and night from evil.

---

* Devotees.   † Surya, the Sun.

2. O Jatavedas with the teeth of iron, enkindled with thy flame attack the demons.
Seize with thy tongue the foolish gods' adorers : rend, put within thy mouth the raw-flesh eaters.

3. Apply thy teeth, the upper and the lower, thou who hast both, enkindled and destroying.
Roam also in the air, O king, around us, and with thy jaws assail the wicked spirits.

14. With fervent heat exterminate the demons; destroy the fiends with burning flame, O Agni.
Destroy with fire the foolish gods' adorers ; blaze and destroy the insatiable monsters.

15. May gods destroy this day the evil-doer : may each hot curse of his return and blast him.
Let arrows pierce the liar in his vitals, and Visva's net enclose the Yatudhana.*

16. The fiend who smears himself with flesh of cattle, with flesh of horses and of human bodies,
Who steals the milch-cow's milk away, O Agni,—tear off the heads of such with fiery fury.

20. Guard us, O Agni, from above and under, protect us from behind us and before us ;
And may thy flames, most fierce and never wasting, glowing with fervent heat, consume the sinner.

Hymn 90. PURUSHA.†

["This pantheistic hymn, which is generally called the Purusha-sukta, is of comparatively recent origin, and appears to be an attempt to harmonize the two ideas of sacrifice and creation. It contains the only passage in the Rig-Veda which enumerates the four castes."—Griffith. In the Rig-Veda the castes issuing from the mouth, arms, thighs and feet is probably only an allegory. In Manu and the Puranas it is represented as a literal statement of fact.]

1. A thousand heads had Purusha, a thousand eyes, a thousand feet.
He covered earth on every side, and spread ten fingers' breadth beyond.

2. This Purusha is all that yet hath been and all that is to be ;
The lord of immortality which waxes greater still by food.

3. So mighty is his greatness ; yea, greater than this is Purusha.
All creatures are one-fourth of him, three-fourths eternal life in heaven.

4. With three-fourths Purusha went up : one-fourth of him again was here
Thence he strode out to every side over what eats not and what eats.

---

* Rakshasas.
† Purusha represents Man personified and regarded as the soul and original source of the universe, the personal and life-giving principle in all animated things. —Griffith.

5. From him Viraj* was born; again Purusha from Viraj was born.
As soon as he was born has spaced eastward and westward o'er
the earth.

6. When gods prepared the sacrifice with Purusha as their offering,
Its oil was spring, the holy gift was autumn ; summer was
the wood.

7. They balmed as victim on the grass Purusha born in earliest
time.
With him the deities and all Sadhyas† and Rishis sacrificed.

8. From that great general sacrifice the dripping fat ‡ was gathered
up.
He formed the creatures of the air, and animals both wild and
tame.

9. From that great general sacrifice Richas and Soma-hymns were
born :
Therefrom the metres were produced, the Yajus had its birth
from it.

10. From it were horses born, from it all creatures with two rows of
teeth :
From it were generated kine, from it the goats and sheep were
born.

11. When they divided Purusha how many portions did they make ?
What do they call his mouth, his arms ? What do they call his
thighs and feet ?

12. The Brahman was his mouth, of both his arms was the Rajanya
made.
His thighs became the Vaisya from his feet the Sudra was
produced.

13. The Moon was gendered from his mind, and from his eye the Sun
had birth ;
Indra and Agni from his mouth were born, and Vayu from his
breath.

14. Forth from his navel came mid-air; the sky was fashioned from
his head ;
Earth from his feet, and from his ear the regions. Thus they
formed the worlds.

15. Seven fencing-logs§ had he, thrice seven layers of fuel were
prepared,
When the gods, offering sacrifice, bound, as their victim Purusha.

16. Gods, sacrificing, sacrificed the victim : these were the earliest
holy ordinances.
The mighty ones attained the height of heaven, there were the
Sadhyas, gods of old, are dwelling.

* Viraj is said to have come, in the form of the mundane egg from Adi-Purusha,
the primeval Purusha. Or Viraj may be the female counterpart of Purusha.—Griffith.
† A class of celestial beings, probably ancient divine sacrificers.
‡ The mixture of curds and butter.
§ Pieces of wood laid round a sacrificial fire to keep it together.

Hymn 121.   Ka.

This hymn is claimed to be written by the son of Prajapati.

[Ka, meaning who ? that is, the unknown god, has been applied as a name to Prajapati, and to other gods, from a forced interpretation of the inter-rogative pronoun which occurs in the refrain of each verse of the hymn. —Griffith.]

1. In the beginning rose Hiranyagarbha,* born only lord of all created beings.
    He fixed and holdeth up this earth and heaven. What god shall we adore with our oblation ?†

2. Giver of vital breath, of power and vigour, he whose command-ments all the gods acknowledge :
    Whose shade is death, whose lustre makes immortal. What god shall we adore with our oblation ?

3. Who by his grandeur hath become sole ruler of all the moving world that breathes and slumbers ;
    He who is lord of men and lord of cattle. What god shall we adore with our oblation ?

4. His, through his might, are these snow-covered mountains, and men call sea and Rasa‡ his possession :
    His arms are these, his thighs are these heavenly regions. What god shall we adore with our oblations ?

5. By him the heavens are strong and earth is steadfast, by him light's realm and sky-vault are supported :
    By him the regions in mid-air were measured. What god shall we adore with our oblations ?

6. To him, supported by his help, two armies enbattled look while trembling in their spirit,
    When over them the risen sun is shining. What god shall we adore with our oblation ?

7. What time the mighty waters came, containing the universal germ, producing Agni,
    Thence sprang the gods' one spirit into being. What god shall we adore with our oblation ?

8. He in his might surveyed the floods containing productive force and generating Worship.
    He is the god of gods, and none beside him. What god shall we adore with our oblation ?

9. Ne'er may he harm us who is earth's begetter, nor he whose laws are sure, the heaven's creator,
    He who brought forth the great and lucid waters. What god shall we adore with our oblation ?

---

* The gold germ, the Sun-god, as the great power of the universe.
† Also translated " Worship we Ka the god with our oblation."
‡ The mythical river of the sky.

10. Prajapati !* thou only comprehendest all these created things, and none beside thee.
Grant us our hearts' desire when we invoke thee : may we have store of riches in possession.

Hymn 129. CREATION.

This hymn is claimed to be written by Prajapati, the Supreme.

[Here says Max Müller we find the conception of a beginning of all things, and of a state previous even to all existence. It is a hymn full of ideas which to many would seem to necessitate the admission of a long antecedent period of philosophical thought.—*Ancient Sanskrit Literature*, p. 559.]

1. There was not non-existent nor existent : there was no realm of air, no sky beyond it.
What covered in, and where? and what gave shelter? Was water there, unfathomed depth of water?

2. Death was not then, nor was there aught immortal : no sign was there, the day's and night's divider.
That One Thing,† breathless, breathed by its own nature : apart from it was nothing whatsoever.

3. Darkness there was : at first concealed in darkness this All was indiscriminated chaos.
All that existed then was void and formless : by the great power of Warmth was born that Unit.

4. Thereafter rose Desire in the beginning, Desire, the primal seed and germ of Spirit.
Sages who searched with their heart's thought discovered the existent's kinship in the non-existent.

5. Transversely was their severing love extended : what was above it then, and what below it?
There were begetters, there were mighty forces, free action here and energy up yonder.

6. Who verily knows and who can here declare it, whence it was born and whence comes this creation?
The gods are later than this world's production. Who knows then whence it first came into being?

7. He, the first origin of this creation, whether he formed it all or did not form it,
Whose eye controls this world in highest heaven, he verily knows it, or perhaps he knows not.

Hymn 145. SAPATNIBADHANAM.

[The hymn is a spell to rid a jealous wife of a more favoured rival. The Rishi is Indrani, the consort of Indra.—Griffith.]

1. From out the earth I dig this plant, an herb of most effectual power,

---

* Lord of life, creatures or creation. Savitar and Soma Pavamana are also so called. Prajapati was afterwards the name of a separate god, the bestower of progeny and cattle, and sometimes invoked as the Creator.—Griffith.
† The unit out of which the universe was developed.

Wherewith one quells the rival wife and gains the husband for oneself.

2. Auspicious, with expanded leaves, sent by the gods, victorious plant,
   Blow thou the rival wife away, and make my husband only mine.

3. Stronger am I; O stronger one, yea, mightier than the mightier; And she who is my rival wife is lower than the lowest dames.

4. Her very name I utter not: she takes no pleasure in this man,
   Far into distance most remote drive we the rival wife away.

5. I am the conqueror, and thou, thou also art victorious:
   As victory attends us both we will subdue my fellow-wife.

6. I have gained thee for vanquisher, have grasped thee with a stronger spell.
   As a cow hastens to her calf, so let thy spirit* speed to me, hasten like water on its way.

Hymn 162.

[This hymn is by Rakshoha, Slayer of Rakshasas, a son of Brahma. The subject is the prevention of miscarriage. Stanzas 1, 2 are directed against diseases, and 3—6 against evil spirits which attack women who are about to become mothers.—Griffith.]

Hymn 163.

[This hymn is supposed to be a charm to cure consumption. The first and last stanzas are quoted :]

1. From both thy nostrils, from thine eyes, from both thine ears and from thy chin,
   Forth from thy head and brain and tongue I drive thy malady away.

6. From every member, every hair, disease that comes in every joint,
   From all thyself, from top to toe, I drive thy malady away.

Hymn 169. Cows.

1. May the wind blow upon our Cows with healing: may they eat herbage full of vigorous juices.
   My they drink waters rich in life and fatness: to food that moves on feet be gracious, Rudra.

2. Like-coloured, various-hued, or single-coloured, whose names through sacrifice are known to Agni,
   Whom the Angirasas produced by fervour,—vouchsafe to these, Parjanya, great protection.

3. Those who have offered to the gods their bodies, whose varied forms are all well known to Soma,—
   Those grant us in our cattle-pen, O Indra, with their full streams of milk and plenteous offspring.

---

* The husband's.

4. Prajapati, bestowing these upon me, one-minded with all gods and with the Fathers,
Hath to our cow-pen brought auspicious cattle : so may we own the offspring they will bear us.

Hymn 175. PRESS-STONES.*

1. May Savitar the god, O Stones, stir you according to the Law : Be harnessed to the shafts, and press.
2. Stones, drive calamity away, drive ye away malevolence : Make ye the cows our medicine.
3. Of one accord the upper stones, giving the Bull† his bull-like strength,
Look down with pride on those below.
4. May Savitar the god, O Stones, stir you as Law commands for him, Who sacrifices, pouring juice.

Hymn 191. AGNI.

[This is the last hymn of the Rig-Veda. The subject is agreement in an assembly.]

1. Thou, mighty Agni, gatherest all that is precious for thy friend ·
Bring us all treasures as thou art enkindled in libation's place.
2. Assemble, speak together : let your minds be all of one accord,
As ancient gods unanimous sit down to their appointed share.
3. The place is common, common the assembly, common the mind,
so be their thought united.
A common purpose do I lay before you, and worship with your general oblation.
4. One and the same be your resolve, and be your minds of one accord.
United be the thoughts of all that all may happily agree.

ATHARVA VEDA.

Next to the Rig-Veda this is the most important of the Vedas. As already mentioned, the Yajur Veda and the Sama Veda consist almost entirely of selections from the Rig-Veda. The proportion is much less in the Atharva Veda. One-sixth of the work is in prose. The number of the hymns is about 700, and of the verses about 6,000, of which about a sixth are found in the Rig-Veda. Professor Whitney, who edited the work in America, thus describes its character :

"In the earlier hymns of the other Vedas the gods are approached with reverential awe indeed, but with love and confidence also ; the demons, embraced under the general name *rakshas*, are objects of horror whom the gods ward off and destroy : the

---

* The stones used in pressing soma.   † Soma.

divinities of the Atharvan are regarded rather with a kind of cringing fear, as powers whose wrath is to be deprecated, and whose favour curried for. It knows a whole host of imps and hobgoblins, and addresses itself to them directly, offering them homage to induce them to abstain from doing harm. The *mantra* or prayer, which in the older Veda is the instrument of devotion, is here rather the tool of superstition; it wrings from the unwilling hands of the gods the favours which of old their good-will to men induced them to grant, or by simple magical power obtains the fulfilment of the utterer's wishes. The most prominent characteristic of the Atharva is the multitude of incantations which it contains. These are pronounced either by the person who is himself to be benefited, or, more often, by the sorcerer for him, and they are directed to the procuring of the greatest variety of desirable ends. Most frequently, perhaps, long life or recovery from grievous sickness, is the object sought; in that case a talisman, such as a necklace, is sometimes given, or, in numerous instances some plant endowed with marvellous virtues is to be the immediate means of the cure; further, the attainment of wealth or power is aimed at, the downfall of enemies, success in love or in play, the removal of petty pests, and so on, even down to the growth of hair on a bald pate. Hymns of a speculative character are not wanting, yet their number is not so great as might naturally be expected.

"The Atharva Veda forms an intermediate step rather to the gross idolatries and superstitions of the ignorant mass, than to the sublimated pantheism of the Brahmans."*

There is yet no complete English translation of the Atharva Veda; but Muir, in his *Sanskrit Texts*, gives numerous quotations from them, and translates a few hymns in full. The following are some extracts from his work. There are some spells even in the Rig-Veda, but the Atharva Veda abounds with them.

Book IV.   Hymn   2.   The Ox, or Kettle.

[A kettle was used for boiling milk. The four-legged kettle may have suggested the figure of an ox.]

1. The ox has established the earth and the sky; the ox has established the broad atmosphere.
   The ox has established the six vast regions; the ox has pervaded the entire universe.
2. The ox is Indra. He watches over the beasts. As Sakra (or mighty) he measures the threefold paths,
   Milking out the worlds, whatever has been or shall be, he performs all the functions of the gods.
3. Being born as Indra among men, the kindled and glowing kettle works. . . .

---

* Oriental and Linguistic Studies, 1st Series, pp. 20, 21.

5. That which neither the lord of the sacrifice nor the sacrifice rules, which neither the giver nor the receiver rules, which is all-conquering, all-supporting, and all-working,—declare to us the kettle, what quadruped it is.*

Book IV. Hymn 34. THE PLEASURES OF A FUTURE STATE.

[Muir quotes the following verses as illustrative of the sensual ideas on this point.]

2. Boneless, pure, cleansed by the wind, shining, they go to a shining region; Agni does not consume their generative organ; in the celestial world they have abundance of sexual gratification.

3. Want never comes upon those who cook the vishtarin oblation. (Such a man) abides with Yama, goes to the gods, and lives in blessedness with the Gandharvas, the quaffers of Soma.

4. Yama does not steal away the generative power of those who cook the vishtarin oblation.   (Such a man) becomes lord of a chariot on which he is borne along; becoming winged, he soars beyond the sky."†

Book III. 19. THE ADVANTAGES OF PRINCES EMPLOYING A PUROHIT.

1. May this prayer of mine be successful; may the vigour and strength be complete, may the power be perfect, undecaying, and victorious of those of whom I am the *purohita*.

2. I fortify their kingdom, and augment their energy, valour, and force.   I break the arms of their enemies with this oblation.

3. May all those who fight against our wise and prosperous (prince) sink downward, and be prostrated.   With my prayer I destroy his enemies and raise up his friends.

4. May those of whom I am the *purohita* be sharper than an axe, sharper than fire, sharper than Indra's thunderbolt.

5. I strengthen their weapons; I prosper their kingdom rich in heroes.   May their power be undecaying and victorious.   May all the gods foster their designs.

6. May their valorous deeds, O Maghavat, burst forth; may the noise of the conquering heroes arise; may their distinct shouts, their clear yells, go up; may the gods, the Maruts, with Indra as their chief, march forward with their host.

7. Go, conquer, ye warriors; may your arms be impetuous.   Ye with the sharp arrows, smite those whose bows are powerless; ye whose weapons and arms are terrible (smite) the feeble.

8. When discharged, fly forth, O arrow, sped by prayer, vanquish the foes, assail, slay all the choicest of them; let not one escape.‡

---

* *Sanskrit Texts*, Vol. V. p. 399.   † *Ibid*, pp. 307, 308.   ‡ *Ibid*, Vol. II. pp. 283, 284.

Book V. 18. THE GUILT OF OPPRESSING AND ROBBING BRAHMANS.

1. King, the gods have not given thee (this cow) to eat. Do not, O
    Rajanya, seek to devour the Brahman's cow, which is not to be
    eaten.
2. The wretched Rajanya, unlucky in play, and self-destroyed, will
    eat the Brahman's cow, saying, ' Let me live to-day (if I can) not
    (live) to-morrow,
3. This cow, clothed with a skin, contains deadly poison, like a
    snake. Beware, Rajanya, of this Brahman's (cow) ; she is ill-
    flavoured, and must not be eaten.
4. She takes away his regal power, destroys his splendour, consumes
    him entire like a fire which has been kindled. The man who
    looks upon the Brahman as mere food to be eaten up, drinks
    serpent's poison.
5. Indra kindles a fire in the heart of that contemner of the god
    who smites the Brahman, esteeming him to be inoffensive,
    and foolishly covets his property. Heaven and earth abhor
    the man who (so) acts.
6. A Brahman is not to be wronged, as fire (must not be touched)
    by a man who cherishes his own body. Soma is his (the Brah-
    man's) kinsman, and Indra shields him from imprecations.
15. Like a poisoned arrow, O king, like a serpent, O lord of cows,—
    such is the dreadful shaft of Brahman, with which he pierces
    his enemies.*

Book III. 10. FOR CONCORD IN A FAMILY.

1. I impart to you concord, with unity of hearts and freedom from
    hatred : delight in another, as a cow at the birth of a calf.
2. May the son be obedient to his father, and of one mind with his
    mother : may the wife, at peace with her husband, speak to
    him honeyed words.
3. Let not brother hate brother, nor sister sister; concordant and
    united in will speak to one another with kind words.
4. We perform in your house an incantation, creating concord
    among its inmates, and one through which the gods will not
    desert you, nor mutual hatred exist. †

Book IX. 2. KAMA.

[Kama, desire for good, is celebrated as a great power superior to all the
gods ; and is supplicated for deliverance from enemies. In some parts of the
Atharva Veda he is identified with Agni, but in others he is said to be
distinct.]

1. With oblations of butter I worship Kama, the mighty slayer of
    enemies. Do thou, when lauded, beat down my foes by thy
    great might.

---

* *Sanskrit Texts*, Vol. I. pp. 285, 286.
† *Sanskrit Texts*, Vol. V. pp. 439, 440.

2. The sleeplessness which is displeasing to my mind and eye, which harasses and does not delight me, that sleeplessness I let loose upon my enemy. Having praised Kama, may I rend him.

3. Kama, do thou, a fierce lord, let loose sleeplessness, misfortune, childlessness, homelessness, and want, upon him who designs us evil.

4. Send them away, Kama, drive them away; may they fall into misery, those who are my enemies. When they have been hurled into the nethermost darkness, do thou, Agni, burn up their dwellings.

19. Kama was born the first. Him neither gods nor Fathers, nor men have equalled. Thou art superior to these, and for ever great. To thee, Kama, I offer reverence.

24. Even Vata (the Wind) does not vie with Kama, nor does Agni, nor Surya, nor Chandramas (the Moon).*

Book XIX. 54. Kala, Time.

[Time is described as the source and ruler of all things.]

1. From Time the waters were produced, together with divine knowledge, *tapas*, and the regions. Through Time the sun rises and again sets.

2. Through Time the wind blows; through Time the earth is vast. The great sky is embraced in Time.

3. Through Time the hymn formerly produced both the past and the future. From Time sprang the Rik verses. The Yajus was produced from Time.

4. Through Time they created the sacrifice, an imperishable portion for the gods. On Time the Gandharvas and Apsarases, on Time the worlds are supported.

5.-6. Through Time this Angiras and Atharvan rule over the sky. Having through divine knowledge conquered both this world and the highest world, and the holy worlds and the holy ordinances, yea all worlds, Time moves onward as the supreme god.†

Book V. 30. To recall from Death.

[Muir quotes from hymns containing incantations designed to save persons suffering from dangerous diseases, and on the point of death, from death; or rather perhaps to try to recall their spirits after their separation from the body.]

1. From thy vicinity, from thy vicinity, from a distance, from thy vicinity (I call) to thee: remain here; do not follow, do not follow, the early Fathers. I firmly hold back thy breath.

2. Whatever incantations any kinsman or stranger has uttered against thee,—with my voice I declare thy release and deliverance from them all.

---

* *Sanskrit Texts*, Vol. V. pp. 405, 406.   † *Sanskrit Texts*, Vol. V. p. 409.

3. Whatever hurt thou hast done, or curse thou hast spoken, in thy folly, against man or woman, with my voice, etc.

4. If thou liest there in consequence of any sin committed by thy mother, or thy father, with my voice, etc.

5. Receive the medicine which thy father, mother, sister and brother offer to thee   I make thee long-lived.

6. Remain here, O man, with thy entire soul; do not follow the two messengers of Yama; come to the abodes of the living.

7. Return when called, knowing the outlet of the path, the ascent, the advance, the road of every living man.

8. Fear not : thou shalt not die ; I make thee long-lived. I have charmed out of thy members the consumption by which they are wasted.

9. The consumption which racks and wastes thy limbs, and sickens thy heart, has flown away to a distance like a hawk, overcome by my word.

10. The two sages, Alert and Watchful, the sleepless and the vigilant, these the guardians of thy life, are awake both day and night.

11. May this adorable Agni rise here to thee as a sun.
Rise up from deep death, yea, even from black darkness.

12. Reverence to Yama, reverence to Death, reverence to the Fathers, and to those who guide us. I place in front of this (sick) man, for his security, Agni, who knows how to carry him across.

13. Let his breath, let his soul, let his sight come, and then his strength ; let his body acquire sensation, and stand firm upon its feet.

14. Provide him, Agni, with breath and with sight; restore him, furnished with a body, and with strength. Thou hast the knowledge of immortality; let him not depart, or become a dweller in a house of clay.

15. Let not thy inhaled breath cease ; let not thy exhaled breath vanish. Let the sun, the lord, raise thee up from death by his rays.

16. This tongue speaks within, bound, convulsive. By thee I have charmed away the consumption, and the hundred torments of the fever.

17. This world is the dearest, unconquered by the gods. To whatever, death thou wast destined when thou wast born, O man, —we call after thee, do not die before thou art worn out by old age.*

The other three hymns are of a similar character. Hymn VII. 53 begins as follows :

1. Brihaspati, thou hast delivered us from dwelling in the realm of Yama, from the curse. The Asvins—they who, O Agni, are the two physicians of the gods,—they have repelled death from us by their powers.

---

* *Sanskrit Texts*, Vol. V. pp. 441, 442.

2. Continue associated, ye two breaths, inspired and expired ; forsake not his body : may they, united, remain with thee here. Live prosperously a hundred autumns. Agni is thy brilliant protector and lord.*

The following are a few verses from Hymn 1, Book VIII.

1. Reverence to Death the Ender! May thy inhaled and exhaled breaths gladly rest here. May this man ·remain here united with his spirit in the domain of the sun, in the world of deathlessness.

4. Rise up hence, O man. Casting off the fetters of death, do not sink downward. Do not depart from this world, from the sight of Agni and the Sun.

7. Let not thy soul go away thither, let it not disappear ; do not wander away from the living ; do not follow the Fathers. May all the gods preserve thee.

9. Let not the two dogs sent by Yama, the black and the brindled (seize thee). Come hither ; do not hesitate ; do not remain here with averted mind.

18. Let this man remain here, O gods, let him not depart hence to the other world. We rescue him from death with a charm of boundless efficacy.†

The following verses are from the second hymn of the same Book :

1. Seize this boon of immortality ; may long life, which cannot be cut off, be thine. I restore to thee breath and life ; do not depart to the mist (*rajas*) or to darkness (*tamas*) ; do not die.

2. Come hither to the light of the living ; I rescue thee that thou mayst survive a hundred autumns. Loosing the bands of death and imprecation, I lengthen out thy existence.

5. Let this man live and not die. We restore him. I make for him a remedy. Death do not kill the man.

11. I give thee thy breaths, death at thy full age, long life and health. I drive away all the messengers of Yama, who roam about, sent by the son of Vivasvat.

12. We remove afar Evil, Nirriti, Grahi, and flesh-devouring Pisachas, and hurl all wicked Rakshasas, as it were into darkness.

The instrument would seem to be a certain plant. The hymn concludes as follows :

28. Thou, the medicament named Pūtudra (Butea frondosa), art the body of Agni, the deliverer, the slayer of Rakshases, and of rivals, and thou art the chaser away of diseases.‡

---

* *Sanskrit Texts*, Vol. V. p. 443.   † *Ibid*, pp. 444, 445.
‡ *Sanskrit Texts*, Vol. V. pp. 447 449.

THE BRAHMANAS.

The Brahmanas, as already explained, are that part of the Veda which is intended to guide the Brahmans in Vedic ceremonies. Like the hymns, they are held to be *Sruti*.

Max Müller thus estimates their character :

" The Brahmanas represent no doubt a most interesting phase in the history of the Indian mind, but judged by themselves as literary productions, they are most disappointing. No one would have supposed that at so early a period, and in so primitive a state of society, there could have risen up a literature which for pedantry and downright absurdity can hardly be matched anywhere. There is no lack of striking thoughts, of bold expressions, of sound reasoning, and curious traditions in these collections. But these are only like the fragments of a *torso*,* like precious gems set in brass and lead. The general character of those works is marked by shallow and insipid grandiloquence, by priestly conceit, and antiquarian pedantry. It is most important to the historian that he should know how soon the fresh and healthy growth of a nation can be blighted by priestcraft and superstition. It is most important that we should know that nations are liable to these epidemics in their youth as well as in their dotage. These works deserve to be studied as the physician studies the twaddle of idiots, and the raving of madmen. They will disclose to a thoughtful eye the ruins of faded grandeur, the memories of noble aspirations. But let us only try to translate these works into our own language, and we shall feel astonished that human language, and human thought should ever have been used for such purposes."†

The estimate of the Brahmanas by Professor Eggeling, the translator of the Satapatha Brahmana, is much in the same terms. He says in the Introduction :

" The translator of the Satapatha Brahmana can be under no illusion as to the reception his production is likely to meet with at the hand of the general reader. In the whole range of literature few works are probably less calculated to excite the interest of any outside the very limited number of specialists than the ancient theological writings of the Hindus, known by the name of Brahmanas. For wearisome prolixity of exposition, characterised by dogmatic assertion and a flimsy symbolism rather than by serious reasoning, their works are perhaps not equalled anywhere."

Specimens will be given from two of the principal Brahmanas.

The AITAREYA BRAHMANA of the Rig-Veda contains " the earliest speculations of the Brahmans on the meaning of the sacrificial prayers, and on the origin, performance, and sense of the Rites of the Vedic Religion." The Sanskrit text, with an English translation, was published by the late Dr. Haug, Superintendent of Sanskrit Studies in the Poona College.

---

* The trunk of a statue deprived of head and limbs.
† *Ancient Sanskrit Literature*, pp. 389, 390.

The work, as translated by Dr. Haug, begins as follows :

" Agni, among the gods, has the lowest, Vishnu the highest place ; between them stand all the other deities.

They offer the Agni-Vishnu rice-cake (*purudasa*) which belongs to the *Dikshaniya Ishti* (and put its several parts) on eleven potsherds (*kapala*). They offer it (the rice-cake) really to all the deities of this (Ishti) without foregoing any one. For Agni is all the deities, and Vishnu is all the deities. For these two (divine) bodies, Agni and Vishnu, are the two ends of the sacrifice. Thus when they portion out the Agni-Vishnu rice-cake, they indeed make at the end (after the ceremony is over) prosper (all) the gods of this (ceremony).

Here they say : if there be 11 potsherds on which portions of the rice-cake are put, and (only) two deities, Agni and Vishnu, what arrangement is there for the two, or what division ?

(The answer is) The rice-cake portions on 8 potsherds belong to Agni ; for the *Gayatri* verse consists of 8 syllables, and the Gayatri is Agni's metre. The rice-cake portions on the 3 potsherds belong to Vishnu ; for Vishnu (the sun) strode thrice through the universe. This the arrangement (to be made) for them ; this is the division.

He who might think himself to have no position (not to be highly respected by others) should portion out (for being offered) *Charu* (boiled rice) over which ghee is poured. For on this earth no one has a firm footing who does not enjoy a certain (high) position. The ghee (poured over this *Charu*) is the milk of the woman; the husked rice grains (of which Charu consists) belong to the male; both are a pair. Thus the Charu on account of its consisting of a pair (of female and male parts) blesses him with the production of progeny and cattle, for his propagation (in his descendants and their property.) He who has such knowledge propagates his progeny and cattle.

He who brings the New and Full Moon oblations, has already made a beginning with the sacrifice, and made also a beginning with (the sacrificial worship of the) deities. After having brought the New or Full Moon oblations, he may be inaugurated in consequence of the offering made at these (oblations) and the sacrificial grass (having been spread) at these (oblations, at the time of making them). This (might be regarded) as one Diksha (initiatory rite).

The Hotar must recite 17 verses for the wooden sticks to be thrown into the fire (to feed it). For Prajapati (the Lord of all creatures) is seventeen-fold, the months are twelve, and the seasons five by putting *Hemanta* (winter) and *Sisira* (between winter and spring) as one. So much is the year. The year is Prajapati. He who has such a knowledge prospers by these verses (just mentioned) which reside in Prajapati."

Vol. II. pp. 1—6.

According to the foregoing, the offering of boiled rice on which ghee has been poured, secures to the worshipper children and cattle.

The SATAPATHA BRAHMANA is called the Brahmana " of a hundred paths," because it consists of a hundred lectures (Adhyayas.)

The first Kanda treats of New and Full Moon Sacrifices. The first 11 verses show how purification is to be obtained the day before the sacrifice begins. The remainder of the first Brahmana is as follows:

" 12. By way of his first act on the following morning he (Adhvaryu priest) betakes himself to the water, and brings water forward : for water is (one of the means of) sacrifice. Hence by this his first act he approaches (engages in) the sacrifice ; and by bringing (water) forward, he spreads out (prepares) the sacrifice.

13. He brings it forward with those mysterious words : ' Who (or Prajapati) joins (or yokes) thee (to this fire) ? He joins thee. For what (or, for Prajapati) does he join thee ? For that (or him) he joins thee !' For Prajapati is mysterious ; Prajapati is the sacrifice : hence he thereby yokes (gets ready for the performance) Prajapati, his sacrifice.

14. The reason why he brings forward water is, that all this (universe) is pervaded by water ; hence by this his first act he pervades (or gains) all this (universe).

15. And whatever here in this (sacrifice) the Hotri or the Adhvaryu, or the Brahman or the Agnidhra or the sacrificer himself, does not succeed in accomplishing, all that is thereby obtained (or made good).

16. Another reason why he brings forward water is this : whilst the gods were engaged in performing sacrifice, the Asuras and Rakshas forbade (*raksh*) them saying, ' He shall not sacrifice !' and because they forbade (*raksh*) , they are called Rakshas.

17. The gods then perceived this thunderbolt, to wit, the water : the water is a thunderbolt, for the water is indeed a thunderbolt; hence wherever it goes, it produces a hollow, (or depression of ground) ; and whatever it comes near, it burns up. Therefore they took up that thunderbolt, and in its safe and foeless shelter they spread (performed) the sacrifice. And thus he (the Adhvaryu priest) likewise takes up this thunderbolt, and in its safe and foeless shelter spreads the sacrifice. This is the reason why he brings forward water.

18. After pouring out some of it (into the jug) he puts it down north of the Garhapatya fire. For water (*ap*) is female and fire (*agni*) is male ; and the Garhapatya is a house : hence a copulative production of offspring is thereby effected in this house. Now he who brings forward the water takes up a thunderbolt ; but when he takes up the thunderbolt, he cannot do so unless he is firmly placed ; for otherwise it destroys him.

19. The reason then why he places it near the Garhapatya fire is, that the Garhapatya is a house, and a house is a safe resting-place ; so that he thereby stands firmly in a house, and therefore in a safe resting-place ; in this way that thunderbolt does not destroy him,—for this reason he places it near the Garhapatya fire.

20. He then carries it north of the Ahavaniya fire. For water is female and fire is male : hence a copulative production of offspring is thereby effected. And in this way alone a regular copulation can take place, since the woman lies on the left (or north) side of the man.

21. Let nobody pass between the water (and the fire), lest by passing between them he should disturb the copulation which is taking place. Let him set the water down without carrying it beyond (the north side

of the fire, *i. e.*, not on the eastern side) ; nor should he put it down before reaching (the north side, *i. e.*, not on the western side). For, if he were to put the water down after carrying it beyond,—there being, as it were, a great rivalry between fire and water,—he would cause this rivalry to break forth on the part of the fire ; and when they (the priests and the sacrificer (touch the water of this (vessel), he would, by carrying it and setting it down beyond (the northern side), cause the enemy to spirt in the fire. If, on the other hand, he were to put it down before gaining (the northern side), he would not gain by it the fulfilment of the work for which it had been brought forward. Let him therefore put it down exactly north of the Ahavaniya fire.

22. He now strews sacrificial grass all round (the fires), and fetches the utensils, taking two at a time, viz., the winnowing basket and the Agnihotra ladle, the wooden sword and the potsherds, the wedge and the black antelope skin, the mortar and the pestle, the large and the small millstones. These are ten in number ; for of ten syllables consists the Viraj (metre) and radiant (*Viraj*) also is the sacrifice : so that he thereby makes the sacrifice resemble the Viraj. The reason why he takes two at a time is, because a pair means strength ; for when two undertake anything, there is strength in it. Moreover, a pair represents a productive copulation, so that a productive copulation (of these respective objects) is thereby effected."*

The directions for the New and Full Moon Sacrifices occupy 273 pages. Even the specimen given shows that they abound with wearisome repetitions ; while the logic is absurd, as in 14, 16, 18, &c. The Second Kanda treats of the establishment of Sacred Fires, the Worship of Fires, &c. The directions about the Agnihotra, or Morning and Evening Milk Offerings, are quoted below :

Fourth Kanda.

II. The Agnihotra or Morning and Evening Libations; and the Agny Upasthâna or Homage to the Fires.

1. Prajapati alone, indeed, existed here in the beginning. He considered, ' How may I be reproduced ?' He toiled and performed acts of penance. He generated Agni from his mouth ; and because he generated him from his mouth, therefore Agni is a consumer of food : and, verily, he who thus knows Agni to be a consumer of food, becomes himself a consumer of food.

2. He thus generated him first (Agre) of the gods ; and therefore (he is called) Agni, for Agni (they say) is the same as Agre. He, being generated, went forth as the first (pûrva) ; for of him who goes first, they say that he goes at the head (Agre). Such, then, is the origin and nature of that Agni.

3. Prajâpati then considered, ' In that Agni I have generated a food-eater for myself ; but, indeed, there is no other food here but myself, whom, surely, he would not eat.' At that time this earth had, indeed, been rendered quite bald ; there were neither plants nor trees. This, then, weighed on his mind.

---

* *Sacred Books of the East*, Vol. XII, pp. 7-11.

4. Thereupon Agni turned towards him with open mouth ; and he (Prajâpati) being terrified, his own greatness departed from him. Now his own greatness is his speech : that speech of his departed from him. He desired an offering in his own self, and rubbed (his hands) ; and because he rubbed (his hands), therefore both this and this (palm) are hairless. He then obtained either a butter-offering or a milk-offering ;— but, indeed, they are both milk.

5. This (offering), however, did not satisfy him, because it had hairs mixed with it. He poured it away (into the fire), saying, ' Drink, while burning (osham dhaya)!' From it plants sprang : hence their name ' plants (oshadhayah).' He rubbed (his hands) a second time, and thereby obtained another offering, either a butter-offering or a milk-offering ; —but, indeed, they are both milk.

6. This (offering) then satisfied him. He hesitated : ' Shall I offer it up ? Shall I not offer it up ?' he thought. His own greatness said to him, ' Offer it up !' Prajâpati was aware that it was his own (Sva) greatness that had spoken (âha) to him; and offered it up with ' Svâhâ !' This is why offerings are made with ' Svâhâ !' Thereupon that burning one (viz., the sun) rose ; and then that blowing one (viz., the wind) sprang up ; whereupon, indeed, Agni turned away.

7. And Prajâpati, having performed offering, reproduced himself, and saved himself from Agni, Death, as he was about to devour him. And, verily, whosoever, knowing this, offers the Agnihotra, reproduces himself by offspring even as Prajâpati reproduced himself; and saves himself from Agni, Death, when he is about to devour him.

8. And when he dies and when they place him on the fire, then he is born (again) out of the fire, and the fire only consumes his body. Even as he is born from his father and mother, so is he born from the fire. But he who offers not the Agnihotra, verily, he does not come into life at all : therefore the Agnihotra should by all means be offered.

9. And as to that same birth from out of doubt ;—when Prajâpati doubted he, while doubting, remained steadfast on the better (side), insomuch that he reproduced himself and saved himself from Agni, Death, when he was about to devour him : so he also who knows that birth from out of doubt, when he doubts about anything, still remains on the better (side).

10. Having offered, he rubbed his (hands). Thence a Vikankata tree sprung forth ; and therefore that tree is suitable for the sacrifice, and proper for sacrificial vessels. Thereupon those (three) heroes among the gods were born ; viz., Agni, that blower (Vâyu,) and Sûrya : and, verily, whosoever thus knows those heroes among the gods, to him a hero is born.

11. They then said, ' We come after our father Prajâpati : let us then create what shall come after us !' Having enclosed (a piece of ground), they sang praises with the Gâyatri stanza without the ' Hin :' and that (with) which they enclosed was the ocean ; and this earth was the praise ground (Astâva).

12. When they had sung praises, they went out towards the east, saying : ' We (will) go back thither !' The gods came upon a cow which had sprung into existence. Looking up at them, she uttered the sound ' Hin.' The gods perceived that this was the ' Hin' of the

Sâman (melodious sacrificial chant) ; for heretofore (their song was) without the ' Hin,' but after it was the (real) Sâman. And as this same sound ' Hin' of the Sâman was in the cow, therefore the latter affords the means of subsistence ; and so does he afford the means of subsistence whosoever thus knows that ' Hin' of the Sâman in the cow.

13. They said, ' Auspicious, indeed, is what we have produced here, who have produced the cow : for, truly, she is the sacrifice, and without her no sacrifice is performed ; she is also the food, for the cow, indeed, is all food.'

14. This (word ' go'), then, is a name of those (cows), and so it is of the sacrifice : let him, therefore, repeat it, (as it were saying, ' Good, excellent !' and verily, whosoever, knowing this, repeats it,) as it were saying, ' Good, excellent !' and, verily, whosoever, knowing this, repeats it (as it were) saying, ' Good,' excellent ! with him those (cows) multiply, and the sacrifice will incline to him.

15. Now, Agni coveted her. ' May I pair with her,' he thought. He united with her, and his seed became that milk of hers : hence, while the cow is raw, that milk in her is cooked (warm) : for it is Agni's seed, and therefore also, whether it be in a black or in a red (cow) it is ever white, and shining like fire, it being Agni's seed. Hence it is warm when first milked, for it is Agni's seed.

16. They (the men) said, "Come, let us offer this up !' ' To whom of us shall they first offer this ?' (said those gods).—' To me !' said Agni ; ' To me !' said that blower (Vâyu),—To me ! said Surya. They did not come to an agreement ; and not being agreed, they said, ' Let us go to our father Prajâpati ; and to whichever of us he says it shall be offered first, to him they shall first offer this.' They went to their father Prajâpati, and said, ' To whom of us shall they offer this first ?'

17. He replied, ' To Agni : Agni will forthwith cause his own seed to be reproduced, and so you will be reproduced.' ' Then to thee,' he said to Sûrya ; and what of the offered (milk) he then is still possessed of, that shall belong to that blower (Vâyu) !' And, accordingly, they in the same way offer this (milk) to them till this day : in the Evening to Agni, and in the Morning to Sûrya ; and what of the offered (milk) he then is still possessed of, that, indeed, belongs to that blower.

18. By offering, those gods were produced in the way in which they were produced, by it they gained that victory which they did gain : Agni conquered this world, Vâyu the air, and Sûrya the sky, and whosoever knowing this, offers the Agnihotra, he, indeed, is produced in the same way, in which they were then produced, he gains that same victory which they then gained ;—indeed, he shares the same world with them, whosoever, knowing this, offers the Agnihotra. Therefore the Agnihotra should certainly be performed.

Every intelligent reader of the foregoing must admit that the severe criticism of Professors Max Müller and Eggeling is deserved.

The foregoing extracts more resemble the " twaddle of idiots" than the utterances of sensible men.

REVIEW.

Some general remarks may now be made based on the preceding pages.

THE RELIGION OF THE VEDAS POLYTHEISTIC.

Classification of the Gods.—"It is difficult," says Max Müller, " to treat of the so-called gods celebrated in the Veda according to any system, for the simple reason that the concepts of these gods and the hymns addressed to them sprang up spontaneously and without any pre-established plan . . . Many functions are shared in common by various gods, no attempt having yet been made at organising the whole body of the gods, sharply separating one for the other, and subordinating all of them to several, or, in the end, to one supreme head."*

Yaska, in his Nirukta, the oldest commentary on the Vedas now in existence, says : "There are three deities, viz., Agni, whose place is on earth ; Vayu, or Indra, whose place is in the air ; and Surya, the sun, whose place is in the sky." "These gods might all be one as a priest receives various names at various sacrifices." "Or," says he, "it may be, these gods are all distinct beings, for the praises addressed to them are distinct, and their appellations also." The former "was certainly not the idea of most of the Vedic Rishis themselves, still less of the people who listened to their songs at fairs and festivals."

Yaska, in the latter part of his work, divides the deities into the three orders of terrestrial, aerial, and celestial.

Number.—The gods are generally spoken of as being " thrice-eleven" in number. "Ye gods, who are eleven in the sky, who are eleven on earth, and who in your glory are eleven dwellers in the (atmospheric) waters, do ye welcome this our offering." "Agni, bring hither according to thy wont, and gladden the three and thirty gods with their wives."

The 33 gods did not include them all. Hymn viii. 35, 3 makes the following additions :

> With all the deities, three times eleven, here in close alliance with the Maruts, Brigus, Floods ;
> Accordant, of one mind with Surya and with Dawn,
> O Asvins, drink the Soma-juice.

In Book iv. 9, 9 the gods are mentioned as being much more numerous : " Three hundred, three thousand, thirty and nine gods have worshipped Agni."

Monotheism is a belief in the existence of one God only ; *polytheism* is a belief in a plurality of gods. Max Müller says, " If we must employ technical terms, the religion of the Veda is poly-

---

* *India : What can it Teach us ?* pp. 148, 149.

theism, not monotheism." The 27th hymn of the first Mandala of the Rig-Veda concludes as follows :

" Glory to gods, the mighty and the lesser, glory to gods the younger and the elder ;
Let us, if we have power, pay the gods worship; no better prayer than that, ye gods, acknowledge."

As already mentioned, the gods are repeatedly said to " be thrice-eleven in number." Whitney says : " The great mass of Vedic hymns are absorbed in the praise and worship of the multi-farious deities of the proper Vedic pantheon, and ignore all concep-tion of a unity of which these are to be accounted the varying manifestations."

There are different kinds of polytheism. The ancient Greeks and Romans had a more or less organised system of gods, different in power and rank, and all subordinate to a supreme God, a Zeus or Jupiter. In the Veda, the gods worshipped as supreme by each sect stand still side by side, no one is always first, no one is always last. Even gods of a decidedly inferior and limited character assume occasionally in the eyes of a devoted poet a supreme place above all other gods.

" It would be easy to find," says Max Müller, " in the numer-ous hymns of the Veda, passages in which almost every single god is represented as supreme and absolute. In the first hymn of the second Mandala, Agni is called the ruler of the universe, the lord of men, the wise king, the father, the brother, the son, and friend of men ; nay, all the powers and names of the others are distinctly ascribed to Agni. . . . Indra is celebrated as the strongest god in the hymns as well as in the Brahmanas, and the burden of one of the songs of the tenth book is ; Vis'vasmâd Indra uttarah. " Indra is greater than all." Of Soma it is said that he was born great, and that he conquers every one. He is called the king of the world; he has the power to prolong the life of men, and in one sense he is called the maker of heaven and earth, of Agni, of Surya, of Indra and Vishnu.

" If we read the next hymn, which is addressed to Varuna, we perceive that the god here invoked is, to the mind of the poet, supreme and all-mighty."*

Max Müller has coined a word, henotheism,† to express what he seems to regard as a " peculiar character of the ancient Vedic religion." It denotes that each of several divinities is regarded as supreme, and worshipped without reference to the rest. The same applies largely to modern Hinduism. Each person may have his special god, ishta devata, but whom he may change for another if

---

* Ancient Sanskrit Literature, pp. 533, 534.
† Henos, one, theos, god.

required.   At the same time he may believe in many others.   Henotheism is simply a form of polytheism.

Only one being can be supreme, but a Hindu does not find any
difficulty in accepting the most contradictory statements.   As well
may it be said that all the boys in a class are first.

The hymns of the Rig-Veda were composed by many authors,
extending over a period of several centuries.   Hence the theology
is often inconsistent.   The polytheism of some hymns is very marked and distinct.   In others it is hazy.   Some hymns, in the absence
of all others, might be regarded as monotheistic.

Some suppose that the Indo-Aryan worship in *pre*-Vedic times
was monotheistic.   Max Müller says :

"There is a monotheism which precedes the polytheism of the Veda,
and even in the invocation of their innumerable gods, the remembrance
of a God, one and infinite, breaks through the midst of an idolatrous
phraseology, like the blue sky that is hidden by passing clouds."

The great Heaven-Father, Dyaus Pitar, *may* at a remote period
have been the only object of worship.   In Vedic times, however,
polytheism prevailed.

Deities sprung from the same source had a tendency, after a
very short career of their own, to run together.   Dyaus was the
sky as the ever-present light.   Varuna was the sky as the all-
embracing.   Mitra was the sky as lighted up by the morning.
Surya was the sun as shining in the sky.   Savitri was the sun as
bringing light and life.   Vishnu was the sun as striding with three
steps across the sky ; Indra appeared in the sky as the giver of
rain, Rudra and the Maruts passed along the sky in thunderstorms ;
Vata and Vayu were the winds of the air ; Agni was fire and light.

Hence it happened constantly that what was told of one deity
could be told of another likewise ; the same epithets are shared by
many, the same stories are told of different gods.

Some of the old poets go so far as to declare that one god is
identical with others.   In the Atharva Veda (XIII. 3, 13) we read :
" In the evening Agni becomes Varuna ; he becomes Mitra when
rising in the morning ; having become Savitri he passes through
the sky ; having become Indra he warms the heaven in the middle."
Surya, the sun, is identified with Indra and Agni; Savitri with
Mitra and Pushan ; Indra with Varuna : Dyaus, the sky, with
Parjanya, the rain-god.   One poet says (Rig-Veda I. 164, 46) :
" That which is *one*, sages name it in various ways—they call it
Agni, Yama, Matarisvan."   Another poet says : " The wise poets
represent by their words Him who is one with beautiful wings in
many ways."

" The formation of dual deities," says Max Müller, " seems
quite peculiar to the Veda.   The names of two gods who shared
certain functions in common were formed into a compound with a

dual termination, and this compound became the name of a new deity. Thus we have hymns not only to Mitra and Varuna, but to Mitrâvarunau as one ; may, sometimes they are called the two Mitras and the two Varunas." *

Sometimes all the gods were comprehended by one common name, *Visve Devas*, the All-gods, and prayers were addressed to them in their collective capacity.

Dr. John Muir, who has given special attention to the subject, says that the hymns, "are the productions of simple men, who, under the influence of the most impressive phenomena of nature, saw everywhere the presence and agency of divine powers, who imagined that each of the great provinces of the universe was directed and animated by its own separate deity, and who had not yet risen to a clear idea of one supreme creator and governor of all things. This is shown not only by the special functions assigned to particular gods, but in many cases by the very names which they bear, corresponding to those of some of the elements or of the celestial luminaries." †

Pantheism Developed.—The tendency towards unity shown by some of the Vedic poets, did not end in *monotheism*, but in *pantheism*, that the universe, as a whole, is God. Both the hymns and the Brahmanas teach a polytheistic religion. They form the *Karmakanda*, 'the department of works.' The Upanishads, philosophical treatises at the end of some of the Brahmanas, form the *Jnanakanda*, ' the department of knowledge.' According to the Upanishads there is only one real Being in the universe, which Being also constitutes the universe. This pantheistic doctrine is everywhere traceable in some of the more ancient Upanishads, although often wrapped up in mysticism and allegory. It is clearly expressed in the well-known formula of three words from the Chhandogya Upanishad, *ekam evadvitiyam*, ' one only without a second.'

Rammohun Roy, as already mentioned, despised the hymns of the Vedas ; he spoke of the Upanishads as the Vedas, and thought that they taught monotheism. The Chhandogya formula was also adopted by Keshab Chunder Sen. But it does not mean that there is no second God, but that there is no second any thing—a totally different doctrine.

Later Development of Polytheism.—While the Vedic poets were generally satisfied with "thrice-eleven" or thirty-three deities, in the Puranas they were converted into 33 crores,—a number greater than every man, woman and child in the country. But along with this pantheistic views are also held.

The Religion of the Vedas Polytheistic.—The Rev. Nehemiah Goreh thus states the case :

---

* Hibbert Lectures, p. 291,　　　† Studie , p. 142.

" The most ignorant idolaters will tell you, if you will ask them, that there is only one God, that is, the Supreme Being, and they will never say that there is more than one God. But if any one would say that the Hindus of the present time worship many gods also though they may acknowledge that there is only one God, and that they worship idols, and therefore they cannot be mono-theists ; then I would ask, Was not the same the case with the authors of those ancient hymns of the Rig-Veda ? They may have spoken sometimes here and there of God, but the chief objects of their devotion were Agni, Váyu, Indra, and many other real or imaginary beings. And does the worship of a god in an idol appear to any one worse than the worship of fire and wind ? Why so ? Because idols seem to be very mean things, but fire and wind are grander and finer elements ? Then such a one ought not to find much fault with any that worships gods in images made of gold and silver.

" We, then, all believed that there was only one God, and called Him Omnipotent, Omniscient and so on, and learned writers of our most modern philosophical and religious books propound elaborate arguments to prove the existence of such a God, and yet we, and they, worshipped, at the same time, a multitude of gods also. It is then really incomprehensible to me why any one should say that there is monotheism in the Rig Veda, because in some rare passages of it God seems to be spoken of, and why he should not think that there is monotheism in all, even the most modern, books of Hinduism, and why he should not call every Hindu a monotheist."*

CHARACTER OF THE VEDIC GODS.

More than 2,000 years ago, Aristotle, a famous Greek philoso-pher, said, " men create the gods after their own image, not only with regard to their form, but also with regard to their manner of life." The gods of the Hindus are typical of themselves at different periods in their history. In Vedic times Indra is the soma-drink-ing martial god who recovers the celestial cows from the fort of Pani, and helps the Aryans in their wars against the aborigines. In the Puranas, " Indra is a gorgeous king of a luxurious and somewhat voluptuous court, where dance and music occupy most of his time. Indra is said to have attained his proud position by his austere penances, and is in constant fear lest any mortals on earth attain the same rank by the same means."†

The Vedic gods were like the early Aryans, especially Indra, the highest of them. Like themselves, he is represented as intensely fond of the soma juice, and as delighting in war. He was a poly-gamist, for Hymn x. 145 is the exultation of Indrani over her rival

---

* *The Supposed and Real Doctrine of Hinduism.* pp. 14, 15.
† Dutt's *Ancient India*, Vol. III. p. 278.

wives. In Hymn viii. 85, 4, Indra is, nevertheless, styled the " holiest of the holy." The Rev. Nehemiah Goreh says :

" The Shadvinsha Bráhmana of the Sáma Veda prescribes a ceremony in which the god Indra is to be invoked in these words, ' O adulterous lover of Ahalya !'* Now, that the Veda should prescribe the worship of a god who is believed to be an adulterer itself indicates a terrible corruption of the moral sense, but what is still more terrible is the fact that this god is to be invoked by those words as by an endearing appellation, and so this act of his adultery is supposed to be a matter of glory to him ! Men whose moral sense was corrupted in such a manner could not have had proper notions of holiness."†

Max Müller says, " Some of the poets of the Veda ascribe to the gods sentiments and passions unworthy of the deity, such as anger, revenge, delight in material sacrifices." As already mentioned, Varuna as the only Vedic deity who is described as possessing high moral attributes. Even he gradually disappears, and his character is changed. There is not a hymn addressed to him in the Tenth Book. The Mahabharat describes him as having carried off Bhadra, the wife of Utathya.

Still, though the moral standard of the Vedic gods, with the exception mentioned, is low, they are on the whole far superior to the later creations of Hindu mythology.

THE RELATION OF THE WORSHIPPERS TO THE GODS.

Varuna, from his majesty and purity, was regarded with awe by the early Aryans ; but he was dethroned by Indra, who was looked upon both as a mighty god and as one who would join with them in drinking the soma juice.

The Rev. K. S. Macdonald has the following remarks on the light in which the gods were generally regarded: "In one word the relation was very familiar. There is little or no sense of love or fear, no sense of the holy or the pure or the spiritual. They treat the gods as of themselves, only more powerful, subject to the same weaknesses, the same desires, the same appetites. The Soma the clarified butter, the horses, etc., in which the worshippers delighted were supposed to be sources of still greater pleasure to their gods. The strength, the stimulus which they themselves experienced, or imagined they experienced, from their drinking of the Soma juice, they supposed their gods to receive in still greater measure.... The worshipper offers even to Varuna sweet things which the god is sure to like, and then appeals to him :‡ " Once more together let us speak, because my meath is brought ; priest-like, thou eatest

---

*अहल्यायै जार ।
† The Supposed and Real Doctrines of Hinduism, p. 29.
‡ The Vedic Religion, pp. 136, 138.

what is dear to thee." 1. 25, 17. In another hymn Vasishtha addresses Indra : " Vasishtha hath poured forth his prayers, desiring to milk thee like a cow in goodly pasture." VII. 18. 4. Agni is thus reasoned with in one of the hymns :

> 25. " Son of strength, Agni, if thou wert the mortal, bright as Mitra ! worshipped with our gifts !
> And I were the immortal god,
> 26. "I would not give thee up, Vasu, to calumny or sinfulness, O bounteous one.
> My worshipper should feel no hunger or distress, nor, Agni, should he live in sin." VIII. 19.

Barth says, " The idea that it is from the offering the gods derive their strength recurs at every step in the Hymns."*

> "O Ushas, nobly-born, daughter of heaven, whom the Vasishthas with their hymns make mighty. vii. 77, 6.
> " May these our viands, bounteous ones ! that flow in streams like holy oil,
> With Kanvas hymns, increase your might. viii. 7, 19."
> " As rivers swell the ocean, so, hero, our prayers increase thy might." viii. 88, 8.

Worship a Bargain.—There is little love or gratitude expressed in the hymns. The gods and the worshippers are like traders in a bargain. "I give thee this for that." Indra is thus addressed. " Be thou no trafficker with us, (i. 33-3) do not give sparingly, nor demand too much."

> " Whoso with toil and terrible brings the fuel, serving the majesty of mighty Agni,
> " He kindling thee at evening and at morning, prospers, and comes to wealth, and slays his foeman." iv. 12. 2.
> " The pourer of libations gains the home of wealth, pouring his gift conciliates hostilities, yea, the hostilities of the gods.
> " Pouring he strives, unchecked and strong, to win him riches thousand fold.
> Indra gives lasting wealth to him who pours forth gifts, yea, wealth he gives that long shall last." I. 133. 7.

This is very clearly shown in the Brahmanas. Barth quotes the following from the Taittiriya Sanhita :

" Does he wish to do harm (to an enemy) ? Let him say (to Surya) : Strike such an one, afterwards will I pay thee the offering. And (Surya) desiring to obtain the offering, strikes him." vi. 4, 5, 6.
"When filled, O divider ! fly yonder ; when well filled, fly back to us ! As at a stipulated price, let us exchange force and vigour, O Indra ! give me and I shall give thee ; bring me, I shall bring thee." 1. 8, 4, 1.

---

* *The Religions of India*, p. 36.

The Dr. A. K. S. Macdonald says : " Cannon Rawlinson points out the relation as almost the very opposite to what one would expect—the worshipper being the lord and master, the worshipped being the servant, if not the slave : ' The offerings of praise and sacrifice, and especially the offering of the Soma juice, were considered not merely to please the god who was the object of them, but to lay him under a binding obligation, and almost to compel him to grant the request of the worshippers.' ' Who buys this— *my* Indra,' says Vamadeva, a Vedic poet, ' with ten milch kine ? When he shall have slain his foes, then let the purchaser give him back to me again ;' which the commentator explains, as follows : ' Vamadeva, *having by much praise got Indra into his possession or subjugation*, proposes to make a bargain when about to dispose of him ;' and so he offers for ten milch kine to hand him over temporarily, apparently to any person who will pay the price, with the proviso that when Indra has subdued the person's foes, he is to be returned to the vendor !"*

In later times this idea was still more strongly developed. The performance of austerities for a continued period was supposed to constrain the gods to grant the desired boon, although fraught with peril and even destruction to themselves.

THE PRAYERS OF THE VEDAS.

Prayer is an essential part of religion. Belief in God leads a man to ask Him for such blessings as he thinks himself to need.

Prayer is an index both to a man's own character and to the supposed nature of the deity he worships. Most people are worldly, and their prayers are only for temporal blessings, for wealth, for sons, recovery from sickness, deliverance from earthly enemies, &c. Only a few are spiritually minded, and seek for pardon of sin, holiness, and communion with God.

The Vedic Aryans had a firm belief in the virtue of prayer. The Vedas are largely a collection of prayers.

The hymns usually begin by praising the gods for their supposed excellencies, their great deeds, sometimes even their personal beauty. The following are some examples :

Indra is then addressed :

" To Indra Dyaus the Asura hath bowed him down, to Indra mighty earth with wide extending tracts, to win the light, with widespread tracts.

" All gods of one accord have set Indra in front, preëminent."

I. 131. 1.

" Thou, god without a second." I. 32. 12.

---

* The Vedic Religions, p. 137.

Indra is praised for his capacity to drink Soma :

"Then Indra at a single draught drank the contents of thirty pails,
Pails that were filled with Soma juice." VII. 66. 4.

Indra thus boasts of his greatness after drinking Soma :

11. "One of my flanks is in the sky ; I let the other trail below ;
Have I not drunk of Soma-juice ? "
12. I, greatest of the mighty ones, am lifted to the firmament :
Have I not drunk of Soma-juice ? " X. 119.

Some of his achievements under its influence have already been quoted.

Agni is thus addressed :

" Agni I hold as herald, the munificent, the gracious, son of strength,
who knoweth all that live, as holy singer, knowing all." 1. 127. 1.
" To Agni I present a newer mightier hymn, I bring my words
and song unto the son of strength,
Who, offspring of the waters, bearing precious things, sits on the
earth, in season, dear invoking priest." I 143. 1.

The Maruts are thus addressed :

" Come hither Maruts, on your lightning-laden cars, sounding with
sweet songs, armed with lances, winged with steeds." 1. 88, 1.

The gods are sometimes praised for their beauty, " One of the epithets most commonly applied to Indra, " says Muir, is *susipra*, or *siprin*, in the interpretation of which Sayana wavers between ' the god with handsome cheeks or nose.' Agni is called " lord of the lively look." II. 7, 8.

The " broad-tressed Sinivali is thus described : "

" With lovely fingers, lovely arms, prolific Mother of many sons—
Present the sacred gifts to her, to Sinivali queen of men." II. 32, 7.

BLESSINGS ASKED.

The Rev. Dr. K. S. Macdonald says :
" One thing is very clear to every reader of the Veda, that the desires of the hymnists were ever towards cows, horses, offspring (sons), long life on earth, victory over their earthly enemies, etc. ; that the requests for spiritual blessings, or an inheritance in heaven, or immortality, were very few in number, and not very clearly expressed. The visible and sensible, as far as their hopes and wishes were concerned, occupied their thoughts, almost to the complete exclusion of the invisible and the spiritual." *

Wealth.—This, in one form or another, is the subject of nearly every prayer, or forms one of the petitions, " Bring us the wealth

---

* *The Vedic Religion*, pp. 48, 49.

for which we long" (VIII. 45, 42) is the conclusion in many hymns.

The ancient Aryans were largely a pastoral people. Professor Bhattacharyya infers this from "cows, the recovery of cows, the plunder of cows, the increase of cows and gifts of cows being described in the Rig-Veda in such permutations and combinations."[*] Cows and horses form the refrain in the following hymn addressed to Indra :

1.   " O Soma-drinker, ever true, utterly hopeless though we be,
    Do thou, O Indra, give us hope of beauteous horses and of kine,
    In thousands, O most wealthy one.
2.   O Lord of strength, whose jaws are strong, great deeds are thine,
    the powerful :
    Do thou, O Indra, give us hope of beauteous horses and of kine,
    In thousands, O most wealthy one." I. 29.

The following are other requests :

    " O Indu, Soma, send us now great opulence from every side,
    Pour on us treasures thousandfold." IX. 40. 40. 3.
    " Pour out on us abundant food, when thou art pressed, O Indu,
       wealth
    In kine and gold and steeds and strength." IX. 41, 4.
    " Will ye then, O Maruts, grant us riches, durable, rich in men
       defying onslaught,
    A hundred, thousand-fold, ever increasing ? I. 64, 15.
    " Knowing our chief felicity, O Agni bring hither ample riches
       to our nobles." VII. 1, 24.
    " O wondrous Indra, bring us wondrous riches." VII. 20. 7.

At the commencement of ploughing, the following verse was repeated with an offering of fire :

    " Auspicious Sita, come thou near : we venerate and worship
       thee,
    That thou may bless and prosper us and bring us fruits abund-
       antly." IV. 57. 6.

A hymn to Varuna, in which deliverance from sin is sought, ends with, "King, may I never lack well-ordered riches." II. 2. 8. 11.

Rain.—This is frequently asked. Indra is chiefly adored because he slays with his bolts the demon who withholds the rain. Parjanya is thus addressed :

    " Lift up the mighty vessel, pour down water, and let the liberat-
      ed streams rush forward.
    Saturate both the earth and heaven with fatness, and for the
      cows let there be drink abundant." V. 83. 8.

---

[*] Tagore Law Lectures, p. 112,

Sons.—The following are a few examples :

"Men yearn for children to prolong their line, and are not disappointed in their hope." I. 68. 4.

"May the wealth-giver (Agni) grant us wealth with heroes (sons).

May the wealth-giver grant us food with offspring." I. 96. 8.

"Help is to wealth, exceeding good and glorious, abundant, rich in children and their progeny." II. 2. 12.

"To us be born a son and spreading offspring, Agni, be this thy gracious will to us-ward." III. 6. 11.

"Brihaspati, may we be lords of riches, with noble progeny, and store of heroes." IV. 50. 6.

Long Life.—The Aryans, coming from a cold country, first reckoned their years by "winters." Probably in later hymns "autumns" are substituted.

"Grant unto us to see a hundred autumns ; ours be the happy lives of our forefathers." II. 27, 10.

"Long let our life, O Agni, be extended." IV. 12. 6·

"Accept, O Maruts, graciously this hymn of mine that we may live a hundred winters through its power." V. 54, 15.

"Be gracious, Indra, let my days be lengthened." VI. 47, 10.

Preservation from Danger.—Amidst constant wars with the aborigines, this request frequently occurs in the hymns. But safety is also sought from other dangers, as snake bites.

"In thy kind grace (Indra) and favour may we still be strong : expose us not to any foe's attack.

With manifold assistance guard and succour us, and bring us to felicity." VIII. 3, 2.

"May wealthy Indra as our good protector, lord of all treasures, favour us with succour,

Baffle our foes, and give us rest and safety. VI. 47, 12.

"Savitar, god, send far away all sorrows and calamities,

And send us only what is good." V. 82, 5.

"Give us not up to any evil creature, as spoil to wolf or she-wolf, O ye holy," VI. 51, 6.

"May they, Earth, Aditi, Indra, Bhaga, Pushan increase our laud, increase the fivefold people.

"Giving good help, good refuge, goodly guidance, be they our good deliverers, good protectors." VI. 51, 11.

"Not to the fanged that bites, not to the toothless : give not us up, thou conqueror to the spoiler." I. 190, 5.

Destruction of Enemies.—Next to wealth, this is one of the most frequent petitions. Some prayers include all who are un-friendly ; others single out individuals.

"Destroy this ass, O Indra, who in tones discordant brays to thee."

" Slay each reviler, and destroy him who in secret injures us."
I. 29, 5, 7.

" O Agni, radiant one, to whom the holy oil is poured, burn up
Our enemies whom fiends protect." I. 12, 5.

" Cast thy dart knowing, thunderer, at the Dasyu ;" I. 103, 3.

" Whatever mortal with the power of demons fain would injure us.
May he, impetuous, suffer harm by his own deeds." VIII. 18, 13.

"Crunch up on every side the dogs who bark at us : slay ye our
foes, O Asvins." I. 182, 4.

" Consume for ever all demons and sorcerers, consume thou each
devouring fiend." I. 36, 20.

" Drive from us with thy tongue, O god, the man who doeth evil
deeds,
The mortal who would strike us dead." VI. 16, 32.

1. Annihilate the fools, slay them and burn them up; Chase them
away from us, pierce the voracious ones.

2. Against the foe of prayer, devourer of raw flesh, the vile fiend,
fierce of eye, keep ye perpetual hate.

10. The fiend, O Agni, who designs to injure the essence of our food,
kine, steeds, or bodies,
May he, the adversary, thief, and robber, sink to destruction,
both himself and offspring.

11. " May he be swept away, himself and children. May all the three
earths press him down beneath them.
May his fair glory, O ye gods, be blighted, who in the day or
night would fain destroy us." VII. 104.

Quotations have been given from Hymn 87 Book X. addressed
to Agni, the Slayer of Rakshasas.

Pardon of Sin.—Prayers of this nature chiefly occur in the
hymns to Varuna, the principal of which have been quoted. A
few other extracts may be given :

" Aditi, Mitra, Varuna, forgive us however we have erred and
sinned against you." II. 27. 14.

" Prolong our days of life (ye Asvins), wipe out our trespasses."
I. 157. 4.

" Most youthful god (Agni) whatever sin, through folly, here in
the world of men we have committed,
Before great Aditi make thou us sinless : remit, entirely, Agni,
our offences." IV. 12. 4.

" Let us not suffer for the sins of others, nor do the deed which
ye, O Vasus, punish." VI. 51. 7.

" What secret sin or open stirs their (Maruts) anger, that we
implore the swift ones to forgive us." VII. 58. 5.

" May he, the bounteous god (Brihaspati) may find us sinless,
who giveth at a distance like a father." VII. 97, 2.

" Save us (Visvedevas) from uncommitted and committed sin,
preserve us from all sin to-day for happiness." X. 63. 8.

Future World.—The references to this are few, and chiefly found in the Ninth and Tenth Books. The great desire of the Aryans was to enjoy the present life.

" The givers of rich meeds are made immortal; the givers of rich fees prolong their life time." 1. 125, 6.

" May I attain to that his well loved mansion when men devoted to the gods are happy." I. 154, 5.

" We pray for rain, your boon (Mitra-Varuna) and immortality." V. 63, 2.

" When I and Indra mount high up to the bright one's place and home,

" We, having drunk of meath, will reach his seat whose friends are three times seven." VIII. 38, 7.

" We have drunk Soma and became immortal ; we have attained the light, the gods discovered." VIII. 48, 3,

" High up in heaven abide the guerdon-givers ; they who give steeds dwell with the Sun for ever.

They who give gold are blest with life eternal : they who give robes protect their lives, O Soma." X. 107, 2.

The hymn of the Rig-Veda, says Muir, " contain, as far as I am aware, no permanent mention of the future punishment of the wicked. Nevertheless Yama is to some extent an object of terror."[*]

ARE THE VEDAS A DIVINE REVELATION ?

Supposed Wisdom of the Ancients.—An error has prevailed in all countries and in all ages to regard persons who lived long ago as the ancients—very old and very wise,—while people now living are looked upon as children. The very opposite is the case. *We are the ancients ;* those who lived long ago are the children. The world is thousands of years older now than it was then.

In Vedic times there were no books, and printing was unknown. All the valuable knowledge which has been gained in any quarter of the globe during the last twenty-five centuries is now at command. During these many years, lakhs of learned men have been adding to our stores. Every fresh discovery is now flashed by the electric telegraph, and by means of newspapers is at once made known to the whole civilised world.

The late distinguished Indian statesman, Sir Madhava Row, says in a Convocation Address :

" Avoid the mischievous error of supposing that our ancient fore-fathers were wiser than men of the present times. It cannot be true. Every year of an individual's life he acquires additional knowledge. Knowledge thus goes on accumulating year by year. Similarly every generation adds to the knowledge of the previous generation. Under such a process the accumulation of knowledge in a century is very large.

---

[*] *Sanskrit Texts*, Vol. V. 302.

To assert therefore that men possessed more knowledge scores of centuries ago than at the present day is manifestly absurd.

Even assuming intellectual equality between the ancients and moderns, men of modern times have had enormous advantages over those of ancient times for the acquisition of knowledge. Our field of observation, our facilities for observation, our instruments of observation, our highly elaborated methods of calculation, our means of publishing the results of observation, of getting the results scrutinized, questioned, compared, discussed and variously verified, are infinitely greater than those of remote generations. The explorations of the ancients were fragmentary and superficial.

The whole world is now one field of observation. An enormous intellectual committee of the whole civilized human race is ceaselessly sitting from generation to generation, and is ceaselessly working for the collection and augmentation of human knowledge.

Calmly and carefully reflect and you are certain to agree with me. Hesitate not therefore to prefer modern knowledge to ancient knowledge. A blind belief in the omniscience of our forefathers is mischievous, because it perpetuates errors and tends to stagnation."*

An adult deserves no credit for being wiser than when a young child. The present generation should be,

" The heir of all the ages, in the foremost files of time."

The Vedas represent the comparative *Childhood of the World.*

Estimates of the Vedas.—Two classes of persons entertain the most exalted notions of the Vedas. First those who *know nothing of them.* This includes the great mass of the people of India, educated and uneducated. According to the Latin proverb, " Everything of which we are ignorant is taken for something magnificent." The other class consists of these who *know nothing else.* Such are the pandits, frogs in a well, and men like Dayanand Sarasvati. The latter held that whatever was not to be found in the Vedas was false or useless ; whatever was found in the Vedas was beyond the reach of controversy.

Max Müller thus describes the conclusion arrived at by intelligent Indians :

" The friends of Rammohan Roy, honest and fearless as they have always proved themselves to be, sent some young scholars to Benares to study the Vedas and to report on their contents. As soon as their report was received, Debendranath Tagore, the head of the Brahma-Samaj, said at once that, venerable as the Vedas might be as relics of a former age, they contained so much that was childish, erroneous, and impossible as to make their descent from a divine source utterly untenable."†

Mr. K. K. Bhattacharyya, late Professor of Sanskrit in the Presidency College, Calcutta, in his Tagore Law Lectures,

---

* Madras Convocation Addresses, 8vo. 231 pp. 8 As. Post-free. Sold by Mr. A. T. Scott, Tract Depôt, Madras.   † *Biographical Essays,* pp. 168, 169.

describes the thousand hymns of the Rig-Veda as a "dreary wilderness, at but distant intervals redeemed by slight flashes of satire or quaint flights of fancy." (p. 119.)

Professor Max Müller has spent many years, in editing the Rig-Veda, with the commentary of Sayana. He is not likely to undervalue it—rather the reverse. He himself makes the following confession in his "Preface to the Sacred Books of the East" :—

" Scholars also who have devoted their life either to the editing of the original texts or to the careful interpretation of some of the sacred books, are more inclined, after they have disinterred from a heap of rubbish some solitary fragments of pure gold, to exhibit these treasures only than to display all the refuse from which they had to extract them. I do not blame them for this, perhaps I should feel that I was open to the same blame myself, for it is but natural that scholars in their joy at finding one or two fragrant fruits or flowers should gladly forget the brambles and thorns that had to be thrown aside in the course of their search." Page x.

In his Lecture on the Vedas he expresses the following opinion of the hymns :—

"The historical importance of the Veda can hardly be exaggerated, but its intrinsic merit, and particularly the beauty or elevation of its sentiments, have by many been rated far too high. Large numbers of the Vedic hymns are childish in the extreme : tedious, low, common-place. The gods are constantly invoked to protect their worshippers, to grant them food, large flocks, large families, and a long life ; for all which benefits they are to be rewarded by the praises and sacrifices offered day after day, or at certain seasons of the year. But hidden in this rubbish there are precious stones."

" I remind you again that the Veda contains a great deal of what is childish and foolish, though very little of what is bad and objectionable. Some of its poets ascribe to the gods sentiments and passions unworthy of the deity, such as anger, revenge, delight in material sacrifices ; they likewise represent human nature on a low level of selfishness and worldliness. Many hymns are utterly unmeaning and insipid, and we must search patiently before we meet, here and there, with sentiments that come from the depth of the soul, and with prayers in which we could join ourselves."

The hymns which have been quoted in full are some of the most interesting, and scarcely give a fair general idea of the contents.

The repetitions are endless, the same epithets and images are applied first to one and then to another of the gods. *Give us wealth,* is the request that runs through nearly the whole of them.

The following are some of the reasons why the Vedas cannot be accepted as a revelation from the mouth of Brahma, given crores of years ago :

1. *The writers of the hymns, in many cases, claim to be their authors, and internal evidence shows that they were composed when the Aryans were entering India.*

These points have been already noticed so fully (see pp. 13-18) that it is unnecessary to recapitulate what has been said.

2. *The low conceptions given of God show that the writers were not inspired.*

The Vedas unquestionably teach polytheism ; but as every intelligent man is now a monotheist, attempts are made to show that the " thrice eleven" deities mean only one God.

The inconsistent accounts of the gods show that they are mere inventions according to the fancies of the poet.   As already quoted " The father is sometimes the son, the brother is the husband, and she who in one hymn is the mother, is in another the wife."

The Aryans framed their gods after themselves.   They bargained with their gods just as they did with one another ; they flattered them : they offered them sweet things and told them to be good. They themselves were fond of Soma-beer ; so they thought it was so with Indra. Just as the smell of liquor attracts the drunkard, so as soon as Indra knew of some one preparing Soma-beer, he mounted his chariot and drove to the place.   Grant that Indra was fond of Soma-beer, is it to be supposed that the king of heaven could not get it except by coming to some Aryan peasant's home. One hymn says that (the worshipper) brings Indra to drink the Soma by a rapid seizure, like a loaded horse (by a halter). It is said of the Asvins, " ye fly to our oblations like a pair of hawks." (VIII. 35, 9.)

The gods are supposed to have wives like the Hindus, and the disputes of rival wives in modern times are reproduced in the heaven of Indra.

3. *Superstitious beliefs, now exploded, are accepted as true.*— There is the firm faith in magical arts which still prevails among uncivilised nations. To prevent others from learning the hymns, the Brahmans taught that the mispronunciation of a word would bring down the anger of the gods. The influence ascribed to the different metres in which a hymn is composed has been quoted (see pp. 3, 4). The repetition of certain words is supposed to have a magical effect. The same power is ascribed to certain plants. The Hindu belief that eclipses are caused by an Asura seizing the sun and moon, is held, and the sun expresses gratitude to the Rishi Atri for deliverance through his prayer (V. 40. 5-9).

A few charms are found even in the Rig-Veda. The Atharva Veda is largely a collection of them. Stones, bones, shells, herbs, and other so-called fetishes, like those of African negroes, appear in it. In the Yajur-Veda, the queen of a childless king, in order to have a son, is to lie all night embracing a dead horse. No sensible man can now believe any such things.

4. *The worldly character of the hymns shows their origin.*

Bishop Caldwell justly says : " If any person reads the hymns of the Vedas for the first time, he will be struck with surprise at the utterly worldly, unethical, unspiritual tone by which they are generally pervaded." The Rev. Dr. K. S. Macdonald expresses the same opinion :

"In the Veda, man is generally looked upon as essentially of this world. He is constantly represented as taken up with the things of this world, what he sees, hears, tastes, and feels in it,—the glowing of the fire, the flashing of the lightning, the howling of the storm, the rushing of the wind, the splash of the rain, the rising and setting of the sun, the dawning and gloaming of the day, the number of his cows, camels, sons, and horses, the burning of his enemies' towns and the carrying off booty, the slaughter of the Dasyus and Rakshasas, the offering of *ghi* and Soma to Indra and Agni in the hope of receiving more sons and cattle and slaughtering more enemies. These and such like things seem to constitute the whole duty of man as he is represented in the hymns of the Rig-Veda. As a matter of fact, there is no attempt in the Vedas, or indeed in modern Hinduism, to give a correct conception of man's duties."*

The Rishis, from whom better things might have been expected, were as worldly as the common people. Instead of wishing to live ascetic lives, "give us the wealth for which we yearn," is the grand theme of their hymns. Several illustrative quotations have already been given.

The Rishis did not wish to live in huts. One of them prays thus :

"We solicit of the divine protector of the Maruts, of the Asvins, of Mitra, and of Varuna, a spacious dwelling for our welfare. Mitra, Aryaman, Varuna, and Maruts, grant us a secure, excellent, and well-peopled dwelling, a three-fold shelter."

Another Rishi prays not only that Pushan should protect him in all his doings, but also "bestow on us our share of maids." IX. 67, 10.

Besides praying directly for wealth, the Rishis sought to gain it by invoking blessings on those who bestowed gifts, and by cursing those who offered no oblations. Max Müller says :

"There is a whole class of hymns commonly called *danastutis*, or praises of gifts. They are the thanksgivings of certain priests for presents received from their royal patrons. The liberality of their royal patrons is held up to the admiration and imitation of later generations by stories which had to be repeated at the sacrifices."†

The following are some illustrative extracts :

When will he (Indra) trample, like a weed, the man who hath no gifts for him ? I. 84. 8.
"Slay the niggards." I. 184. 2.
"Consumer of the churlish niggard." VI. 61. 1.
"Wealth comes not to the niggard churl." VII. 32. 21.
"For those who give rich meeds are all these splendours, for those who give rich meeds suns shine in heaven."
"Let afflictions fall upon the niggard." I. 125. 6, 7.

---

* *The Vedic Religion*, p. 229.   † *Ancient Sanskrit Literature,* p. 493.

Some of the Rishis either received immense gifts or told great lies.   Brahmatithi says :

37. " As Kasu, Chedi's son, gave me a hundred head of buffaloes, and ten thousand kine.
38. He who hath given me for mine own ten kings like gold to look upon.
39. No man, not any, goes upon the path on which the Chedis walk.
      No other prince, no folk is held more liberal of gifts than they.   VIII.   5.

The Rishi Vasa Asvya thus praises the liberality of Prithusravas, the son of Kanita.

21. " Now let the godless man approach who hath received reward so great
      As Vasa Asvya, when this light of morning dawned, received from Prithusravas, from Kanita's son.
22. Steeds sixty thousand and ten thousand kine, and twenty thousand camels I obtained ;
      Ten hundred brown in hue, and other ten red in three spots; in all ten thousand kine.
23. Ten browns that make my wealth increase, fleet steeds whose tails are long and fair,
      Turn with swift whirl my chariot wheel ;
24. The gifts which Prithusravas gave, Kanita's son munificent.
      He gave a chariot wrought of gold ; the prince was passing beautiful, and won himself most lofty fame.
33. And now to Vasa Asvya here this stately woman* is led forth,
      Adorned with ornaments of gold."   VIII. 46.

5. *The Fatherhood of God and the Brotherhood of Man are not acknowledged.*—The truth of this great doctrine is now generally admitted by intelligent Hindus.   Neither is found in the Vedas.   It is true that the gods are asked to give like a father, but this is very different from the acknowledgment that we derived our being from God and of that endearing relationship expressed by the title " Our Father in heaven."   The Rev. Dr. K. S. Macdonald says :

" There was a recognition of a common relationship between all the Aryans as such, as descended from one common father Manu. The rest of the human race seems to have been regarded as altogether outside the pale of mercy or the ordinary demands of humanity."

" The horizon of the Rishi, is confined almost invariably to himself.   He prays for the happiness of neither wife nor child, not for the good of his village or his clan, nor yet for his nation or people.   His eye is shut to the sufferings of his fellows.   He manifests no common joys, any more than common sorrows."

---

* Probably the wife of the conquered king.

But there is much that is worse than this negative side.   Christianity teaches, " Thou shall love thy neighbour as thyself."   We should forgive and pray for our enemies.   Jesus Christ says : " Love your enemies, bless them that curse you, do good to them that hate you, and pray for them which despitefully use you, and persecute you."

The Aryans not only did not regard the non-Aryan races, and even some Aryans, as brothers ; they simply wished their destruction and to obtain their wealth.

> " Slay ye our Aryan foes, O lord of heroes, slay our Dasa foes :
> Drive all our enemies away :" VI. 60, 6.
> " Slay every one who pours no gift, who hard to reach, delights thee not.
> Bestow on us what wealth he hath ; this even the worshipper awaits." I. 176, 4.
> " Tear thou asunder, as of old, like tangles of a creeping plant,
> Demolish thou the Dasa's might. May we with Indras' help divide the treasure he hath gathered up. Let all the others die away." VIII. 40. 6.

Numerous other passages of similiar import might be quoted.

6. *The Vedas do not contain any satisfactory statement as to the way of salvation or human duty.*

The Rev. Dr. K. S. Macdonald says : " No Rishi, so far as I am aware, has ever claimed to be commissioned by God or by the gods, or by any of the gods, to enlighten men in regard to his will concerning men, or men's duties to God, or to one another.   No one claimed to have any authoritative announcement to make as to whence man came, or whether he is going, what is his chief end here or hereafter."

Libations of the Soma juice and the offering of sacrifices are the chief means prescribed for the attainment of blessings.   No intelligent man of the present time will be satisfied with such recommendations.

Nothing is said about labours of love, or acts of charity towards the poor, the widow, or the orphan.

Points of Superiority over later Hinduism.—Only two of the principal will be mentioned.

1. *The modern Caste System did not exist in Vedic Times.*— Caste is noticed only in a single verse of a comparatively modern hymn.

Max Müller first printed the whole of the Rig-Veda with the commentary of Sayana ; and he has devoted nearly his entire life to its study under the most favourable circumstances.   What does he say ?

" There is no authority whatever in the hymns of the Veda for the complicated system of castes.   There is no law to prohibit the different

classes of the people from living together, from eating and drinking together ; no law to prohibit the marriage of people belonging to different
castes ; no law to brand the offspring of such marriages with an indeli-
ble stigma. There is no law to sanction the blasphemous pretensions of
a priesthood to divine honours, or the degradation of any human being
to a state below the animal." *Chips.* Vol. II.

At present the question of sea-voyages is greatly agitated
among the Hindus. The old Aryans had no such scruples. They
rather gloried in their sea-voyages.

2. *Women occupied a higher position than at present.*—There
were no infant marriages. Women, in some cases at least, were
allowed to choose their husbands. Widows were permitted to
re-marry. Women were not secluded. The wife took part in
sacrifices. So far from women being prohibited from religious
teaching, some of the hymn of the Rig-Veda were written by
female Rishis, *e. g.,* X. 39, 40 by Ghoshâ, VIII. 80 by Apalâ, &c.

Truths in the Vedas.—It is admitted that along with serious
errors, the Vedas contain some great truths, either plainly expressed
or dimly shadowed forth. The following may be mentioned :

1. *Prayer.*—The Aryans were, in their way, a religious people.
They daily acknowledged their dependence upon the gods, and
sought every blessing from them. In this they set us an example.

2. *Praise.*—The gods are praised for what they are, and for
what they have done for man. This feeling of thankfulness is
highly to be commended.

3. *An acknowledgment of God's Omniscience.*—Scoffers have
said, " How doth God know ? and is there knowledge in the Most
High ?" On the contrary, in the Vedas, even the winkings of men
are said to be known to Varuna.

4. *A confession of Sinfulness.*—It is true that these are not
very numerous, but they occur, especially in hymns to Varuna.
Thus in Book X. 89,3, there is the following :

"O bright and powerful god, through want of strength I erred
and went astray :
Have mercy, spare me, mighty lord."

In some later Hindu writings the feeling is more strongly
expressed. The following daily confession is made by some
Brahmans :

Pâpo'ham pâpakarmâham pâpâtma pâpasambhavah |
" I am sin, I commit sin ; my soul is sinful; I am conceived in
sin." This acknowledgment is true, and deserves to be made
daily by every man. Our sins in thought, word, and deed, are
numberless. How to be released from them should be the earnest
desire of every one.

5. *Mediation.*—There are few doctrines in the Christian relig-

ion to which Hindus more object than to mediation, but it is distinctly found in the Vedas. Max Müller calls Agni "the messenger and mediator between God and men." Agni, it is said "goes wisely between these two creations (heaven and earth, gods and men) like a friendly messenger between two hamlets." He announces to the gods the hymns, and conveys to them the oblations of their worshippers.

But mediation is not found merely in the Vedas. In every-day life it is universally acted upon. When any one has offended another, it is a common thing to seek reconciliation through a friend; a favour, such as an office, is often sought through the intervention of a person known to both.

In one sense, however, mediation is not necessary. We can offer our prayers direct to God without the intervention of a priest on earth.

6. *Sacrifice.*—One of the chief doctrines of Christianity is that the Son of God, for man's redemption, became incarnate, and suffered death upon the cross as a sacrifice for sin. The late Rev. Dr. Krishna Mohun Banerjea, for many years one of the Sanskrit Examiners of the Calcutta University, thus shows how this doctrine is shadowed forth in Vedic Hinduism:

The two propositions which he enunciates are :—

1*st.* That the fundamental principles of Christian doctrine in relation to the salvation of the world find a remarkable counterpart in the Vedic principles of primitive Hinduism in relation to the destruction of sin, and the redemption of the sinner by the efficacy of Sacrifice, itself a figure of *Prajápati*, the Lord and Saviour of the Creation, who had given himself up as an offering for that purpose.

2*ndly.* That the meaning of "*Prajápati*," an appellative, variously described as a *Purusha*, begotten in the beginning, as *Viswakarma* the creator of all, singularly coincides with the meaning of the name and offices of the historical reality JESUS CHRIST, and that no other person than JESUS of Nazareth has ever appeared in the world claiming the character and position of the self-sacrificing *Prajápati*, at the same time both mortal and immortal.

The proofs of these propositions are next submitted :—

The first and foremost rites of religion which the Indo-Aryans regularly celebrated, and on which they most firmly relied as the great cure for all the evils of life, and the secret of all success in the world, were *sacrificial rites.* Not idolatrous worship, not observances of caste, not any popular ceremony of our days, but *yajna* (sacrifice) and its connectives were the religious rites cherished by them.

The authorship of the institution is attributed to "Creation's Lord" himself. The world was called into being by virtue of sacrifice and is still upheld by its force, being indeed its "navel." Rig-Veda I. 164, 35.

Sacrifice offered according to the true way—the right path—has been held in the Rik, Yajus, and Saman to be the good ferrying boat or raft by which we may escape from sin. It was expressly declared to be the authorised means both for remission and annulment of sin.

The sacrificer offered the victim in place of himself. The Taittiriya Brahmana says, " The sacrificer is the victim ; it takes the sacrificer to the blessed place." Sacrifice was regarded as the way of deliverance from sin. The Rig-Veda x. 133. 6, says, " Do thou, by means of sacrifice, take away from us all sin." The Tandya Maha Brahmana of the Saman Veda says of sacrifice : " Whatever sins we have committed by day or by night, thou art the annulment thereof. Whatever sins we have committed, knowingly or unknowingly, thou art the annulment thereof. Thou art the annulment of sin—of sin."

Sacrifice was regarded as the destroyer of Death. In the Taittiriya Aranyaka it is said, " O Death ! the thousand myriads of thy bands for the destruction of mortals we annul them all by the mysterious power of sacrifice." Sacrifice opens the way to heaven. " Whosoever desires the felicity of heaven, let him perform sacrifices in the right way."

The secret of this extreme importance attached to sacrifice, and the key to the proper understanding of the whole subject was the self-sacrifice of *Prajápati*, the Lord or Supporter of the Creation, the " *Purusha*, begotten before the world," " the *Viswakarma*, the author of the universe." The idea is found in all the three great Vedas—Rik, Yajus, and Saman—in Sanhitas, Brahmanas, Aranyakas and Upanishads. The Divine *Purusha* who gave himself up as a sacrifice for the Devas, *i. e.*, *emancipated* mortals, had, it is said, desired and got a mortal body *fit for sacrifice*, and himself became *half mortal* and *half immortal*.

The Yajus puts into the mouth of the Divine Self-sacrificer the words : " Let me offer myself in all creatures, and all creatures in myself." The Satapatha Brahmana says, " The Lord of creatures gave himself for them for He became their sacrifice." The Taittiriya Aranyaka contains the following : " They slew Purusha the victim—Purusha who was born from the beginning." The Rig Veda styles him, " the giver of himself, the giver of strength, whose shadow, whose death, is immortality."

The world was condemned and offered for sacrifice, that is to say, was devoted to destruction, for sin ; and the Divine Saviour then offered Himself for its deliverance. The Bible says, " If one died for all, then were all dead." The Veda says conversely : *Because all were devoted to destruction, therefore one died for all.*

All that has just been shown appertaining to the sacrifice of *Prajápati* curiously resembles the Biblical description of CHRIST as God and man, our very Emmanuel (God with us,) mortal and immortal, who " hath given Himself for us, an offering and a sacrifice to God for a sweet smelling savour," of whom all previous sacrifices were but figures and reflections, who by His sacrifice or death hath " vanquished death, and brought life and immortality to light through the gospel."

The Vedic ideal of Prajápati, as we have seen, singularly approximates to the above description of our Lord, and therefore remarkably confirms the saving mysteries of Christianity.

Christian evangelists when they draw our attention to the claims of Gospel truth do not utter things which can be called *strange* to Indian ears. Salvation from sin by the death of a Saviour, who was God and man himself, was a conception which had administered consolation to our ancient *Rishis*, and may yet, in a higher form, and to a greater degree, do the same for all India.

I proceed now to discuss the second proposition. The name *Prajápati* not only means " the Lord of creatures," but also " the supporter, feeder, and deliverer of his creatures." The great Vedic commentator *Sayana* interprets it in that wider sense. The Lord and Master has to feed and maintain his servants and subjects. The name JESUS, in the Hebrew, means the same. The radical terms stands for *help, deliverance, salvation*. And that name was given Him because He would *save* His people from their sins. In the prophecy cited by St. Matthew, He is described as a leader or ruler, who " shall *feed* my people Israel." He is therefore to His people what a shepherd is to his flock—both leader, ruler, and feeder. The same is the import of *pati*; the name *Prajápati*, therefore, singularly corresponds to the name JESUS.

Not a single character in the Hindu pantheon, or in the pantheon of any other nation, has claimed the position of one who offered himself as a sacrifice for the benefit of humanity. There is, as all educated persons must know, only one historical person, JESUS of Nazareth, whose name and position correspond to that of the Vedic ideal—one mortal and immortal—who sacrificed himself for mankind. By the process of exhaustion you may conclude that JESUS is the true *Prajápati*, the true Saviour of the world, " the only name given among men whereby we must be saved."

I think I may therefore declare our second proposition to be also demonstrated. CHRIST is the true *Prajápati*—the true Purusha begotten in the beginning before all worlds, and Himself both God and man. The doctrines of saving sacrifice, the " primary religious rites" of the Rig-Veda,—of the double character, priest and victim, variously called *Prajápati, Purusha* and *Viswakarma*,—of the Ark by which we escape the waves of this sinful world—these doctrines I say, which had appeared in our Vedas amid much rubbish, and things worse than rubbish, may be viewed as fragments of diamonds sparkling amid dust and mud, testifying to some invisible fabric of which they were component parts, and bearing witness like planets over a dark horizon to the absent sun of whom their refulgence was but a feeble reflection.

The Christian, with the wide sympathy which incites him to invite all nations to the faith of Christ, can only rejoice that the JESUS of the Gospels responds to the self-sacrificing *Prajápati* of the Vedas, and that the evangelist's chief work will be to exhibit before his neighbours and fellow-subjects the true Ark of salvation—that true " vessel of sacrifice by which we may escape all sin." He will only have to exhibit for the faith of the Hindus the real personality of the true Purusha, " begotten before the worlds," mortal and yet divine, " whose shadow, whose death is immortality itself."

The Veda tells us of the ark of Salvation by which sin may be escaped, and repeatedly exhorts us to embark in it. The ark of Salvation, with the *Purusha* begotten in the beginning as its head, can be no other than the Church of Christ. In addition then to the exhortations of Christian evangelists, you have your own Veda calling on you to embark on that very Ark, if you desire to be delivered from the waves of sin.*

A RETURN TO VEDIC HINDUISM IMPOSSIBLE.

An appeal to Educated Hindus.

Thoughtful Hindus, dissatisfied with their religion as exhibited in the Epic poems and Puranas, may have hoped to find in the Vedas a pure system which might meet in the wants of their souls. Such an idea can be entertained only by those who are unacquainted with the Vedas or who give the hymns a meaning directly the opposite to the sense in which they were understood by their authors. Among the latter are the Arya Samajists, noticed in the Appendix.

In some respects, it is true, the Vedas may be followed. As already mentioned, caste, characterised by Sir H. S. Maine in his *Ancient Law* as "the most blighting and disastrous of human institutions," is not found in them. Women enjoyed more liberty and took a higher position. In both respects a return to the Vedic system may be made with advantage.

But it is different with regard to still more important questions. Into the lips of one of the old Rishis the words of Tennyson might well be put,

> "What am I ?
> An infant crying in the night,
> An infant crying for the light,
> And with no language but a cry."

The Vedas represent the childhood of religion, and cannot now be our guide.

1. *You cannot go back to the* GODS *of the Vedas.*—You cannot believe in "thrice eleven" deities. Heaven and earth, sun and moon, the clouds, the dawn, can never be endowed in your minds with intelligence, with wrath or mercy. No imagination can make them anything else to you than what they are:—varied, beautiful forms of matter, but matter still. You feel that you should adore the great Creator Himself, and not the objects He has made.

A hymn found in the Bible, sung by a Rajarishi nearly three thousand years ago, expresses the feelings we ought to entertain :

"O Lord, our Lord, how excellent is Thy name in all the earth ! who hast set Thy glory above the heavens. When I consider Thy heavens, the work of Thy fingers, the moon, and the stars which Thou hast ordained,—what is man that thou art mindful of him ? and the son of

---

* The foregoing extracts are abridged from *The Relation between Christianity and Hinduism.* 32 pp. ½ Anna. Sold by Mr. A. T. Scott, Madras and at other Tract Depôts. A fuller explanation is given in Dr. Banerjea's *Arian Witness to Christianity.*

man that thou visitest him ? O Lord, our Lord, how excellent is Thy
name in all the earth ! "

No enlightened man can accept the polytheism of the Vedas.

2. *You cannot offer the* PRAYERS *of the Vedas.*—You need something more than cows and horses, health and wealth, the destruction of public and domestic enemies. It is true that there are petitions for the pardon of sin addressed specially to Varuna, but
there are few and far between.

3. *You cannot make the* OFFERINGS *of the Vedas.*—You cannot
invite Indra to drink the Soma juice " like a thirsty stag ;" you
cannot sacrifice buffaloes, bullocks, cows and sheep ; you cannot
perform the *ashvamedha.* These were but shadows of the true
sacrifice, dimly set forth in what is said of Prajápati.

It must be acknowledged by every thoughtful, intelligent
Hindu, that the religion of the Vedas does not meet the spiritual
wants of man.

A NATIONAL RELIGION.

India is the land of caste and exclusiveness; all beyond the
pale of Aryavarta are impure Mlechhas. This caste feeling, under
the guise of patriotism, has, especially in Bengal, prompted the
cry for a *National* Religion. It is considered degrading for India
to have any other religion than its own.

It may first be remarked that there is no national *science.*
Keshub Chunder Sen justly says : " Is there an astronomy for
the East and another for the West ? Is there an Asiatic optics as
distinguished from European optics ? Science is one. It is one
yesterday, to-day, and for ever ; the same in the East and the West ;
it recognises neither caste, nor colour, nor nationality. It is God's
science, the eternal verity of things."

It is the same with *religion.* If each country had its own god,
there might be different religions ; but all enlightened men are
now agreed that there is only one God, the Creator, Preserver, and
Governor of the Universe. The Brotherhood of Man is similarly
acknowledged :

> " Children, we are all
> Of one great Father, in whatever clime,
> His providence hath cast the seed of life :
> All tongues, all colours."

Since God is one and all men are alike His children, it is reason-
able to suppose that He has given only one religion.

The most enlightened countries in Europe and America accepted a religion first made known to them by Asiatics, and did not
reject it from a false patriotism, saying, " We must have national
religions." An Indian poet says " The disease that is born with
us kills us ; the medicine which is found on some far-off mountain
cures our natal disease."

The cry for a National Religion originates in ignorance and pride. It will pass away. An educated Hindu does not contend for the Geography of his fathers, with its seas of sugar-cane juice, milk, and ghee. He has accepted "foreign" science. The Indian would be considered an idiot who urged his countrymen to stick to the national conveyances; palanquins and bullock carts, and refuse to travel by the "foreign" inventions of railways. A distinguished French Orientalist says that as India has already adopted the science and art of Christian nations, so she will one day spontaneously embrace their faith.

Of all false patriotism that is the worst which seeks by sophistry to defend erroneous religious beliefs because they are national. It promotes hypocrisy and disregard of truth among its advocates, while it is a grievous wrong to their ignorant countrymen, tending to perpetuate the reign of superstition.

The late Sir Madhava Row justly said, " *What is not* TRUE *is not* PATRIOTIC." There is an Indian proverb "Truth conquers." Any belief, any practice, not founded on truth, must eventually fall.

Instead of national religions, it is a far grander idea for the whole human race to fall down together as children at the feet of the true Dyaus-Pitar.

Max Müller says :

" Thousands of years have passed since the Aryan nations separated to travel to the North and the South, the West and the East : they have each formed their languages, they have each founded empires and philosophies, they have each built temples and razed them to the ground ; they have all grown older, and it may be wiser and better ; but when they search for a name for what is most exalted and yet most dear to every one of us, when they wish to express both awe and love, the infinite and the finite, they can but do what their old fathers did when gazing up to the eternal sky, and feeling the presence of a Being as far as far and as near as near can be ; they can but combine the self-same words, and utter once more the primeval Aryan prayer, Heaven-father in that form which will endure for ever, ' Our Father which art in heaven.' " *

A RELIGION WORTHY OF ACCEPTANCE.

It has been shown that an enlightened, thoughtful Hindu cannot accept the creed of the Vedas, considered the highest standards of his religion. It may be compared to a broken cistern which can hold no water to satisfy the thirst. But his attention is directed to a fountain of living water, freely offered to all.

Christianity is worthy of acceptance because it presents a Deity deserving the most profound reverence and the warmest love, while it is also a religion exactly suited to our needs. These points may be noticed more in detail.

---

* *Science of Religion*, p. 173.

1. **The Deity of Christianity.**—God in the Bible, is revealed under two aspects. He is the great *Creator* of the Universe. Hinduism has no Creator in the strict sense of the word. Matter or Maya is held to be eternal, and the nominal Creator merely forms it anew. Souls are also held to be eternal.* The more correct ideas now held by educated Hindus have been derived from Christianity. God is infinite in power, wisdom and goodness. His most glorious attribute is His holiness, in which He differs immeasurably from Hindu divinities.

The second aspect under which God is revealed in the Bible is that of *Father*. We are taught to address Him as " Our Father in heaven." He is rightly so called, because we derived our being from Him, because He supports us as a father supports his children, and because He bears a father's love toward us. We have been disobedient rebellious children, justly deserving to be shut out from His presence ; but He earnestly invites us to return to Him, offering free forgiveness. To those who do so, He stands in a more endearing relation than before.

Our moral sense is outraged when we are asked to worship Indra or Krishna, Vishnu or Siva. On the other hand, the God of Christianity far transcends our loftiest conceptions.

It has also been said that Christianity is suited to our needs. The three great wants of man are the following :

1. **Pardon of Sin.**—The great cry of humanity is, " How shall man be just with his Maker ?" Every one who thinks seriously must confess that he sins daily in thought, word and deed. Hinduism gives contradictory answers to the question, Can sin be forgiven ? Many believe that it can be washed away by bathing in the Ganges or other supposed sacred waters. Even the repetition of the name of a god is thought to have this effect. On the other hand, according to the doctrine of *Karma,* pardon is impossible. Sankar Acharya says that Brahma can no more interfere with *Karma* than he can bring wheat out of rice.

Bramhos, like other intelligent men, acknowledge that sin cannot be removed by bathing, by the products of the cows, &c. ; but they appear to adopt, in some measure, the doctrine of *Karma,* supposing that sin must be punished by " adequate agonies." What suffering this involves who can tell ?

It has been shown that the two great doctrines of mediation and sacrifice are found in Vedic Hinduism. In later books a third doctrine, that of incarnation, is taught. Krishna says in the Bhagavad Gita, " Whensoever religion fades and irreligion prevails, then I produce myself." All are embodied in Christianity. The remarks of the late Rev. Dr. Krishna Mohun Banarjeae already quoted, (pp. 140—143) should be carefully studied.

---

* See *Supposed and Real Doctrines of Hinduism as held by Educated Hindus.* By the Rev. Nehemiah Goreh. 32 pp. ¼ An. Sold by Mr. A. T. Scott, Tract Depôt, Madras.

Christianity shows how pardon may be obtained consistently with God's justice. God is the lawgiver of the universe. He is our King as well as our Father. If sin were pardoned without an atonement, it would be regarded as a slight thing, and men would be tempted to rebel against the Divine Government. God Himself provided Saviour. He so loved men that He gave His only Son the Lord to become incarnate in this world, and die on their account. He bore the punishment due to our sin, He perfectly observed God's laws. He answers for the sins of those who accept Him as their Saviour, and covers them, as it were, with His robe of righteousness. Free pardon is now offered to all who seek it in the name of Jesus Christ.

2. **Holiness.**—While pardon of sin is a great blessing, it is not enough. We all have the disease of sin, which is more loathsome than the worst forms of leprosy. In God's sight, we are, as it were, covered from head to foot with putrid sores. In such a state we can never enter His holy heaven.

Hinduism offers no help in the attainment of holiness. Its principal deities are themselves represented as guilty of great crimes. No prayers for holiness can be addressed to them. No exhortations to lead a holy life are given in any Hindu temple. In some of them there are dancing girls, whose influence can only be corrupting. According to philosophic Hinduism, the highest duty is to refrain from all actions good or bad, and to meditate till a man believes in the blasphemous assertion *Aham Brahmasmi*, I am Brahma.

Christianity, besides pardon, offers to send a physician to cure the disease of sin—the Holy Spirit.

A physician employs medicines; so the Holy Spirit prescribes means for our recovery from sin, though it is He who gives efficacy to them all. They include the study of the Bible and other good books, prayer, public worship, watchfulness against sin, &c.

The progress made is often very slow, for the patients neglect greatly the medicines prescribed. Still, it is begun on earth and completed above.

3. **Heaven.**—The Empress of India has reigned more than fifty years; but before long her crown must be laid aside, and she must lie in the tomb like her long line of ancestors. Short-lived happiness cannot satisfy us. We need an eternity of joy.

Hindus hope to purchase heaven by their supposed good deeds, by giving alms to beggars, &c. One of the most efficacious means prescribed is to take hold of a cow's tail at death, the animal being given to Brahmans.

Every intelligent man can see the worthlessness of such methods; but, in any case, a dying Hindu must leave the world in great alarm about the future. During his innumerable previous books, according to his idea, he may have committed some sin not yet expiated, and when he departs he may go to one of the fearful hells described in the Puranas. Even at best, happiness is only temporary.

Christians do not hope to enter heaven on account of their own supposed good deeds. They confess that their best actions are defiled by sin and need forgiveness. They hope to be saved only through the spotless righteousness of the Lord Jesus Christ. Through Him their sins are forgiven and admission to heaven is obtained. At death the true Christian has no fear. As soon as breath departs, his soul goes to paradise, there to be happy for ever in God's palace.

Concluding Appeal.—About a hundred generations have passed away since some of the Vedic hymns were written. The reader must sooner or later, follow them. It is the highest folly to think only of the world which we must so soon leave, and neglect that in which our eternal lot will be cast. Jesus Christ says, " What shall it profit a man, if he shall gain the whole world, and lose his own soul ?"

With heart-felt sorrow for the past, return to the one true God, saying, " Father I have sinned against Thee, and no more worthy to be called Thy Son," and accept the blessings freely offered through Jesus Christ. You will then be received again into God's family as His adopted child. He will watch over you through life, causing all things to work together for your good, and prepare you for the eternal happiness in store for you.

The doctrines of Christianity are here only very briefly stated. The reader is referred to the books mentioned below * but especially to the New Testament.

Follow the course urged upon you by your learned countryman, Dr. K. M. Banerjea, who now, as it were, addresses you from the tomb :

" If it were possible for the hoary Rishis to reappear in the world, they themselves would exhort you, nay, beseech you, implore you, perhaps also constrain you not to neglect so great a salvation ; not to waver in your duty to acknowledge and embrace the true Prajápati, the true Purusha begotten before the world, who died that you might live, who by death hath vanquished death, and brought life and immortality to light through the Gospel. Denying CHRIST, whether actively or passively, you virtually repudiate every thing that is good. Embracing CHRIST, you will find in Him a strength and comfort which your ancient Rishis would have regarded as a most valuable treasure had they lived in these days. You will find in Him everything worthy of your lineage, worthy of your antiquity, worthy of your traditions, and worthy of your education, and at the same time just to your children and to your successors in life."

---

* *Letters to Indian Youth on the Evidences of Christianity.* By the Rev. Dr. Murray Mitchell. 207 pp. 6 As. Post-free, 7 As.
Elements of Christian Truth. By the same author. 71 pp. 1¼ Annas.
Short Papers for Seekers after Truth. 112 pp. 1 Anna. Sold by Mr. A. T. Scott, Madras and at other Tract Depôts throughout India.

APPENDIX.

THE ARYA SAMAJ.

The great bulk of the Hindus, pandits as well as the common people, in addition to the Vedas properly so called, accept as sacred the Brahmanas, Upanishads, the Laws of Manu, the Itihasas, Puranas, &c., and understand them in the sense in which they have been explained in the commentaries for many centuries.

Western science, in different degrees, is spreading in India. Some Hindus get only a glimmering of it through the vernaculars or through an imperfect knowledge of English. Such men sometimes attempt to jumble together Hindu and Western ideas. The two, in many respects, are absolutely contradictory. Agreement is sought by torturing and twisting the Hindu books, so as to give them an entirely different meaning from the true one. Of men of this class, the late Dayanand Sarasvati, the founder of the Arya Samaj, was a striking example.

A short account will first be given of his life.

Dayanand was born at Morvi, in Kathiawar, in the year 1824. His father was a zealous Saivite. Dayanand, at an early age, studied Sanskrit grammar, and learnt the Vedas by heart. Afterwards his father wished to initiate him in the worship of the Linga; for which purpose he was to fast a whole night in the temple of Siva. When he was left alone he began to meditate. He says :—

" Is it possible, I asked myself, that this idol I see bestriding his bull before me, and who, according to all accounts, walks about, eats, sleeps, drinks, holds a trident in his hand, beats the drum, and can pronounce curses on men, can be the great deity, the Mahadeva, the Supreme Being? Unable to resist such thoughts any longer I roused my father, asking him to tell me whether this hideous idol was the great god of the scriptures. ' Why do you ask?' said my father. ' Because,' I answered, ' I feel it impossible to reconcile the idea of an omnipotent living God with this idol, which allows the mice to run over his body, and thus suffers himself to be polluted without the slightest protest.' Then my father tried to explain to me that this stone image of the Mahadeva, having been consecrated by the holy Brahmans, became, in consequence, the god himself, adding that as Siva cannot be perceived personally in this Kali-Yuga, we have the idol in which the Mahadeva is imagined by his votaries." This explanation, however, was not satisfactory.

When Dayanand was 21 years of age his father wished him to be married against his will ; so he left home secretly. Afterwards he was found and brought back, but again he ran away. For years he wandered about, for a time becoming a Sannyasi. Even when ten years of age he saw the folly of idolatry. When he grew older, he rejected all the Hindu sacred books as inspired except the four Vedas and the Isa Upanishad which is found in the Yajur Veda.*

In 1881, a large convocation of 300 Pandits from Gauda, Navadipa, and Kasi, was held to discuss with Dayanand his opinions. The following resolutions were carried against him :

(1.) That the Brahmanas are as valid and authoritative as the Mantras, and that the other Smritis or law-books are as valid and authoritative as Manu.

(2.) That the worship of Vishnu, Siva, Durga, and other Hindu deities, the performance of the Shraddha ceremonies after death, and bathing in the Ganges, are sanctioned in the Shastras.

(3.) That in the first hymn of the Rig-Veda, addressed to Agni, the primary meaning of Agni is fire, and its secondary meaning is God.

(4.) That sacrifices are performed to secure salvation.

Besides lecturing, Dayanand devoted some of the later years of his life to the publication of books. Before his death he had completed a translation into Hindi of one-half of the Vedas. The principal points of his teaching are embodied in his *Rig-Vedadi Bhashya Bhumika*, ' A Prefatory Exposition of the Rig-Veda and others.' His *Satyarth Prakash*, ' Manifestation of True Meanings,' gives his teaching as to religious and social customs.

Latterly Dayanand became very corpulent. He died at Ajmere in 1883 at the age of 59.†

Dayanand accepted and rejected what he pleased of the Hindu sacred books, and put his own meaning upon them. All who differed from him were denounced as ignorant. All the translations, commentaries, and dictionaries prepared by pandits during the last 2,500 years were wrong ; he alone was right. It was his plan in discussions to have a company of admirers who would join him in loud derisive laughter at his opponents. He tried this when arguing with pandits at Benares. On the second day of the debate, they gathered together a larger number of men, who hooted and laughed at whatever Dayanand said, so that the tables were turned, and he was completely defeated.

Numerous Societies have been formed in North India and the Punjab, called Aryá Samajes, professing to follow Dayanand's interpretation of the Vedas. An Anglo-Vedic College has been established at Lahore, and a weekly newspaper in English, called the *Arya Patrika*, is issued.

---

* See his letter to Raja Sivaprasad, *Athenæum*, Feb. 5, 1881.
† Chiefly abridged from *Biographical Essays*, by Max Müller.

The following are the principal opinions of Dayanand :—
1. **The Eternity of the Vedas.**—Mr. Forman says :

" The pundits are content with putting the origin of these books back near the beginning of the world when Brahm taught Brahma, and Brahma issued each of the four Vedas out of each of his four mouths in turn, teaching them to the holy Rishis who wrote them down. Dayanand laughs at all this. He says Brahma was not a god, but only a great Raja, and that he could not possibly have been the author of the Vedas, for he himself was a student of them. He says the Vedas are eternal absolutely; that they are the knowledge of God, and hence as eternal as God himself, that they have been given in just their present form this world and to other worlds through all eternity, in their long passages from formation to destruction, each occupying hundreds of billions of years. That the edition for the present world was taught by God to the first four men created 100,960,852,975 years ago. These four men were named Agni, Vayu, Suraj and Angira. They, having learned the Vedas from God, each wrote one of the four books."*

Calculations differ as to the exact period of creation. The *Aryan Magazine*, published in 1884, makes the Aryan era 196 crores, 8 lakhs 52,984 years. A writer in the same periodical makes the time yet to pass as 235 crores, 91 lakhs, 47,015 years. Upon this claim to antiquity, the *Indian Spectator* remarks :—

" AGE WITHOUT WISDOM OR PROGRESS.—The Hindu Aryas do not count their existence by centuries but by millions of years. This is their 1,961st million. What a contrast to our miserable 19th century ! But alas and alas ! These millions and billions of years have left the Hindus no wiser than the mushroom Europeans in the Dark Ages. Far better is the 19th century of Europe than the 1,961st millionth year of Aryan India."

Dayanand argues that the Vedas are eternal from the eternity of sound. "Thus take the word *gau*, a cow : he says the sound *g* has always existed, so also the sound *au*; the Four (Agni, Vayu, &c.) only combined these, and in writing gave the word *gau*. He further explains that all space is filled with these sounds ; that when a man speaks he simply chooses whichever of the sounds he wants, and taking them in, arranges them in whatever order he wishes, and so forms words and sentences. That as soon as each sound has performed its duty, it separates from those to which it has been temporarily joined and goes again to its own place in space, ready to be used again when wanted." Dayanand adopted this opinion from the Purva Mimansa of Jaimini. On the above reasoning, every book may be proved to be eternal.

It has been shown that Dayanand's theory of the Vedas being eternal is contradicted by the hymns themselves. Some of the hymns are said to be quite new, others old. The names of the writers are given. It has also been already explained that internal

---

* *The Arya Samaj*, p. 13,

evidence shows that the hymns were composed when the Aryans were entering India, and had frequent wars with the aborigines.

Raja Siva Prasad, of Benares, asked Dayanand why he regarded the Samhita as inspired and not the Brahmanas. The reply was, " Samhita is *per se* (of itself) visible, proved by preception." Dayanand was next asked his reply to, " The disputant says that the Brahmanas are *per se* visible, and proved by perception ;" to which no answer was given.

Like the rest of Hindus, Dayanand considered the inspiration of the Vedas to be self-evident, and not to require any proof. The *Arya Patrika* says of them : " They are engraved in the starry heavens. They are kneaded into the mould of the earth. They are written in the beams of the sun. They are seen in the light of the moon. They are in the flashes of lightning. In short, they are always with God who fills all in all." (*Jan.* 16, 1886).

2. **A Belief in One God.**—Dayanand rejected the 33 crores of Hindu gods and goddesses, and claimed the Vedas to be monotheistic. It has been shown that the Vedas teach polytheism. The deities are again and again said to be thrice-eleven in number. They have different names, parents, wives, and children, and live in different places. If they are all one, it might as well be said that 33 persons now living are all one. In later times pantheism was developed. The well known phrase *Ekam evadvitiyam,* " One only without a second," does not mean that there is no second God, but that there is no second anything.

Monotheism was learned from Christianity.

3. **The Eternity of Souls and Prakriti.**—It has been mentioned that Dayanand mixed up his old ideas as a Hindu with the slight western knowledge he had acquired through the vernaculars. He learned the eternity of souls and his ideas about Prakriti from the Sankhya Darsana of Kapila, of which they are the chief doctrines. Kapila's system is known among Hindus as the Niriswara Sankhya, or *the Sankhya without the Lord,* its founder being accused of atheism.

The *Arya Patrika* reasons thus :—

" If the soul is immortal, how it can be regarded as a created essence is what completely passes our comprehension. The assumption of the immortality of the soul necessitates the assumption of its eternity. If the soul is to exist for ever, it must have been existing from time indefinite. In fact whatever exists at the present time has existed always and shall always exist. Not a single particle of what the universe at present contains can be blotted out of existence. Every thing in the universe is eternal and unperishable. The existence of anything at the present time presupposes its existence in the past, and necessitates its existence in the future." *Jan.* 31, 1888.

The above is a clear statement of the Sankhya doctrine. It

is a fixed Hindu dogma, *navastuno vastusiddhih,* nothing can be produced out of nothing.

The fundamental error of Hinduism is that expressed in the words of the Bible : " Thou thoughtest that I (God) was altogether such an one as thyself." Because a carpenter cannot work without materials, the Almighty God cannot do it. " Ye do err, not knowing the power of God." He does not require, like weak and imperfect man, to stop for materials, but can call them into existence by the mere *fiat* of His will.

If souls are eternal, we are all little gods. But not only men are such, so is every reptile that crawls on the ground, and every insect that flutters in the air. Souls, according to Hinduism, may also pass into plants and even into inanimate objects. Who then can estimate the number of these eternal *svayambhu* essences !

Whether is it more rational to suppose the existence of one Being, infinite in power and wisdom, or to imagine that countless unintelligent atoms and spirits have existed from all eternity ?

The reasoning that if the soul is to live for ever, it must have had an eternal pre-existence, is equally unfounded. This is also a denial of God's power. He can give a future eternal existence to any creature He has called into being.

For further remarks on this point, see *Philosophic Hinduism,* pp. 29-31 and 38, 39.

4. **Transmigration.**—This doctrine is held by the followers of the Arya Samaj, although Max Müller says that the Vedas do not contain a " trace" of it. As one error often requires another to support it, so the false belief in the eternal existence of the soul, required to be accounted for by transmigration.

This dogma is considered in *Popular Hinduism,* (pp. 61—63). Only a few remarks can be made here on the subject.

1. *It is contrary to the course of Nature, in which like always produces like.* Every animal and plant produces animals and plants exactly like itself. According to transmigration, a man in his next birth may be a tiger, a pig, a fly, or a pumpkin.

2. *No one has the slightest recollection of any previous birth.* If the soul is eternal, why does it not recollect anything that happened previous to its present life ?

3. *By transmigration persons virtually become new beings, so that they are in reality punished for the actions of others.* It is said that at every new birth something takes place by which the remembrance of former things is destroyed. In this case the person on whom it is wrought is no longer the same person. One man is really punished for the faults of another of which he is quite ignorant.

The world is not a place where we are rewarded or punished for actions in imaginary former births ; but one where our conduct is tried. We are like the servants of a great King, who has allotted to us different duties, and according as we discharge them, we shall be dealt with at death.

5.   **The Rejection of Sacrifice.**—Dayanand professed the greatest reverence for the Vedas, but his teaching is in direct opposition to their whole tenor.   The remark of Mr. Kunte has been quoted : "No matter what hymn is read, it directly or indirectly cannot but refer to a sacrifice."   As Dr. Clark says : "In life or in death, sacrifice was the pivot on which the whole religion of the Arya turned.   It met him in every phase of life, in every state of being,— it was his all in all."

One great object of sacrifice in the Vedas is the forgiveness of sin.   It is repeated again and again that sacrifice is the "annulment of sin."   Dayanand looks upon this idea as absurd.   Sin cannot be pardoned ; its punishment must be endured.   He says that the Vedas prescribe things to be burned to make an excellent smoke which purifies the air ; also rising, it mixes with and forms clouds and comes down as rain ; the rain thus also being purified by its presence.   The object and effect of sacrifices, as ordered in the Vedas, is the purifying of air and water, and hence the destroying of disease.

Dayanand, when asked why there is a platform prescribed for sacrifice, an excavation, &c., replies : A platform is ordered to be made round, square, three-cornered, &c., in order that it may be an object-lesson in geometry for the people ; a hole is made that it may be lined with brick, and thus the people, in calculating the number of bricks needed for a hole of given dimensions, may have an exercise in arithmetic !

6.   **Caste.**—"Caste," says Mr. Forman, "as held by the Hindus, Dayanand repeatedly denounces as the creation of Brahmans and as a great evil.   Of *eating from the hands of others,* he says that the Hindu is free to eat from the hand of any, excepting only Christians and Muhammadans—and these are excepted because in the composition of their bodies there are mixed bad-smelling particles !   Not only *may* a Hindu eat from the hands of a low-caste man, but men of the higher castes (in his sense of the word) should not cook their own food, but should eat only food cooked by *Shudras* or low-caste men.   For, says he, working over the fire in cooking, heats the head and thus injures the brain ; and the lower people ought to do this for the higher."

7.   **Education of Children.**—After five years of age the sexes are to be kept strictly apart.   The teachers and servants in boys' schools are to be only men, and in girls' schools only women.   The school is to be at least 8 miles from the nearest village.   So long as the children are pupils their parents are not to see them.   Nor are there any letters to pass between children and parents.

The subject of study in these schools is to be only and always the Vedas, for in them alone is truth and only truth.

The study of the Vedas should be prosecuted at the very least 24 years—*i.e.*, from 8 until 32 years of age—better until 50, and better still 56 years of age. The benefits to be derived from these courses of study are as follows :—By the first course, studying each of the first two Vedas 12 years, one attains to freedom from disease and a lengthening of life to 70 or 80 years of age ; by the second course, giving 12 years to each of the first 3 Vedas and 8 years to the last, the life, members, heart and spirit being joined in strength, one becomes a man who causes all enemies to weep, and who nourishes all good men ; by the third course, from 8 to 56 years of age, or "48 years of study as there are 48 letters in the alphabet," giving 12 years to each of the Vedas, one gets his life in his power.

And now the men and women thus educated may go forth well-fitted for life ; let them marry and settle down as householders. When one complies with these conditions, he gains such a hold on life, that he may live on to be 400 years of age. It is rather hard for this theory that Dayanand, who studied the Vedas throughout his life, died at the age of 59.

8. **Marriage.**—Child marriage is denounced. The allowable ages for marriage are for men from 25 to 48, and for women from 16 to 25.

The *Satyarth Prakash*, (pp. 80-83) gives the following directions about marriage. The photographs of all pupils in the boys' school who are old enough to be married, are to be sent to and kept by the Principal of the girls' school, and photographs of the marriageable girls to be in possession of the Principal of the boys' school. When either Principal thinks that one of the pupils should be married, let him, or her, choose from among the photos in hand the one, the original of which would seem by appearance best suited for the match. Then let this photograph be sent to the Principal of the other school, accompanied by a description of age, height, character, family, property, &c. If both Principals agree that the marriage is desirable, the photograph and description of the young man are presented to the young woman, and the photograph of the young woman is presented to the young man. If all is favourable, the parents are to be notified, and the marriage is to take place. The parents may carry on these negociations if they wish to do so.

Second Marriage is forbidden, but what he calls *Niyog* (rejoined) is allowed. Widowers and widows may live together for a time for the sake of producing children. This compact is to last only until the birth of two children, to be given to whichever of the parents desired to have it for the sake of children. If both parents desire children, the compact is to last until the birth of four—two to be taken by each parent. The compact must then end. Dayanand further declares that should any man or woman break this law, as to the limit of Niyog, they are to be cast out from among the Aryas.

Niyog is also allowed in certain cases to men and women whose wives and husbands are living.

9.   **Ideas of Geography.**—The following is an example : In the *Satyarth Prakash*, " Concerning Travel," Dayanand says that Munis and Rishis and other excellent people used to go to other countries.   Viyash Muni and his son Sukhdeo and their disciples went to Pátál, *i. e.*, America (!) and dwelt there.   One day, while living in America, Sukhdeo asked his father, Viyash Ji, some question concerning knowledge. Viyash Ji told him to go to Janakpur in Hindustan, and ask the Raja there.   We then have an account of the countries Sukhdeo passed through on his journey. Going on and on he arrived at Harivarsh, *i. e.*, *Hari*, a monkey, and *Varsh*, country,—*i. e.*, the country of monkeys—*i. e.*, the country of people who are like monkeys, or those who have red mouths and light-coloured hair—*Europe*.   From Europe he went on to Huudish, the country of the Jews ; thence he came into China and thence to India.   Dayanand probably knew scarcely enough of geography to be aware that an explanation of Sukhdeo's choosing so circuitous a route in passing from Europe to Hindustan would have been in place.

Again it is related that Krishna went to America in a ship, and called from there Udalak Muni, and brought him to the sacrifice prepared by Raja Yudhistir.   At one time Arjuna, an Indian Raja of the same date, went to America and fought with the Raja of America.   When the Raja of America was conquered, he gave his daughter, Ulupi by name, to Arjuna !

10.   **Modern Inventions supposed to be found in the Vedas.**— Max Müller says of Dayanand :—

" To him not only was everything contained in the Vedas perfect truth, but he went a step further, and by the most incredible interpretations succeeded in persuading himself and others that everything worth knowing, even the most recent inventions of modern science, were alluded to in the Vedas.   Steam-engines, railways, and steam-boats, all were shown to have been known, at least in their germs, to the poets of the Vedas, for Veda, he argued, means Divine Knowledge, and how could anything have been hid from that ?"[*]

The following is the mode in which Dayanand finds railways in the Vedas :—

Pandits explain *Shwetam Ashwam* to mean the white horse. " But Dayanand sees more in it ; the meaning is the steam horse or steam. In *Ashwi* then (meaning here fire and water, and hence steam) we find the motive power for these vehicles.   Again, *Karashwa, i. e ,* *chhah ghore* (six horses), so the pandits, but Dayanand says, the meaning is, that the vehicles are to contain six compartments for fire and water."[†]

---

[*] *Biographical, Essays* p. 170.
[†] Rev. H. Forman, *The Arya Samaj*, pp. 52, 53.

By similar reasoning, balloons, guns, &c., are discovered in the Vedas.

Dayanand's teachings concerning the sciences and the arts are but a crude combination of the ideas he had imbibed from Hinduism with the most primary and incorrect ideas of the sciences and arts introduced by the English.

It has been shown that in Vedic times cows were killed and their flesh eaten. Modern Hindus worship the cow, and accordingly think it very wrong to eat one of their gods. Dayanand thus argues against the use of animal food :

"He calculates that a cow will give on an average 8 or $8\frac{1}{2}$ maunds of milk in a month, or in a year 99 maunds, in a life time 1,201 maunds, enough with a proper admixture of ghee and sugar to furnish food for a day to 25,740 men. How trivial, in comparison with this, the number that could be fed for a day on that cow's meat. But when you add to this the produce of even the immediate progeny of this cow, how much stronger the comparison and the conclusion from it ! Supposing this cow to have 13 calves and allowing for the early death of one, there remain as producers 6 cows and 6 oxen. The milk given by these cows would feed 1,54,440 men, while the grain produced by the labor of the oxen during their life time would feed once, on a ration of 3 paos to a man, an army of 2, 56,000 men. Thus as the result of one spared cow, you have food sufficient to satisfy the hunger of 4,10,440 men. He then carries out a similar calculation with regard to goats and sheep."

The absurdity of this reasoning is easily apparent. Dayanand balances the number of men that could be fed for one day on the flesh of a cow, with the number that could be fed by a number of cows and oxen for several years requiring large quantities of land. On the same principle a much larger number could be fed by eating the cow. Suppose the flesh of the cow to be equal in nourishment to 30 seers of wheat, and that each seer that is sown produces 10 seers. The increase by eating the cow and sowing the wheat would be as follows :

Sown	30	seers.
1st Crop	300	,,
2nd ,,	3,000	,,
3rd ,,	30,000	,,
4th ,,	300,000	,,
5th ,,	3,000,000	,,
6th ,,	30,000,000	,,
	3,33,33,300	

Allowing one seer a day, 6 crops would yield sufficient grain to feed, not merely four lakhs of men, but upwards of three crores, and all this from eating one cow !

Dayanand's Criticisms on the Bible.—If Dayanand twists and tortures the Vedas, giving them quite a different meaning from the true one, it is not surprising that he should do the same with the Bible. One or two examples may be given.

The Sabbath, or Sunday, was to be kept holy, and it is said God blessed it. Upon this Dayanand remarks, " When He blessed the Sunday, what did He do to Monday and the other days ? He must have cursed them. Such is not the conduct of a wise man ; how can it be the work of God ?"

" Not only are baseless inference drawn from texts, but the passages quoted are sometimes represented as saying something very different from what they do say. In Gen. xxxi. 30, we find Laban asking Jacob, ' Wherefore hast thou stolen my gods ?' But the verse is so quoted as to make it appear that God is the speaker, and not Laban. Then comes the objection, that the ' Christian's God also acknowledges gods of stone, or why should he speak of stealing the gods ?"*

The hostility of Dayanand to Christianity is inherited by his followers. There is a class of vulgar, half-educated men in England, called Secularists. They are the same as the Indian Charvakas. They do not believe in God or in any life after this world. They scoff at all religion, but they especially try to caricature Christianity and to attack it with low abuse. The Arya Samajists, in their ignorance, suppose the Secularist tracts against Christianity to be " unanswerable," and have translated some of them into the vernaculars. Their objections have been known for nearly eighteen centuries ; but, as a rule, they are misrepresentations of Christianity and without weight. In general they are treated with contempt in Europe. A very wise man long ago said, " A scorner seeketh wisdom and findeth it not." Sanskrit writers, before entering upon a subject, usually consider who are " competent" to enter upon the study. Vishvanath Bhattacharyya in the *Nyaya Sutra Vritti*, justly says : " They who desire to know the truth are competent for discussion." Unless there is this desire, all discussion is useless.

Although the Arya Samajists are glad to use Secularist attacks upon Christianity, their own belief in God is ridiculed nearly as much as belief in the Bible.

The Future of the Arya Samaj.—The Hindus are very open to flattery. Even an ordinary man is often addressed as Maharaj ! National vanity is pleased with the thought that their sacred books are eternal, and contain the germs of all knowledge. Dayanand also gave up some of the grosser forms of Hindu superstition. The forecast of Max Müller will doubtless prove correct : " For a time this kind of liberal orthodoxy started by Dayanand may last ; but the mere contact with Western thought, and more particularly with Western scholarship, will most likely extinguish it."†

---

* Rev. J. Gray, in *Indian Evangelical Review* for October, 1886. See the paper for many other examples. † *Biographical Essays*, p. 182.

The Vedas themselves only require to be known to show the absurdity of Dayanand's interpretation of them. His ignorance of geography is simply ridiculous. His want of common sense is shown by his proposed scheme of education. But worst of all is his disgusting doctrine of *niyog*. It alone is sufficient to disprove his claims to be regarded as a true teacher.

The foregoing remarks are chiefly compiled from a pamphlet by the Rev. H. Forman, entitled, " The Arya Samaj, its Teachings and an Estimate of it." It is published by the North India Tract Society, Allahabad, price 1 anna.*

---

* It may also be obtained from the Tract Depôt, Madras.

CPSIA information can be obtained at www.ICGtesting.com
Printed in the USA
LVOW11s0117271115

464317LV00002B/307/P

9 781585 092239